AAUSC 2018 Volume—Issues in Language Program Direction

Understanding Vocabulary Learning and Teaching: Implications for Language Program Development

Johanna Watzinger-Tharp
University of Utah

Kate Paesani
University of Minnesota

Series Editors

Peter Ecke
University of Arizona

Susanne Rott
University of Illinois at Chicago

Editors

Australia • Brazil • Mexico • Singapore • United Kingdom • United States

AAUSC 2018 Volume: Understanding Vocabulary Learning and Teaching: Implications for Language Program Development

Peter Ecke, Susanne Rott, Johanna Watzinger-Tharp and Kate Paesani

Sr. Product Team Manager: Heather Bradley Cole

Product Assistant: Catherine Bradley

Marketing Manager: Sean Ketchem

Production Service: Lumina Datamatics, Inc.

Senior Designer: Sarah Cole

Manufacturing Planner: Fola Orekoya

© 2020, 2019 Cengage Learning, Inc.

Unless otherwise noted, all content is © Cengage

ALL RIGHTS RESERVED. No part of this work covered by the copyright herein may be reproduced or distributed in any form or by any means, except as permitted by U.S. copyright law, without the prior written permission of the copyright owner.

> For product information and technology assistance, contact us at **Cengage Customer & Sales Support, 1-800-354-9706** or **support.cengage.com**.
>
> For permission to use material from this text or product, submit all requests online at
> **www.cengage.com/permissions**.

Library of Congress Control Number: 2018953450

Student Edition:
ISBN: 978-0-357-10668-6

Cengage
20 Channel Center Street
Boston, MA 02210
USA

Cengage is a leading provider of customized learning solutions with employees residing in nearly 40 different countries and sales in more than 125 countries around the world. Find your local representative at **www.cengage.com**

Cengage products are represented in Canada by Nelson Education, Ltd.

To learn more about Cengage platforms and services, visit **www.cengage.com**.

To register or access your online learning solution or purchase materials for your course, visit **www.cengage.com/student**

Printed in the United States of America
Print Number: 01   Print Year: 2018

Contents

Acknowledgments v

AAUSC Editorial Board 2018 vii

Annual Volumes of Issues in Language Program Direction ix

Abstracts xiii

	Introduction	
Peter Ecke (The University of Arizona) & Susanne Rott (The University of Illinois at Chicago)	Vocabulary Learning and Teaching: Variables, Relationships, Materials, and Curriculum Development	1

PART 1: Vocabulary Learning and Use: Variables and Relationships

	Chapter 1	
Nan Jiang (University of Maryland)	Semantic Development and L2 Vocabulary Teaching	10
	Chapter 2	
Ulf Schuetze (University of Victoria)	Supporting Your Brain Learning Words	28
	Chapter 3	
Maria Rogahn, Denisa Bordag, Amit Kirschenbaum, & Erwin Tschirner (University of Leipzig)	Minor Manipulations Matter: Syntactic Position Influences the Effectiveness of Incidental Vocabulary Acquisition During L2 Reading	38
	Chapter 4	
Erwin Tschirner (Universität Leipzig), Jane Hacking, & Fernando Rubio (University of Utah)	The Relationship Between Reading Proficiency and Vocabulary Size: An Empirical Investigation	58

PART 2: Vocabulary Teaching, Materials, and Curricula

Claudia Sánchez-Gutiérrez, (University of California, Davis), Nausica Marcos Miguel (Denison University), & Michael K. Olsen (Tennessee Technological University)

Chapter 5
Vocabulary Coverage and Lexical Characteristics in L2 Spanish Textbooks 78

Jamie Rankin (Princeton University)

Chapter 6
der |die| das: Integrating Vocabulary Acquisition Research into an L2 German Curriculum 99

Nina Vyatkina (University of Kansas)

Chapter 7
Language Corpora for L2 Vocabulary Learning: Data-Driven Learning Across the Curriculum 121

Alla Zareva (Old Dominion University)

Chapter 8
Setting the Lexical EAP Bar for ESL Students: Lexical Complexity of L2 Academic Presentations 146

Joe Barcroft (Washington University in St. Louis)

Chapter 9
The Input-Based Incremental Approach to Vocabulary in Meaning-Oriented Instruction for Language Program Directors and Teachers 164

Editors 181

Contributors 181

Acknowledgments

We would like to thank the members of the AAUSC Editorial Board for their interest in the initial volume proposal and for their feedback, which helped improve the proposal and shape the volume's focus. We are particularly grateful to the series editors, Johanna Watzinger-Tharp and Kate Paesani, for their encouragement and for their editorial and organizational support throughout the planning stage, the review phase, and the copyediting process. Without their guidance, this project would not have been possible.

We would like to thank all colleagues who responded to our call for papers, including those whose manuscripts were not included in this volume. We learned a great deal from their submissions and wish them success in their future work. We want to express our gratitude to the following colleagues who served as reviewers and provided valuable feedback for the authors and us: Joe Barcroft, Carl S. Blyth, Alex Boulton, Cindy Brantmeier, Claudia R. Fernández, Christopher J. Hall, Carol A. Klee, Beatriz Lado, Judith E. Liskin-Gasparro, Lara Lomicka Anderson, Hiram Maxim, Ayman A. Mohamed, Kate Paesani, Lisa C. Parkes, Fernando Rubio, Joshua J. Thoms, Per Urlaub, Johanna Watzinger-Tharp, Wynne Wong, and Gabriela Zapata. Carl Good and Lucas Riddle assisted us with the proofreading of manuscripts.

We are grateful to Provost Andrew Comrie of the University of Arizona for a grant to Peter Ecke through the Provost Author Support Program, which helped to fund this project. Most important, we are indebted to the authors of the nine chapters who became part of this volume. We are confident that their contributions will spark interest and fruitful discussion among language program directors, graduate students, teachers, and researchers interested in second language vocabulary learning and teaching.

Peter Ecke and *Susanne Rott*
Editors

AAUSC Editorial Board 2018

Johanna Watzinger-Tharp, Series Editor	University of Utah
Kate Paesani, Series Editor	University of Minnesota
Heather Willis Allen	University of Wisconsin
Catherine Barrette	Wayne State University
Carl S. Blyth	University of Texas at Austin
Cori Crane	Duke University
Robert L. Davis	University of Oregon
Jane Hacking	University of Utah
Charles J. James	University of Wisconsin
Carol A. Klee	University of Minnesota
Beatriz Lado	Lehman College, CUNY
Glenn Levine	University of California at Irvine
Judith E. Liskin-Gasparro	University of Iowa
Lara Lomicka Anderson	University of South Carolina
Hiram H. Maxim	Emory University
Nicole Mills	Harvard University
Lisa Parkes	Harvard University
Fernando Rubio	University of Utah
Colleen Ryan	Indiana University
Joshua J. Thoms	Utah State University
Per Urlaub	Middlebury College

Annual Volumes of *Issues in Language Program Direction*

2017   ***Engaging the World: Social Pedagogies and Language Learning***
Editors: Sébastien Dubreil and Steven L. Thorne

2016   ***The Interconnected Language Curriculum: Critical Transitions and Interfaces in Articulated K-16 Contexts***
Editors: Per Urlaub and Johanna Watzinger-Tharp

2015   ***Integrating the Arts: Creative Thinking about Foreign Language Curricula and Language Program Direction***
Editors: Lisa Parkes and Colleen M. Ryan

2014   ***Innovation and Accountability in Language Program Evaluation***
Editors: Nicole Mills and John Norris

2013   ***Individual Differences, L2 Development, and Language Program Administration: From Theory to Application***
Editors: Cristina Sanz and Beatriz Lado

2012   ***Hybrid Language Teaching and Learning: Exploring Theoretical, Pedagogical and Curricular Issues***
Editors: Fernando Rubio and Joshua J. Thoms

2011   ***Educating the Future Foreign Language Professorate for the 21st Century***
Editors: Heather Willis Allen and Hiram Maxim

2010   ***Critical and Intercultural Theory and Language Pedagogy***
Editors: Glenn S. Levine and Alison Phipps

2009   ***Principles and Practices of the Standards in College Foreign Language Education***
Editor: Virginia M. Scott

2008   ***Conceptions of L2 Grammar: Theoretical Approaches and Their Application in the L2 Classroom***
Editors: Stacey Katz and Johanna Watzinger-Tharp

2007   ***From Thought to Action: Exploring Beliefs and Outcomes in the Foreign Language Program***
Editor: H. Jay Siskin

2006 *Insights from Study Abroad for Language Programs*
Editor: Sharon Wilkinson

2005 *Internet-mediated Intercultural Foreign Language Education*
Editors: Julie A. Belz and Steven L. Thorne

2004 *Language Program Articulation: Developing a Theoretical Foundation*
Editors: Catherine Barrette and Kate Paesani

2003 *Advanced Foreign-Language Learning: A Challenge to College Programs*
Editors: Heidi Byrnes and Hiram Maxim

2002 *The Sociolinguistics of Foreign Language Classrooms: Contributions of the Native, the Near-native, and the Non-native Speaker*
Editor: Carl S. Blyth

2001 *SLA and the Literature Classroom: Fostering Dialogues*
Editors: Virginia M. Scott and Holly Tucker

2000 *Mentoring Foreign Language Teaching Assistants, Lecturers, and Adjunct Faculty*
Editor: Benjamin Rifkin

1999 *Form and Meaning: Multiple Perspectives*
Editors: James F. Lee and Albert Valdman

1998 *Research Issues and Language Program Direction*
Editor: Kathy Heilenman

1997 *New Ways of Learning and Teaching: Focus on Technology and Foreign Language Education*
Editor: Judith Muyskens

1996 *Patterns and Policies: The Changing Demographics of Foreign Language Instruction*
Editor: Judith E. Liskin-Gasparro

1995 *Redefining the Boundaries of Language Study*
Editor: Claire Kramsch

1994 *Faces in a Crowd: The Individual Learner in Multisection Courses*
Editor: Carol Klee

1993	***The Dynamics of Language Program Direction*** Editor: David P. Benseler
1992	***Development and Supervision of Teaching Assistants in Foreign Languages*** Editor: Joel C. Walz
1991	***Assessing Foreign Language Proficiency of Undergraduates*** Editor: Richard B. Teschner
1990	***Challenges in the 1990s for College Foreign Language Programs*** Editor: Sally Sieloff Magnan

Abstracts

PART 1—Vocabulary Learning and Use: Variables and Relationships

Nan Jiang

Semantic Development and L2 Vocabulary Teaching

Semantic development is an integral part of vocabulary learning and teaching in a second language (L2), as an adequate understanding of a word's meaning is vital to the accurate use of new words. However, semantic development in adult L2 learning can be a challenge for both learners and teachers for at least two reasons. The first is the presence of a semantic system that is specific to a learner's first language (L1). This system often overlaps with the semantic system of the target language in a complicated and subtle way and interferes with the development of the new semantic system. The second is a lack of optimal input, in terms of both quality and quantity, that is necessary for semantic development or restructuring to take place. This chapter begins with the discussion of how two semantic systems may differ, outlining five patterns of semantic overlap across languages. It goes on to review research evidence for the difficulty L2 learners encounter in semantic development, suggesting that they often continue to rely on the semantic system associated with their L1, even at an advanced level of proficiency. The chapter ends with a discussion of pedagogical strategies instructors may use to help facilitate semantic development among L2 learners.

Ulf Schuetze

Supporting Your Brain Learning Words

Encountering, processing, retrieving, and articulating words is a dynamic and fluid process. Several brain regions are involved that are associated with attention, language, memory, and the senses (Baddeley, 2007; Pulvermüller, 1996; Schuetze, 2017). This chapter provides insight into the processes at work in the brain focusing on the formation of the language network; its interaction with the limbic system; and the capacity to direct, switch, and divide attention. Bringing together cognitive psychology and applied linguistics, teaching tips as well as strategies for effective second and foreign language vocabulary acquisition are provided.

MARIA ROGAHN, DENISA BORDAG, AMIT KIRSCHENBAUM, AND ERWIN TSCHIRNER

Minor Manipulations Matter: Syntactic Position Influences the Effectiveness of Incidental Vocabulary Acquisition During L2 Reading

This chapter reports on a study that addresses the role of syntactic prominence, that is, the perceived importance of sentence constituents, in L1 and L2 incidental vocabulary acquisition. In a self-paced reading study with 80 native German speakers and 64 advanced learners of German, we explored the initial stages of vocabulary acquisition. The results revealed an acquisition advantage for the meanings of new words that appeared as subjects in main clauses compared to those that appeared as objects in subordinate clauses in L2, but not in L1. We argue that the acquisition advantage for words with high syntactic prominence in L2 can be attributed to a higher allocation of the readers' attention to prominent sentence constituents. L1 participants did not display this benefit because their high linguistic competence allowed sufficient processing of both subject and object, main and subordinate clauses. The findings demonstrate that syntactic prominence has, so far, been an overlooked factor in incidental vocabulary acquisition, which, however, has important implications for teaching material design and vocabulary presentation.

ERWIN TSCHIRNER, JANE HACKING, AND FERNANDO RUBIO

The Relationship Between Reading Proficiency and Vocabulary Size: An Empirical Investigation

Studies of the vocabulary size needed to be a proficient second-language reader commonly arrive at numbers that are staggering. The figures most often cited are between 8,000 and 9,000 words, as required for reading novels and newspaper articles with sufficient ease and understanding (Nation, 2006). To date, almost all of the empirical research on reading proficiency and vocabulary size has focused on English, but two recent studies (Hacking & Tschirner, 2017; Hacking, Tschirner, & Rubio, in press) reported lexical minimums associated with particular American Council on the Teaching of Foreign Languages (ACTFL) reading proficiency levels. This chapter builds on these data and examines the relationship between the reading proficiency and vocabulary knowledge of L2 learners of German, Russian, and Spanish. It addresses the following research questions: (1) How well does reading proficiency as defined by ACTFL predict vocabulary size measured as the receptive knowledge of various bands of the most frequent 5,000 words in German, Russian, and Spanish? (2) What vocabulary sizes are predicted by ACTFL reading proficiency levels? (3) Do German, Russian, and Spanish differ with respect to the relationship between reading proficiency and vocabulary size? This chapter will also focus on some implications for curriculum development.

PART 2—Vocabulary Teaching, Materials, and Curricula

Claudia Sánchez-Gutiérrez, Nausica Marcos Miguel, and Michael K. Olsen

Vocabulary Coverage and Lexical Characteristics in L2 Spanish Textbooks

This chapter reports on a study that examined the vocabulary coverage of elementary and intermediate Spanish textbooks used in U.S. universities, as well as the lexical characteristics of the words they contain. Concretely, glossaries from 16 textbooks were analyzed to determine the coverage of words found among the 3,000 most frequent words in Spanish, the length and concreteness of the words, and the development of these characteristics between elementary and intermediate textbooks. Results indicate that textbook vocabulary generally does not represent the most frequent words in Spanish and that words in intermediate textbooks are significantly longer and less concrete than words in elementary textbooks. According to these findings, language program directors and teachers should complement textbook glossaries with words drawn from the 3,000 most frequent words of the target language as well as incorporate techniques that ease the learning burden of long and abstract words. This analysis can also guide textbook authors on how to improve vocabulary selection for their textbooks.

Jamie Rankin

der|die|das: Integrating Vocabulary Acquisition Research into an L2 German Curriculum

While there has been broad consensus in L2 research regarding the importance of learning L2 vocabulary, and that high-frequency vocabulary should be the primary focus of that learning at the outset of L2 development, both priorities are strikingly absent from current L2 textbooks on the market. This is true both in terms of the vocabulary items presented (which bear astonishingly little resemblance to the ranked frequency lists now available), and the ways that the textbooks provide (or fail to provide) focused study and systematic review of vocabulary in general. This chapter describes a collaborative project that was designed to address this problem. It narrates the development of a lexically focused curriculum for Beginning German at the college and university level that bases its core (i.e., active) vocabulary on a recently published frequency list of German (Jones & Tschirner, 2006) and describes how the presentation and review mechanisms were designed to reflect recent research on vocabulary acquisition and retention. The intention is not to argue that this particular curriculum should serve as a model, but rather to provide a window into the process of integrating research and instructional *praxis* in a relatively neglected domain of foreign language curriculum development.

Nina Vyatkina

Language Corpora for L2 Vocabulary Learning: Data-Driven Learning Across the Curriculum

Empirical Instructed Second Language Acquisition research on L2 vocabulary has shown that Data-Driven Learning (DDL), or teaching and learning languages with the help of corpora (large, structured electronic collections of texts), is beneficial for L2 vocabulary acquisition. Nevertheless, it is still far from becoming a common pedagogical practice, not least because few pedagogical manuals and user-friendly corpus tutorials have been published to date. This chapter describes how DDL with an open-access German language corpus has been used across the curriculum in a German Studies program at a North American university. I report empirical results and present specific pedagogical suggestions and activities for using a corpus to enhance L2 vocabulary knowledge at all proficiency levels and show how DDL can help learners improve not only the breadth of their L2 vocabulary knowledge (the number of words the basic meaning of which the learner knows) but also the depth of this knowledge, including collocations, frequency, and grammatical patterns. Although this chapter uses a German program as a case study, its pedagogical suggestions can be applied to teaching any language for which open-access electronic corpora are available.

Alla Zareva

Setting the Lexical EAP Bar for ESL Students: Lexical Complexity of L2 Academic Presentations

This study was conducted with three primary goals in mind: (1) to determine how the academic presentations of native speaking (L1) college students and English-as-a–second- or subsequent-language (L2) users compared in their lexical complexity profiles; (2) to establish guiding baselines of several measures associated with lexical complexity, which includes lexical density, lexical sophistication, and lexical diversity as subcomponents of its three-dimensional framework; and (3) to determine the relationship among the subcomponents. The study was based on two corpora of L1 and L2 academic presentations ($N = 70$) delivered by individuals during regular classes. The analyses allowed us to establish not only the common lexical complexity ground shared by the L1 and L2 presentations but also some typical lexical baselines that both L2 learners and instructors should monitor in courses focused on the use of language for academic purposes. The findings are discussed in light of their pedagogical implications for language programs that include in their curricula and assessments the development of presentational competence in a foreign language.

Joe Barcroft

The Input-Based Incremental Approach to Vocabulary in Meaning-Oriented Instruction for Language Program Directors and Teachers

The tenets of input-based incremental (IBI) vocabulary instruction (Barcroft, 2012) include (a) planning for vocabulary-learning opportunities; (b) presenting target words as input in particular ways while considering research findings and theoretical advances on lexical input processing; (c) specifying how different types of tasks promote different types of processing and, in turn, different aspects of vocabulary knowledge; (d) respecting the incremental nature of developing vocabulary knowledge; and (e) promoting learning of all aspects of vocabulary knowledge, including language-specific meanings and usage, over time. This chapter explains how language program directors (LPDs) and instructors can integrate the IBI approach within programs of meaning-oriented instruction in order to increase vocabulary learning in a theoretically grounded and evidence-based manner. The first section of the chapter reviews how meaning-oriented approaches provide necessary ingredients for successful L2 acquisition. The second section reviews some background issues related to what it means to "know" vocabulary. The third section summarizes the specific proposals of the IBI approach to vocabulary instruction, followed in the fourth section by examples of research findings that support them. The fifth section explains how IBI proposals can be seamlessly integrated into language programs focused on meaning, such as communicative language teaching and task-based instruction. The sixth section presents concrete lesson plans that demonstrate the integration of the IBI approach in meaning-oriented lessons at different levels of L2 proficiency. The seventh and final section provides six recommendations for LPDs and teachers on how to incorporate IBI vocabulary instruction within the multiple levels of a language program.

Introduction
Vocabulary Learning and Teaching: Variables, Relationships, Materials, and Curriculum Development

Peter Ecke, The University of Arizona
Susanne Rott, The University of Illinois at Chicago

Vocabulary acquisition is an indispensable part of second language acquisition (L2). It is crucial in the development of overall language proficiency and subskills, such as listening, reading, speaking, and writing (Nation, 2013). Learners and teachers of languages will intuitively agree with Wilkins' (1972) frequently cited statement that "while without grammar very little can be conveyed, without vocabulary nothing can be conveyed" (pp. 111–112). Since Wilkins' statement 45 years ago, the learning of words in another language has become a vibrant and interdisciplinary research area. Subsequent linguistic, cognitive, sociocultural, and classroom-focused studies have brought to light the multidimensional nature of vocabulary learning, knowledge, and use.

Yet, Schmitt (2008) has cautioned that many L2 learners are not aware of the complexity of word knowledge and equate learning a new word merely with learning its spoken and written L2 form and its word meaning. Such a limited understanding of the learning task likely confines students' focus to pronunciation, spelling, and L1 to L2 correspondences, thereby diminishing the time and effort they spend on learning words.

What is it that L2 learners need to learn of a specific word?

Although lexical research has resulted in many insights about the learning of L2 words, a theoretically grounded and evidence-based framework to effectively integrate lexical development in an L2 curriculum is still lacking. Nevertheless, most lexical researchers subscribe to a set of empirical findings that testify, in particular, to the challenge of developing a functional lexicon in an instructed learning environment. A functional lexicon generally refers to the ability to access and retrieve words automatically for comprehending and producing ideas in all four modalities. Such an advanced fluency requires knowledge of multiple aspects of word knowledge that Nation (2001) described as follows:

Word form includes:

- the spoken form (pronunciation), written form (spelling), and word parts (e.g., prefixes and suffixes).

Word meaning includes:

- the availability of the context-specific meaning of a word form (e.g., *file* refers to organizing papers in the context of paperwork, whereas *file* refers to a surface-smoothing tool in the context of fixing or building something);
- the knowledge of concept and referents (e.g., in English the concept of *riding* includes the riding of a horse, bike, and bus); and
- the ability to access associations of words that could be used in a particular context (angry, irate, furious, outraged).

Word use includes the understanding of:

- grammatical functions (e.g., the verb *love* always requires an object, whereas the construction *in love* does not, and if an object is used with the latter the preposition *with* is required);
- conventionalized expressions, such as collocations (one *rides a bike* and does not **drive a bike*); and
- constraints in usage (*a priori* is used in written texts and less in oral discourse).

How much of a vocabulary do L2 learners have to learn?

Researchers and practitioners agree that L2 students need to learn thousands of words in order to become functionally proficient in a language. However, researchers have yet to provide empirical evidence for how many words L2 learners must learn in order to acquire advanced language abilities for specific languages. Research-based estimates for L2 English provide a general idea of what vocabulary knowledge could be required for certain tasks. Corpus studies suggest that 8,000–9,000 word families are necessary for comprehending academic texts in English (Hazenberg & Hulstijn, 1996), while 5,000–7,000 words may be sufficient for oral discourse (Nation, 2006). Although some of the words for reading and oral discourse might overlap, many might not because certain words are only used in written discourse and colloquialisms are only encountered in oral interaction. Thus, it is still quite unclear how many words learners of languages other than English need to know in order to reach a certain proficiency level. Research that correlates L2 learners' overall language proficiency or proficiency in specific language skills with vocabulary knowledge (see Tschirner, Hacking, and Rubio, this volume) may generate data that could allow for more refined estimates of the word knowledge that is needed at different proficiency levels. Such data will help language program directors specify the vocabulary knowledge that L2 learners are expected to achieve within their programs and curricula.

What are the challenges that L2 learners encounter when learning new words?

One aspect that complicates the calculation of how many words or word families need to be learned is the fact that many words have multiple meanings (polysemy) and many words are used in conventionalized multiword expressions (e.g., collocations, lexical phrases, and phraseologisms etc.). When L2 users encounter words in new contexts, knowing the core meaning of a word is not sufficient, in particular if there is no literal correspondence in any of the other languages they know. For example, if the salesperson in a coffee shop asks, "Room?" the question is not whether the coffee should be charged to the room or whether the coffee should be brought to a specific room, but rather whether the cup should be filled to the brim or if there should be *room for milk*. In other words, L2 learners also have to learn the sociopragmatic meaning of *room*. *Room* not only refers to the walled, physical space in a building but also to the space at the top of a coffee mug. Similarly, the context of use determines the meaning of a word, such as for the phrasal verb *put down*. Students might first learn this phrase's core meaning of physical placement, as in *put the fork down* (place the fork on the table) or *put the baby down* (put the baby in the crib to sleep), before learning its metaphorical extensions, such as *put the dog down* (euthanize the dog) or *put someone down* (talk negatively about them). For learners of English, the task is to expand and refine the meaning of the multiword form *put down*. In contrast, native speakers of English who are learning another language might need to learn word forms for which the form–meaning pair overlaps between their L1 and the L2. English learners of L2 German, for example, can frequently rely on such a correspondence. Both languages have corresponding verbal forms for the physical placement of *putting down*. Germans use the verb *hinlegen* for the context of *putting down the baby and the fork*. In contrast, they use *einschläfern* in the context of euthanizing a dog and *herabsetzen* for talking negatively about a person. Boogards (2001) demonstrated that the learning effort is higher for learning a new form as compared to learning an additional meaning for an already familiar form. That is, depending on the L1, other languages a student knows, and the target L2, the learning effort required for individual polysemous words can vary widely. Determining which of the conventionalized expressions are congruent between the L1(s) and the target language is mostly unpredictable for learners.

Nonetheless, L2 learners start acquiring individual word forms by automatically adopting one meaning that they assume corresponds to a translation equivalent from the L1 or another L2 (Hall & Ecke, 2003). While this assumption will often be correct, it can lead to the construction of erroneous lexical representations if there is no equivalence, or no precise equivalence, in meaning or in the grammatical function of the word pairs in question (Hall, Newbrand, Ecke, Sperr,

Marchand, & Hayes, 2009; Jiang, this volume). Formal similarity of new words with known L1 or L2 words (as in cognates or false cognates/false friends) will often strengthen learners' postulation of meaning equivalence (Hall, 2002). This will make it relatively easy to learn cognates, but it can also lead to errors if there is a difference in meaning and/or grammatical specification between the word pairs perceived as equivalents. For example, the Spanish word *tuna* does not refer to the fish *tuna* as in English but to the cactus species *prickly pear*. The German verb *warten* (wait) does not subcategorize the preposition *für* (for) as in English *waiting for*. Instead, it requires the preposition *auf* (on). Such cases of partial similarity and difference are predestined to cause problems for L2 learners. Models of L2 vocabulary acquisition have sketched out the underlying processes that affect success or failure in the learning of new individual words in second and subsequently learned languages as well as the role played by formerly established lexical representations from L1 and L2 in the acquisition process (e.g., Ecke, 2015; Hall & Ecke, 2003; Jiang, 2000). Learners detect and use similarity between new and known words and use this similarity effectively to reduce the learning burden. Based on partial similarity, they assume overall equivalence, which will help them build and use temporary representations but may also result in the construction and use of deviant lexical structures (errors). While textbooks frequently explain how useful cognates are for comprehending and using the target language, they generally neglect to point out that learners need to attend to congruent, partially congruent, and incongruent aspects between the target language and other languages they know. Providing students the tools to notice word aspects helps them to learn words more effectively.

For efficient learning (and encoding in memory) a thorough understanding of the letter-sound correspondences of the target language is crucial. Gardner (2013) has provided the example of learning the French word for appetizer *hors d'oeuvres*. He explains that if learners are not familiar with the French letter-sound correspondence they might encode the word as *horse devors* instead of using the correct pronunciation *ordurves*. If the word is initially encoded incorrectly, restructuring to accommodate the correct pronunciation will require additional learning effort. Meanwhile, learners might miss valuable input opportunities to strengthen the lexical entry in long-term memory. Likewise, learners' incorrect pronunciation might lead to miscommunication. Consequently, an early focus on the letter-sound correspondence of the L2 can help students encode and learn words independently.

How do L2 learners successfully acquire thousands of words?

Considering the large number of words that L2 learners need to master, the general assumption is that students need to become independent learners by either immersing themselves into the target culture through study abroad (e.g., Kinginger, 2013), engaging in mass reading (e.g., Luppescu & Day, 1993), or watching TV shows (e.g., Peters, 2018). The three types of language immersion, however, can only be fruitful if learners have a basic vocabulary they can draw on (e.g., Grabe & Stoller, 2002) to comprehend the majority of the input and infer the meanings of unfamiliar word forms. For the comprehension of written texts, the ballpark figure that has generally been accepted as a baseline vocabulary is 3,000 word families (Nation, 2006). The advantage of learning words in natural use contexts and thereby encountering and processing multiple form, meaning, and use patterns (Nation, 2001) can be offset by the need to frequently encounter and process a given word. Repeated, long-term exposure to new words can be enhanced through explicit learning exercises using targeted instructional materials. In order to maximize learning time spent on each word, it is useful to create varied materials that target the learning of specific word aspects most useful for each word. The aspect of fluency (in comprehension and production) should play an important role in teaching and materials design, because fluency requires repeated practice opportunities.

What are the challenges for L2 vocabulary teaching and program development?

It becomes obvious that language program directors have to keep many specific linguistic and learning aspects in mind when outlining an effective lexical curriculum. Therefore, choosing a textbook for a language program sequence can only be the starting point for building a goal-oriented program. Obviously many textbooks are written for a generic learner population with general learning goals. Yet student populations are becoming increasingly diverse. Students might know multiple languages, have studied abroad, have friends who speak the target language, or, in turn, might not have any experience with the target language community at all. Also, the length of study can vary widely among students. While some students might just start as beginners in the program, others might have studied the target language previously in other learning settings. Although previous learning experiences cannot predict future learning, there is certainly a difference between learners who start completely anew with a language and learners who can reactivate some words, grammar, pronunciation, reading, speaking, and writing experiences. Naturally, a diverse student population potentially leads to a set of varied learning goals, such as for career advancement, a specific profession, travel, heritage exploration, or academic study. Consequently, decisions need to be made about which words to teach and which word aspect(s) to focus on first.

Few textbooks distinguish between words that mainly serve comprehension purposes and need to be known receptively and words that need to be learned for productive use. Instead, normally all words are treated equally in L1–L2 word pair lists. Thematic sets of words are often chosen because of topics that serve the learning of a particular grammatical structure. For example, in German the learning of reflexive verbs is frequently introduced with the topic of daily hygiene, a topic with very low communicative relevance because shaving, showering, and putting on lotion and makeup are rarely discussed in public and with people who are not close acquaintances. Likewise, textbooks usually do not address word learning strategies for students who already speak multiple languages. Accordingly, Nation (2007) has pointed out that teachers and curriculum developers need to fine-tune learning affordances provided in textbooks and create lexical assignments that target a specific student population and institution-specific program goals.

What is the contribution of this volume?

Given the essential nature of vocabulary in language learning and use and the magnitude of the lexical learning task, it seems surprising that none of the 28 past volumes of *Issues in Language Program Direction* have focused on vocabulary learning and teaching in second language programs. We will fill this gap with this volume and a series of contributions that present research findings to a broad audience that goes beyond researchers working in the field of vocabulary acquisition. Like previous AAUSC volumes, this collection of articles is addressed primarily to language program directors, teacher trainers, graduate students, teaching assistants, and language teachers as well as second language textbook authors and material developers. The volume provides insights into vocabulary learning mechanisms and discusses how these insights are relevant to improved vocabulary development, classroom teaching, material and textbook design, and curriculum development. The studies in this volume provide only a glimpse into the lexical research work that lies ahead.

We have grouped the nine contributions into two (related) parts: (a) Vocabulary Learning and Use: Variables and Relationships and (b) Vocabulary Teaching, Materials, and Curricula. In the first chapter, "Semantic Development and L2 Vocabulary Teaching," Nan Jiang explains what the process of developing a new semantic system involves. Using error examples from learners of Chinese and other languages, he demonstrates how challenging it is to assign the correct meaning to new L2 word forms. He shows in what ways the L1 and L2 semantic systems may differ, explains how the L1 system will often interfere with the development of an L2 system, and provides suggestions for pedagogical strategies that instructors may use to facilitate the assignment of meaning to new L2 word forms.

In the second chapter, "Supporting Your Brain Learning Words," Ulf Schuetze discusses how vocabulary learning is affected by memory, selective attention, and the senses. He reviews relevant research findings from cognitive psychology, neuropsychology, and applied linguistics, and based on these, provides suggestions for effective vocabulary learning and teaching.

In the third chapter, Maria Rogahn, Denisa Bordag, Amit Kirschenbaum, and Erwin Tschirner present the empirical study "Minor Manipulations Matter: Syntactic Position Influences the Effectiveness of Incidental Vocabulary Acquisition During L2 Reading." The study investigates how a word's position in a sentence may affect incidental vocabulary learning through reading. It reveals an acquisition advantage for the meanings of new words that appear as subjects in main clauses compared to those that appear as objects in subordinate clauses in German as an L2. The finding has important implications for material development and effective vocabulary presentation: presenting new to-be-learned words in subject position is likely to be more effective than presenting them in less prominent positions in a sentence.

In the fourth chapter, "The Relationship Between Reading Proficiency and Vocabulary Size: An Empirical Investigation," Erwin Tschirner, Jane Hacking, and Fernando Rubio investigate the relationship between the reading proficiency and vocabulary knowledge of L2 learners of German, Russian, and Spanish. They found that the Advanced Mid/Advanced High levels of reading proficiency at the ACTFL scale were associated with a vocabulary size of 4,000 to 5,000 words for all three languages, far fewer than the 8,000 to 9,000 words that vocabulary researchers commonly assume to be necessary at this level (Nation, 2006). The finding is encouraging, as it implies that knowing 4,000–5,000 words at the end of a four-semester course sequence may be sufficient for students to comprehend a wide variety of texts. The authors recommend that language program directors provide a well-articulated sequence of vocabulary learning objectives throughout beginning, intermediate, and advanced-level courses and that the first courses should focus on the teaching of the 1,000 most frequent words.

In the fifth chapter, "Vocabulary Coverage and Lexical Characteristics in L2 Spanish Textbooks," Claudia Sánchez-Gutiérrez, Nausica Marcos Miguel, and Michael K. Olsen demonstrate that current textbooks are far from providing the adequate, articulated, and frequency-oriented approach to vocabulary teaching that is recommended by Tschirner et al. in chapter four. Sánchez-Gutiérrez and colleagues analyzed glossaries from 16 Spanish textbooks to determine the books' coverage of the 3,000 most frequent words in Spanish, the length and concreteness of the included words, and how these attributes varied between elementary and intermediate textbooks. Whereas words in intermediate textbooks were shown to be significantly longer and less concrete than words in elementary textbooks, thereby demonstrating a reasonable progression in complexity, the textbooks (at both levels) did a poor job presenting learners with the 1,000 most frequent Spanish words. The study is a call for textbook authors and language program directors to take word frequency seriously and as a guiding criterion for the selection and presentation of vocabulary in teaching materials.

Like the authors of the previous chapter, Jamie Rankin in chapter six is concerned with the inadequate provision of high-frequency words, this time, however, in German textbooks (see Lipinski, 2010). In "*der|die|das*: Integrating Vocabulary Acquisition Research into an L2 German Curriculum" Rankin describes a collaborative project that addresses the lack of high-frequency words in textbooks. In the project, the student and teacher participants develop a lexically focused curriculum for beginning German that selects its core vocabulary from a frequency list of German (Jones & Tschirner, 2006). It also describes how the presentation and review mechanisms were designed and informed by research on vocabulary acquisition and retention. It is an example of how vocabulary research may inform and reform instructional praxis and L2 curriculum development.

Nina Vyatkina's contribution in chapter seven is another example of how research-informed (data-driven) learning can be integrated into language program curricula. In "Language Corpora for L2 Vocabulary Learning: Data-Driven Learning Across the Curriculum" the author describes how learning with an open access German language corpus has been used across the curriculum in a German Studies program at a U.S. university. She reports empirical results that show how data-driven learning can help learners improve the breadth and depth of their L2 vocabulary knowledge. She also suggests pedagogical activities with corpora to enhance L2 vocabulary knowledge at different proficiency levels. Although she uses a German program as a case study, her pedagogical suggestions can be applied to the teaching of any language for which open access corpora are available.

In chapter eight, "Setting the Lexical EAP Bar for ESL Students: Lexical Complexity of L2 Academic Presentations," Alla Zareva investigates the productive vocabulary of very advanced learners of English as a second language and how this vocabulary compares to that of L1 users. She explores what constitutes lexical complexity and to what extent its subcomponents—lexical density, lexical sophistication, and lexical diversity—are related in the vocabulary of academic presentations. Zareva finds that the lexical complexity of the L2 learners and L1 users under investigation is similar and that each of the subcomponents of lexical complexity adds unique information to the overall lexical complexity profiles of student presentations. She recommends the three-dimensional approach to lexical complexity as well as the use of free software to assess lexical complexity for learners, teachers, and material developers.

In chapter nine, "The Input-Based Incremental Approach to Vocabulary in Meaning-Oriented Instruction for Language Program Directors and Teachers," Joe Barcroft describes the tenets of input-based incremental (IBI) vocabulary instruction (Barcroft, 2012). These include (a) planning for vocabulary-learning opportunities; (b) presenting target words as input in particular ways while considering research findings and theoretical advances on lexical input processing; (c) specifying how different types of tasks promote different types of processing and, in turn, different aspects of vocabulary knowledge; (d) respecting the incremental nature of developing vocabulary knowledge; and (e) promoting learning of all aspects of vocabulary knowledge, including language-specific meanings and usage, over time. This chapter explains how language program directors and instructors can integrate the IBI approach in their programs to increase vocabulary learning in a theoretically grounded and evidence-based manner.

We hope that the contributions of this volume will spark reflection and discussion among researchers, program directors, teachers, and graduate students and contribute to the implementation of research-informed practices in curriculum design, material development, and the teaching and learning of second language vocabulary.

References

Barcroft, J. (2012). *Input-based incremental vocabulary instruction.* Alexandria, VA: TESOL International.

Boogards, P. (2001). Lexical units and the learning of foreign language vocabulary. *Studies in Second Language Acquisition, 23,* 321–343.

Ecke, P. (2015). Parasitic vocabulary acquisition, cross-linguistic influence, and lexical retrieval in multilinguals. *Bilingualism: Language and Cognition, 18,* 145–162.

Gardner, D. (2013). *Exploring vocabulary: Language in action.* New York, NY: Routledge.

Grabe, W., & Stoller, F. L. (2002). *Teaching and researching reading.* Harlow, UK: Longman.

Hall, C. J. (2002). The automatic cognate form assumption: Evidence for the Parasitic Model of vocabulary development. *International Review of Applied Linguistics, 40,* 69–87.

Hall, C. J., & Ecke, P. (2003). Parasitism as a default mechanism in vocabulary acquisition. In J. Cenoz, B. Hufeisen, & U. Jessner (Eds.), *The multilingual lexicon* (pp. 71–85). Dordrecht, Netherlands: Kluwer.

Hall, C. J., Newbrand, D., Ecke, P., Sperr, U., Marchand, V., & Hayes, L. (2009). Learners' implicit assumptions about syntactic frames in new L3 words: The role of cognates, typological proximity and L2 status. *Language Learning, 59,* 153–202.

Hazenberg, S., & Hulstijn, J. H. (1996). Defining a minimal receptive second-language vocabulary for non-native university students: An empirical investigation. *Applied Linguistics, 17,* 145–163.

Jiang, N. (2000). Lexical representation and development in a second language. *Applied Linguistics, 21,* 47–77.

Jones, R. L., & Tschirner, E. (2006). *Frequency dictionary of German.* London, United Kingdom: Routledge.

Kinginger, C. (2013). Identity and language learning in study abroad. *Foreign Language Annals, 46,* 339–358.

Lipinski, S. (2010). A frequency analysis of vocabulary in three first-year textbooks of German. *Die Unterrichtspraxis, 43,* 167–174.

Luppescu, S., & Day, R. R. (1993). Reading, dictionaries, and vocabulary learning. *Language Learning, 43,* 263–287.

Nation, I. S. P. (2001). *Learning vocabulary in another language.* Cambridge, UK: Cambridge University Press.

Nation, I. S. P. (2006). How large a vocabulary is needed for reading and listening? *Canadian Modern Language Review, 63,* 59–82.

Nation, I. S. P. (2007). The four strands. *Innovation in Language Learning and Teaching, 1,* 2–13.

Nation, I. S. P. (2013). *Learning vocabulary in another language* (2nd ed.). Cambridge, UK: Cambridge University Press.

Peters, E. (2018). The effect of out-of-class exposure to English language media on learners' vocabulary knowledge. *International Journal of Applied Linguistics, 169,* 142–168.

Schmitt, N. (2008). Instructed second language vocabulary learning. *Language Teaching Research, 12,* 329–363.

Wilkins, D. (1972). *Linguistics in language teaching.* London, UK: Arnold.

Chapter 1
Semantic Development and L2 Vocabulary Teaching

Nan Jiang, University of Maryland

Introduction

From a psycholinguistic perspective, vocabulary learning involves three cognitive processes: (1) the establishment of a lexical entry in the learner's mental lexicon for a word; (2) the incorporation of accurate information about a word's form, meaning, and syntactic properties in the lexical entry; and (3) the development of the ability to access the lexical entry automatically. The first process enables a learner to recognize a visual or auditory input as a word, the second process allows a learner to use a word accurately and appropriately, and the third process lets a learner use a word efficiently in spontaneous communication.

From a pedagogical perspective, these also represent the tasks a teacher faces in vocabulary teaching in a second language (L2). A teacher has to help learners (1) create a working vocabulary that fits a student's need (i.e., help establish sufficient lexical entries) and (2) develop the ability to use the vocabularies accurately, appropriately, and automatically.

A central aspect of vocabulary learning is to understand the meanings of a word accurately. The importance of adequate semantic development is obvious, as one cannot use an L2 word accurately without an accurate understanding of its meaning. For example, a Chinese learner of English as a second language (ESL) will have difficulty in using the English words *hat* and *cap* accurately if he or she does not know how they differ semantically. However, research suggests that semantic development can be a long and slow process. Even many advanced learners may not understand the meanings of some high-frequency words accurately. Many factors such as learning strategies, L2 proficiency, form overlap, and cognate status may affect semantic development in L2 (e.g., Elgort & Warren, 2014; Hall, 2002; Laufer, 1990; Nassaji, 2003). In this chapter, I focus on the role of first language (L1) semantic structures in L2 semantic development. I begin with a discussion of the complex semantic relationships between languages, go on to review research on L2 semantic development with a particular attention to how L1–L2 semantic differences affect this development, and end with a discussion of pedagogical strategies that may facilitate semantic development in classroom instruction.

Complex Semantic Relationship across Languages

Every language has a unique semantic system underlying its lexical system that reflects its linguistic and cultural heritage. Hence, when any two languages are considered, a complex picture of semantic overlap emerges. There are cases where the concept or meaning underlying a word in one language and its translation in another may be identical, particularly in the case of typologically or historically related languages. However, such complete overlap of meaning is usually an exception rather than a norm. Instead, a word in one language may have no counterpart in another, reflecting the presence of a lexicalized meaning that is unique to the former. A word in one language may differ significantly or subtly in meaning with its closest translation in another, or a semantic distinction may be made in one language but not in another. I outline five patterns of semantic overlap between languages from the perspective of an L2 learner before discussing the significance of such differences for vocabulary learning.

New meanings.

A meaning may be lexicalized in one language but not in another. This difference often reflects the linguistic and cultural heritages of a language. Numerous examples can be found in any language. The Chinese word *qing* refers to a color that lies between blue and green, but the color may not be lexicalized in other languages. The Chinese verb *chao* denotes a method of preparing Chinese dishes such as *chow mein* (chow = chao; mein = noodle). This does not have an English counterpart, so Yuen Ren Chao had to create the English compound *stir-fry* for his wife, Buwei Yang Chao, when she was writing her book *How to Cook and Eat in Chinese* (Yang Chao, 1945). There are many such meanings lexicalized in Chinese but not in English, such as *yuebing* (moon cake), *yaoguai* (monster-like creatures), *jianghu* (sometimes used to refer to a fictional community of kung fu warriors such as depicted in the movie *Crouching Tiger*). On the flip side, the meanings of humor, logic, and romance were not lexicalized in Chinese until they were borrowed as loanwords into Chinese as *youmo*, *luoji*, and *langman*, respectively. (The first of these was coined by the Chinese writer Yutang Lin in 1924.) Likewise, English words such as *fun*, *smirk*, and *fancy* do not find ready translations in many other languages. All these examples illustrate unique lexicalized meanings in a language.

From an L2 learner's perspective, this means the presence of L2 words that do not have a direct translation in the learner's L1. Vocabulary learning under such circumstances entails the learning of a new meaning or concept.

New distinctions.

A semantic distinction may be made in one language but not in another. For example, the two English nouns *criterion* and *standard* are usually translated into *biaozhun* in Chinese, representing a semantic distinction made in English but not in Chinese. More examples include English pairs such as *problem/question, suspect/doubt, real/true, begin/start*. On the flip side, some semantic distinctions are made in Chinese but not in English, as seen in pairs of Chinese words that are usually translated into a single English word, such as *zhichi/zhicheng* (support), *sunhai/sunhuai* (damage), and *shushu/jiujiu* (uncle). The first two of these examples illustrate the abstract/concrete distinction made in Chinese but not in English, such that the first member of the pair refers to an abstract meaning (such as support one's decision or damage a relationship) and the second member to a concrete meaning (such as support a falling wall or damage a piece of furniture). The last example illustrates a distinction made in the very complicated Chinese kinship term system with the former referring to one's father's brother and the latter to one's mother's brother. Similar examples include Dutch word pair *zetten/leggen* (both meaning *put*), French word pair *balle/ballon* (both meaning *ball*), and the Spanish pair *rincón/esquina* (both meaning *corner*) for English speakers, and the English word pair *language/tongue* (both meaning *kieli* in Finnish), and *interfere/interrupt* (both meaning *lehafria* in Hebrew). A new distinction does not have to be always binary. For example, the English words *male* and *female* are used to refer to humans, animals, and plants, but there are three Chinese counterparts for each of them: *male = nan, xiong, gong; female = nü, ci, mu* because different words have to be used to describe human beings, animals, and plants in Chinese.

These examples illustrate cases where two or more meanings are differentiated in one language but not in another, at least at the lexicosemantic level. From a learner's perspective, such cases call for the development of new distinctions at both the lexical and semantic levels. Learning the forms of two new words, for example, *criterion* and *standard*, is relatively easy, but knowing how the two words differ in meaning can be very challenging.

Partial overlap or semantic crossovers.

Two or more meanings in one language may partially overlap with two or more meanings in another language such that they cover similar semantic space, but the space is carved differently in two languages. This can be best illustrated in object classification. Chinese tends to classify objects by function, while English does so by shape. Thus, the Chinese word *bi* refers to all instruments used to write, draw, or paint, including what is usually referred to as a brush in English, that is, brushes for painting. Both Chinese and English distinguish a bottle (*ping*) from a bucket (*tong*), but the same object, for example, the five-gallon water bottle, is often referred to as a bottle in English but as a *tong* (bucket) in Chinese. A further example of how the same set of containers were classified and named differently in English, Spanish, and Chinese can be found in Malt, Sloman, Gennari, Shi, and Wang (1999) and Malt, Sloman, and Gennari (2003). Such partial overlaps also exist in other semantic domains. For example, the German words *auf*, *an*, and *über* seem to cover the same semantic space of six English expressions: *on*, *upon*, *onto*, *on top of*, *over*, and *above* (Ijaz, 1986).

Where some semantic crossovers exist, L2 learners have to restructure the semantic space of individual words so that it becomes consistent with that of native speakers (NS) of the target language.

Developed domain.
Languages may also differ in how well developed a semantic domain is. A well-developed semantic domain contains many subtle semantic distinctions. For example, there are a few dozen verbs in English that can express the basic meaning of human movement on foot, that is, walk, but they are differentiated in the manner of walking, such as *toddle* (child, unsteady steps), *limp* (foot hurt, unsteady steps), *trudge* (heavy steps), *march* (even steps), *shuffle* (sad), *swagger* (proud), *hasten* (fast), *edge* (slow), and *wander* (without aim). Thus, semantic distinctions are made on the basis of step, attitude, speed, and aim in English. Still finer distinctions may exist among *wander*, *stroll*, *saunter*, *roam*, *amble*, and *ramble* as a set and *waddle*, *hobble*, *toddle*, *stumble*, *falter*, *limp*, and *stagger* as another even when they share the meaning of aimless walking and unsteady steps, respectively. In Chinese, all these would be translated into a single verb *zou*. The manner of movement has to be indicated by an adverbial phrase. On the flip side, for the meaning of hold or carry, which is a less developed semantic domain in English, Chinese has more than ten verbs that are differentiated based on which part of the body is involved in holding or the positional relationship between the object and the body, for example, *tuo* (palm), *ding* (head), *bao* (both hands), *na* (one hand), *kang* (shoulder, over), kua (shoulder, under), *bei* (back).

From an L2 learner's perspective, semantic development under such circumstances involves the development of a rich network of related meanings that are differentiated and lexicalized in a way not instantiated in the L1.

Idiosyncratic differences.
When the basic meanings are shared between a translation pair, sometimes certain peculiar difference may exist along a semantic dimension. For example, the Chinese word *huiyi* can be best translated as *meeting* in English, and *kaihui* as *have a meeting*. However, a meeting can take place between two people in English, but it takes three or more people to *kaihui*: two people have a talk, not a meeting, in Chinese. For another example, the English word *leader* is often translated into *lingdao* in Chinese, but *lingdao* always refers to a person who leads, thus with a semantic feature of [+HUMAN]. A leader in English can be a mother duck followed by her ducklings or a section of a fishing line that connects

the hook or lure with the main line. The most interesting example I can find is the Chinese word *shafa*, which is a direct borrowing from *sofa* in English. While *sofa* usually refers to an upholstered seating for two or more people (otherwise it is a chair), the Chinese *shafa* includes an upholstered seat for one person as well, so the meaning of [+MULTIPLE PROPLE] is lost. Because of the high degree of semantic overlap between members of such translation pairs, these peculiar differences often go unnoticed.

These differences are not always arbitrary in that they reflect the linguistic and sociolinguistic characteristics of individual languages. For example, the broader meaning of the word *leader* is related to the fact that it is a derivation from the verb *lead*, which has a very broad meaning (e.g., 24 senses listed at dictionary.com). Its Chinese translation is a verb–verb compound whose component verbs usually take a human as its agent. At the same time, these semantic differences are idiosyncratic in the sense that they occur at an unexpected semantic conjuncture from a learner's perspective or are often difficult to be described systematically.

While by no means exhaustive, these five patterns represent a majority of semantic relationships between two languages at the lexical level that an L2 learner faces in learning L2 words. With such differences in mind, semantic development refers to the process whereby a learner's semantic representation for an L2 word increasingly approximates that of NS of the target language, which is necessary for effective communication with NS. This may mean the development of a new concept or meaning, the learning of a new distinction, the remapping of the semantic space, or the fine adjustment of the specific semantic features associated with a word.

Evidence for and Causes of Slow Semantic Development

Even though semantic development has received relatively less attention in second language acquisition (SLA) research in comparison to the acquisition of other aspects of language, there is already quite consistent evidence showing that semantic development can be a slow and long process in adult L2 learning.

One line of evidence is the lexical errors L2 speakers make. Such errors are common in L2 performance in both classroom and experimental settings. In the former case, a Finnish speaker was found to use *language* instead of *tongue* in saying *He bit himself in the language* (Ringbom, 1983); Hebrew speakers were found to confuse between *interrupt* and *interfere* (Olshtain & Cohen, 1989); and Arabic speakers would use the word *oven* where *bakery* was appropriate, for example, *I go to the oven in the morning to buy bread* (Zughoul, 1991). All such errors have a semantic basis, as they involved a semantic distinction made in English but not in the learner's native language.

In one of the earliest experimental studies that was designed to specifically examine semantic development, Ijas (1986) explored the learning of six English expressions *on, upon, onto, on top of, over,* and *above* by German and Urdu ESL speakers. These latter languages do not make similar semantic distinctions as English does, such as the +/−movement distinction between *on* and *onto* or the +/− contact distinction between *on* and *over*. In a sentence completion task where the participants were asked to choose one of the six English words to complete a sentence, the ESL participants were found to have quite some difficulties in choosing the right word. For example, Urdu ESL speakers had considerable difficulty in differentiating *on* and *over*. The author attributed such non-native-like performance to the fact that such distinctions were not made in the participants' L1 and concluded that "native language conceptual patterns appear to be powerful determinants of the meaning ascribed to L2 words and they seem to be very rigid and difficult to permeate" (p. 447).

In two studies that employed a similar sentence completion task, NS of English and Chinese ESL speakers were asked to fill in the blank in a sentence by choosing between two English words that shared the same Chinese translation, such as *doubt* and *suspect* and *standard* and *criterion*. Two ESL speaker groups were tested: (1) those who were studying at an American university at the time of testing (Jiang, 2004a) and (2) those who had graduated from their graduate programs in the United States and were working as either professors or corporate employees (Jiang, 2007). The average length of residence in the United States was 2.7 and 10.5 years, respectively, for the two groups. The overall accuracy scores for the NS group and the two ESL groups were 94%, 65%, and 85%, respectively. The high accuracy shown by the English NS testified the validity of the test materials. The difference between the two ESL groups suggested that significant progress can be achieved with more experiences in the target language. At the same time, a statistically significant difference between the NS and the advanced ESL groups demonstrated that the development of native-like semantic structures, while achievable based on the trajectory shown in the data of the two ESL groups, takes a long time.

Another line of evidence can be found in the different patterns of performance between NS and L2 speakers where no error is involved. In Ijas (1986), for example, German ESL speakers considered *on* and *on top of* more closely related than English NS did. In Jiang (2002), Chinese ESL speakers considered two English words that shared the same Chinese translation to be more related in meaning than pairs that did not share the same translation, while English NS showed no difference on the same set of stimuli. In a study reported by Malt and Sloman (2003), NS and L2 speakers were compared in two tasks—object classification and object naming—involving two sets of objects: bottles and dishes. The results revealed considerable differences between L2 speakers and NS. Even the most experienced L2 group was significantly deviant from NS in their naming patterns for both sets of objects, and in their typicality rating scores for five of the six categories. A further example of non-native-like performance can be found in a study reported by Saji and Imai (2013). They tested learners of Chinese as an L2 whose native language was Korean or Japanese. These latter two languages have fewer "hold/carry" verbs than Chinese does, which means that some semantic distinctions made in Chinese were absent in these languages in this particular domain. The participants in the study were asked to watch a set of video clips and then write down the most appropriate Chinese verb for describing each action. The results showed that in comparison to adult NS, the L2 speakers used significantly fewer verbs, and they tended to use more general verbs, and verbs that had a translation in their L1s. These results indicated that they had not developed a native-like semantic structure in the domain.

The third line of evidence comes from experimental studies that employed reaction time as primary data. In two studies, where advanced ESL speakers were asked to judge whether two English words were related in meaning, they were found to respond to English word pairs faster when they shared the same L1 translations than when they had different translations, while English NS showed no such difference (Jiang, 2002, 2004b). One explanation of this finding was that an L2-specific distinction, such as between *double* and *suspect*, was not learned among these learners. As a result, both words were mapped to the same L1 meaning, *huaiyi* in the case of Chinese ESL speakers. As a result, the two English words shared the same semantic content, which led the L2 speakers to respond to such pairs faster in the semantic judgment task. In a study reported by Elston-Güttler and Williams (2008), German ESL speakers were asked to decide whether an ending word was appropriate to complete a sentence. The critical stimuli included sentences such as *His shoes were uncomfortable due to a bubble.* The correct response should be "no." However, the ending word *bubble* shared the same German translation *Blase* with the English word *blister*, which was appropriate for this sentence. These researchers found that German ESL speakers took longer to reject such ending words than words that did not share a German translation with an appropriate word. This finding also suggested a lack of new L2 semantic distinctions among these participants.

Further evidence for slow semantic development with or without specific references to L1 influence can also be found in studies reported by Schmitt (1998), Haastrup and Henriksen (2000), Paribakht (2005), and Gullberg (2009).

The studies reviewed above consider semantic development under various semantic overlap patterns, such as new distinctions (Elston-Güttler & Williams, 2008; Jiang, 2002, 2004a, 2004b, 2007; Zughoul, 1991), partial overlaps (Ijas, 1986; Malt & Sloman, 2003), and developed domain (Saji & Imai, 2013). The results were quite consistent: semantic development is limited even among advanced L2 speakers, and many L2 word forms continue to be mapped to L1 meanings.

Before any pedagogical strategies can be discussed, it is important to understand why semantic development is slow even when plenty of L2 input is available. There are at least three reasons. The paramount reason is the presence of an existing L1 semantic system. When an L2 word is first introduced to a learner, he or she is likely to understand its meaning within the existing semantic system. Regardless of the method used to convey the meaning, for example, by providing a translation, a picture, or a linguistic context, learners are more likely to find an existing meaning to be mapped with the new L2 lexical form rather than create a new meaning immediately. In this process, the learners may follow a semantic equivalence hypothesis, in Ijas' (1986) words, assuming that the meaning of an L2 word should be the same as that of its L1 translation. The initial mapping of L2 word form to L1 meaning has been widely recognized and documented (e.g., Blum & Levenston, 1978; Ellis, 1997; Giacobbe, 1992; Ringbom, 1983; Strick, 1980). It is the cornerstone of vocabulary acquisition models such as the parasitic model of vocabulary acquisition (Hall, 2002; Hall & Ecke, 2003; Ecke, 2015) and the psycholinguistic model of L2 lexical development of Jiang (2000).

Under such circumstances, semantic development does not only involve the learning of new meanings, but it also requires overcoming the initial form–meaning mappings or the modification of the existing semantic content to gradually approximate that of the target language. We may refer to this process as one of semantic restructuring. For example, an English-speaking learner of Chinese has to develop a new semantic distinction between concrete and abstract verbs while learning the Chinese words *zhichi* and *zhicheng*, both meaning support. Semantic restructuring also means adding a new semantic feature of [+HUMAN] while learning the Chinese word *lingdao*, thereby overcoming the initial mapping of the word to the meaning of the English word *leader* that does not have this feature. Thus, semantic development in adult L2 learning is essentially a process of semantic restructuring. As is the case with the learning of other aspects of language, for example, phonology, altering an existing mental representation may be more difficult than establishing a new one.

The second reason is the limited effectiveness of language input and experience for semantic restructuring under many circumstances. Language input may be a major driving force for the acquisition of syntactic knowledge (such as word order) and lexical knowledge (such as collocations) as it contains direct positive evidence for the target structures. It nevertheless is often less effective for semantic restructuring as it often lacks clear and powerful cues for indicating how an L2 word differs from its L1 translation in meaning or how two L2 words are semantically different. Because the basic meaning of an L2 word and its L1 translation is often the same, for example, the English word *bird* and its translation in another language, an L2 learner can use an L2 word successfully both receptively and productively by relying on the initial mapping to the L1 meaning. A Chinese ESL learner, for example, may become quite experienced and proficient in English without encountering any instance of this word being used to refer to a chicken, which is acceptable in English but not in Chinese (thus, the meaning of the Chinese translation of this word, *niao*, is semantically narrower).

Take the two English words *criterion* and *standard*, for another example. A Chinese ESL learner can successfully understand the meaning of both words within their existing semantic system, as the Chinese meaning of their shared translation *biaozhun* covers both meanings. It is difficult to imagine a linguistic context that would indicate how the two words differ in meaning or show that one word is appropriate and the other is not. As a final example, it took me more than 10 years of living in the United States to discover on my own that a meeting can take place between two people in the English context. All these examples illustrate cases in which L2 input does not contain powerful cues for L2 learners to discover L2-specific semantic structures. The limited usefulness of input or context for semantic development may be also seen in the low success rate for inferring word meaning based on context (e.g., Nassaji, 2003). Thus, increased L2 experiences do not automatically lead to semantic restructuring. Instead, they often reinforce the initial connection between L2 form and L1 meaning, which may be the reason why semantic development tends to fall far behind the development of other aspects of language among L2 speakers (e.g., Altenberg & Granger, 2001; Jiang, 2007).

Finally, semantic differences can be extremely complicated and subtle, which adds further difficulty to the daunting task of semantic restructuring. Take the pair *obvious* and *apparent*, for example. They may both refer to something that is easily perceivable and thus are semantically related, but they are not identical in that what is obvious is closer to being factual than what is apparent. This difference may lead English NS to prefer one over the other in some sentence context. For example, while developing test materials for a project, I asked 10 English NS to choose between the two words for a set of sentences. For the sentence, *there is also an _____ willingness, at least for now, to cross party lines to accomplish their goals*, seven of them preferred *apparent* over *obvious*, while the remaining three considered both words appropriate. However, under other circumstances, this difference may be less important so that the two words can be used interchangeably. This was reflected in the performance of the same 10 English NS for the sentence *despite his _____ affinity with his many beautiful subjects, Demarchelier claims not to understand women at all*. Three chose *obvious*, four chose *apparent*, and three accepted both as equally appropriate. To further complicate the matter, such semantic differences are often very difficult to articulate and explain for instructional purposes. For example, English NS intuitively know the differences between *criterion* and *standard*, but conveying the semantic differences to non-NS in a clear and convincing way is quite a different matter.

In sum, semantic development often involves altering the existing semantic structures so that L2 word forms become linked to L2-specific meanings. However, language input usually lacks clear and powerful cues to indicate how an L2 meaning is different from an L1 meaning or how two L2 words differ in meaning, particularly when semantic differences are very subtle. As a result, L2 experiences do not always automatically lead to successful semantic development.

Teacher Training and Pedagogical Considerations

Following this analysis, I want to propose that pedagogical intervention is particularly important for facilitating semantic restructuring and that the key to successful pedagogical intervention is to help learners see how the meanings between an L2 word and its L1 translation differ, or how the meanings of two L2 words differ. Knowledge of such differences, whether in an explicit or implicit form, will help trigger the process of semantic restructuring. The following discussion of pedagogical considerations is based on this premise.

Teachers' awareness and knowledge.
Successful semantic restructuring on the part of the learner begins with the awareness and knowledge of the semantic differences between a learner's L1 and the target language on the part of the teacher. A teacher should understand that it is quite common for a word and its translation to have subtle semantic differences. His or her knowledge of such differences between a learner's L1 and L2 is essential in facilitating semantic development through classroom explanation and material development. For example, such knowledge allows a teacher to anticipate where learners are likely to have difficulty and take pedagogical measures accordingly. Unfortunately, many L2 teachers do not know their learners' L1s or they face learners of mixed L1 backgrounds, particularly in an international setting such as ESL teaching in the United States. In this sense, these teachers are ill-equipped to help learners overcome the influence of their L1 semantic structures, which contributes to slow semantic restructuring.

However, even with little knowledge of a learner's L1, a meaning-conscious L2 teacher can develop a sense of how the two languages differ from the errors and inaccuracies in a learner's language use. When an English-speaker learner of Spanish uses *esquina* and *rincón* (both meaning *corner* in English) incorrectly and interchangeably, a Spanish teacher can make a reasonable guess that this pair may represent a new semantic distinction not present in English. The same is true if an ESL teacher finds a Russian ESL speaker to confuse between *scientist* and *scholar* (both sharing the Russian translation учёный). When a Chinese ESL speaker uses the word *brick* to refer to a tile in English or uses the word *pen* to refer to a painting brush, it is also reasonable to think that the two languages may differ in the classification of these objects with only partial overlap in meaning. A teacher's awareness of such semantic differences is the first step in any deliberate pedagogical intervention. This should be considered in teacher training and language program administration.

Explicit explanation.
Many semantic differences can be pointed out to learners explicitly if such knowledge is available on the part of the teacher. The differences between the Spanish words *esquina* and *rincón*, between the French words *balle* and *ballon*, and between

the English words *doubt* and *suspect*, and the difference between the English word *sofa* and its Chinese translation all illustrate examples of semantic differences that can be clearly and easily explained but may take years to be discovered by the learners on their own.

Admittedly, explicit knowledge about semantic differences obtained this way may take a long time to become integrated for automatic application in language use. However, such knowledge can be beneficial even before it becomes integrated. With conscious awareness of the semantic differences across and within languages on the part of the learner, additional encounters with an L2 word may help reinforce this knowledge rather than reinforce the initial mapping of L2 word forms with L1 meanings. Such knowledge may also guide a learner in paying attention to the linguistic cues in the input that are relevant to semantic differences that could have been ignored otherwise. This knowledge also allows learners to express themselves more accurately in L2 production. In short, compared to letting learners make their own discoveries, explicit knowledge may serve as a shortcut or as a cane for the learners to use while walking through the muddy water of meaning, thus speeding up the process of semantic restructuring.

Enhanced input.

However, many semantic differences cannot be described or articulated easily and clearly. Consider explaining the semantic differences between *criterion* and *standard* to some ESL speakers. An English native speaker usually intuitively knows they are different in meaning but may find it extremely difficult to explain the difference in a way that is helpful to an ESL speaker. Dictionary definitions do not usually provide sufficient information, either. For example, both *apparent* and *obvious* are defined as easily or readily seen in some dictionary. The definition of *true* being not false and *real* being not imaginary makes sense to a native speaker but is hardly useful for an L2 learner.

Where semantic differences evade description, a teacher may develop instructional materials that allow learners to make their own discovery implicitly through enhanced input. Enhanced input has been an important concept in instructed L2 learning (Sharwood Smith, 1991, 1993) both theoretically and practically. Drawing learners' attention to a specific linguistic feature or target structure by making the input salient has been shown to be effective in facilitating learning (e.g., Doughty, 1991; Jourdenais et al., 1995). By enhanced input, I mean materials that are developed to target a particular semantic difference or distinction. An ESL instructor, for example, can construct sentences for which only *criterion* or *standard* is appropriate for his or her students. With a sufficient number of such sentences that are used in an intensive manner, a learner may be able to develop his or her own feeling about the differences between the two words. A teacher may also use language corpora for developing such materials. For example, one may identify 20 sentences with *standards* and another 20 sentences with *criteria* from a corpus and use these sentences (or revised versions of such sentences to reduce difficulty) as materials. There are at least three advantages of using such materials. First, they provide intensive input that may serve to accelerate a learner's exposure to a target word. Take the word *criterion* (or its more frequently used plural form *criteria*), for example. According to the Celex corpus, *criteria* has a frequency of 11 occurrences per million words. This means a learner has to read a million words worth of materials to encounter the word 11 times if one relies on natural input. Additionally, a learner's encounter with a target word in naturalistic language experience is most likely to occur in a dispersed fashion. In contrast, an instructor can provide 20 examples in a class meeting. Second, a learner's encounter with a target word is likely to occur without connection to its related word, *standards* in this example. Having sentences containing two semantically confusing words in the same learning context provides a favorable condition for learners to discover the semantic differences on their own. Third, as a semantic development session and with the purpose of these materials clearly explained, a teacher can focus the learners' attention on discovering the semantic differences between two target words. Under such circumstances, such input is more likely to lead to implicit learning of the semantic distinction involved than reinforce the initial form–meaning mapping. In short, the effectiveness of such enhanced input lies in its intensity, its contrastive nature, and in a clear semantic development focus or purpose associated with its use.

The use of L1 translations.

Many people believe that the use of the target language should be maximized and that the L1 use should be limited in L2 teaching, particularly in communicative language teaching (see Augustyn, 2013, Edstrom, 2006, Ford, 2009, Storch & Wigglesworth, 2003, and Turnbull & Arnett, 2002 for discussion). In vocabulary teaching, however, two things should be kept in mind while considering L1 use. First, as illustrated by the errors from Ecke (2015), Hall and Ecke (2003), Olshtain and Cohen (1989), Ringbom (1983), and Zughoul (1991), many L1 transfer errors occur at the semantic rather than lexical level. It is the incorrect understanding of the meaning, rather than the activation of its L1 word form, that leads to lexical inaccuracies, even though form confusion occurs (Laufer, 1989). Second, one is very unlikely to succeed in minimizing L1 influence by avoiding the use of L1 translations. When a new L2 word is first introduced, a learner is likely to understand its meaning within the existing L1 semantic system. For Chinese ESL learners, for example, the word *bird* will be mapped to the Chinese meaning of *niao* when its meaning is understood. Due to the strong link between semantic and lexical representations in a learner's mind, the Chinese translation *niao* will be activated as soon as the meaning is understood, even when a picture is used in conveying the meaning. A quick test can be done to demonstrate this. If I teach you the Chinese word *yanjin* by showing you this picture 👓 and you understand the meaning of the word being glasses, I would predict its English translation *glasses* will appear in your head. Thus, regardless of whether an L1 translation is used in introducing an L2 word, it will be activated anyway.

Following this analysis, I want to suggest that there is no need to avoid L1 translations, particularly in the case of words whose meanings are difficult to convey by means of pictures, gestures, or actions. Where visual aids are less helpful, providing L1 translations offers a quick and unambiguous way of semanticization for the purpose of initial introduction to a word. Many others have made similar suggestions (e.g., Augustyn, 2013; Cook, 1999; Nation, 2003). Additionally, the L1 translation may also serve the role of an anchor for the new L2 word to be attached to the firm basis of the existing memory. This may explain why students often showed better vocabulary retention rates when L1 translations were involved (e.g., Grace, 1998; Laufer & Girsai, 2008; Zhao & Macaro, 2016. See Jiang, 2004b for more discussion).

What is important, though, is to follow up this initial introduction with ample language experiences and enhanced input to help learners (1) see the semantic difference between an L2 word and its L1 translation or between two L2 words, and (2) establish a direct connection between an L2 word and semantic or conceptual representations so that the activation of L1 translations may play a decreasing role in L2 use. Thus, from a teacher's perspective, the emphasis should not be on avoiding using L1 translations, but on providing sufficient and targeted language experiences to promote semantic development.

The timing of attention to meaning.

Several studies showed that attention to meaning at the initial stage of word introduction may inhibit the anchoring of the lexical form in the lexicon. These studies compared word learning outcomes for words that were introduced under two conditions: with or without attention to meaning. Attention to meaning was achieved in these studies by asking students to perform pleasantness rating (Barcroft, 2002), ask meaning-related questions about the new words (Barcroft, 2003) or generate synonyms (Barcroft, 2009), or by presenting new words in semantically related sets (e.g., Bolger & Zapata, 2011; Erten & Tekin, 2008; Finkbeiner & Nicol, 2003). Learning outcomes, as assessed in tasks such as free recall and translation, were usually worse in such conditions, as compared to conditions where no attention was given to meaning. Another study showed no advantage for semantic involvement at the initial stage (Khoii & Sharififar, 2013). This raises the issue of the timing of attention to meaning. It may be advantageous for learners to focus on registering a new word form in the memory (accompanied by a quick L1 translation or some visual aids for semanticization) at the initial stage of word learning, as dividing their attention between form and meaning may interfere with the establishment of the lexical form in the memory, as pointed out by Barcroft (2002). Semantic restructuring can be a target for subsequent learning experiences.

The use of language corpora.

Where explicit description is difficult, semantic differences can also be shown through how words are used. This is where language corpora become useful. They provide information about the linguistic contexts in which a word frequently appears, for example, types of words they collocate with and the syntactic environments they appear in, which may provide clues about subtle semantic differences among a set of semantically related words.

A published study provides a good example to illustrate how corpus information can be used for this purpose. Liu (2010) examined the semantic differences among five semantically related English words: *chief, main, major, primary,* and *principal*. This study is highly relevant in the present context as these words often represent a new semantic distinction that is not present in another language. For example, they are often translated into a single word in Chinese, *zhuyao* (and potentially in other languages), and, as a result, are difficult for Chinese ESL speakers to distinguish. To understand the semantic structures of these words, Liu identified tokens of these words in the Corpus of Contemporary American English and examined (1) what types of nouns they are used to modify, (2) how often they are used to modify these nouns, and (3) in what syntactic structures they occur. Among the many findings from the study, the results showed that even though all these words share the basic meaning of being the first or the most important, they differ in the attributes they are more frequently associated with, for example, *principal* with the amount of work or contribution as in *principal investigator*, *chief* with rank or position as in *chief executive*, and *main* with concrete objects as in *main street*. It was also found that even though all five adjectives can be used to modify abstract nouns, the extent of importance seems to differ, with *main* being the most important followed by *primary, chief, principal, major* in descending importance. These words also differ in how often they are used in formal versus less formal contexts, with *primary* being the most formal followed by *principal, chief, major*, and *main* in that order. Such corpus-based analysis provides a rich array of information about often subtle semantic differences among words. More examples of such corpus-based studies of semantic distinctions can be found in Divjak's (2006) study of five Russian near-synonyms related to the meaning of intending, Divjak and Gries' (2006) study of nine Russian near-synonyms related to the meaning of trying, Gries' (2001) study of pairs of English adjectives ending with the suffixes *ic* and *ical* (e.g., economic and economical), Gries and Otani's (2010) study of two sets of English adjectives *big/great/large* and *little/small/tiny*.

It is comforting to know that individual teachers can also make use of such information without going for a full-fledged study. When an instructor is not clear about how two words differ in meaning, some information may be obtained by searching these words in a corpus and examining the linguistic contexts in which they appear (see Vyatkina, Chapter 7). Take the pair *real* and *true*, for example. A search in the British National Corpus showed that the word *real* goes with nouns such as *answer, difficulty, problem,* and *issue* in both their singular and plural forms much more frequently than the word *true*. In contrast, *true* goes with the noun *color* much more frequently than *real*. While this information may not help reveal exactly how the two words differ semantically, it enhances a learner's performance in using these words correctly. Several corpora are available for free use online, such as the Corpus of Contemporary American English at http://corpus.byu.edu/coca/ and the British National Corpus at the Phrases in English site at http://phrasesinenglish.org/index.html. Such corpora and tools are also available in other languages, such as Spanish (http://www.corpusdelespanol.org/), Portuguese (http://www.corpusdoportugues.org/), French (https://www.sketchengine.co.uk/frtenten-corpus/; https://lextutor.ca/conc/fr/), German (http://www.sfs.uni-tuebingen.de/GermaNet/), Chinese (http://www.aihanyu.org/cncorpus/index.aspx), Japanese (http://www.kotonoha.gr.jp/shonagon/), and Korean (https://ithub.korean.go.kr/user/corpus/corpusSearchManager.do).

Conclusion

Semantic development is an essential part of vocabulary learning and teaching. L2 learners can use L2 words accurately only to the same extent that they understand the meaning of these words accurately. Because of the differences in semantic structures between a learner's L1 and L2, and because of the often inevitable involvement of a learner's L1 semantic system in L2 learning, semantic development requires the restructuring of a learner's existing semantic system. Semantic restructuring is dependent on a learner's discovery or (implicit or explicit) awareness of the semantic differences between the two languages or between two L2 words. However, due to a lack of clear and powerful cues in the language input for signifying such differences, semantic restructuring can be slow and difficult if learners are left to discover semantic differences on their own. Thus, pedagogical intervention is particularly important. However, in practice, the semantic component of vocabulary teaching is often neglected. Among the three elements of vocabulary teaching: form, meaning, and usage, meaning is often given the least attention. In some cases, meaning is neglected because conveying a word's meaning seems so easy. An L1 translation is all it takes for the teaching of meaning. Under other circumstances, meaning is neglected because explaining meaning is so difficult. Teachers are often not equipped for the task, and textbooks and reference books are often less than useful. By focusing on semantic development in discussing L2 vocabulary teaching, I hope to draw attention to this often-neglected aspect of vocabulary teaching, emphasize the importance of pedagogical intervention, and encourage teachers to find their own strategies for facilitating semantic development among learners.

References

Altenberg, B., & Granger, S. (2001). The grammatical and lexical patterning of MAKE in native and non-native student writing. *Applied Linguistics, 22*(2), 173–195.

Augustyn, P. (2013). No dictionaries in the classroom: Translation equivalents and vocabulary acquisition. *International Journal of Lexicography, 26*(3), 362–385.

Barcroft, J. (2002). Semantic and structural elaboration in L2 lexical acquisition. *Language Learning, 52*(2), 323–363.

Barcroft, J. (2003). Effects of questions about word meaning during L2 Spanish lexical learning. *The Modern Language Journal, 87*(4), 546–561.

Barcroft, J. (2009). Effects of synonym generation on incidental and intentional L2 vocabulary learning during reading. *TESOL Quarterly, 43*(1), 79–103.

Blum, S., & Levenston, E. A. (1978). Universals of lexical simplification. *Language Learning, 28*(2), 399–415.

Bolger, P., & Zapata, G. (2011). Semantic categories and context in L2 vocabulary learning. *Language Learning, 61*(2), 614–646.

Cook, V. (1999). Going beyond the native speaker in language teaching. *TESOL quarterly, 33*(2), 185–209.

Divjak, D. (2006). Ways of intending: Delineating and structuring near synonyms. In S. T. Gries & A. Stefanowisch (Eds.), *Corpora in cognitive linguistics: Corpus-based approaches to syntax and lexis* (pp. 19–56). Berlin/New York: Mouton DeGruyter.

Divjak, D., & Gries, S. T. (2006). Ways of trying in Russian: Clustering behavioral profiles. *Corpus Linguistics and Linguistic Theory, 2*(1), 23–60.

Doughty, C. (1991). Second language instruction does make a difference. *Studies in Second Language Acquisition, 13*, 431–469.

Ecke, P. (2015). Parasitic vocabulary acquisition, cross-linguistic influence, and lexical retrieval in multilinguals. *Bilingualism: Language and Cognition, 18*(2), 145–162.

Edstrom, A. (2006). L1 use in the L2 classroom: One teacher's self-evaluation. *Canadian Modern Language Review, 63*(2), 275–292.

Elgort, I., & Warren, P. (2014). L2 vocabulary learning from reading: Explicit and tacit lexical knowledge and the role of learner and item variables. *Language Learning, 64*(2), 365–414.

Ellis, N. C. (1997). Vocabulary acquisition: Word structure, collocation, word-class, and meaning. In N. Schmitt & M. McCarthy (Eds.), *Vocabulary: Description, acquisition and pedagogy* (pp. 122–139). Cambridge: Cambridge University Press.

Elston-Güttler, K. E., & Williams, J. N. (2008). First language polysemy affects second language meaning interpretation: Evidence for activation of first language concepts during second language reading. *Second Language Research, 24*(2), 167–187.

Erten, İ. H., & Tekin, M. (2008). Effects on vocabulary acquisition of presenting new words in semantic sets versus semantically unrelated sets. *System, 36*(3), 407–422.

Finkbeiner, M., & Nicol, J. (2003). Semantic category effects in second language word learning. *Applied Psycholinguistics, 24*(3), 369–383.

Ford, K. (2009). Principles and practices of L1/L2 use in the Japanese university EFL classroom. *JALT Journal, 31*(1), 63–80.

Giacobbe, J. (1992). A cognitive view of the role of L1 in the L2 acquisition process. *Second Language Research, 8*(3), 232–250.

Grace, C. A. (1998). Retention of word meanings inferred from context and sentence-level translations: Implications for the design of beginning-level CALL software. *The Modern Language Journal, 82*(4), 533–544.

Gries, S. T. (2001). A corpus linguistic analysis of English -ic vs. -ical adjectives. *ICAME Journal, 25*, 65–108.

Gries, S. T., & Otani, N. (2010). Behavioral profiles: A corpus-based perspective on synonymy and antonymy. *ICAME Journal, 34*, 121–150.

Gullberg, M. (2009). Reconstructing verb meaning in a second language. How English speakers of L2 Dutch talk and gesture about placement. *Annual Review of Cognitive Linguistics, 7*, 222–245.

Haastrup, K., & Henriksen, B. (2000). Vocabulary acquisition: Acquiring depth of knowledge through network building. *International Journal of Applied Linguistics, 10*(2), 221–240.

Hall, C. J. (2002). The automatic cognate form assumption: Evidence for the parasitic model of vocabulary development. *IRAL, 40*(2), 69–88.

Hall, C. J., & Ecke, P. (2003). Parasitism as a default mechanism in L3 vocabulary acquisition. In J. Cenoz, B. Hufeisen & U. Jessner (Eds.), *The multilingual lexicon* (pp. 71–85). Dordrecht: Kluwer Academic Publishers.

Ijaz, I. H. (1986). Linguistic and cognitive determinants of lexical acquisition in a second language. *Language Learning, 36*, 401–451.

Jiang, N. (2000). Lexical development and representation in a second language. *Applied Linguistics, 21*, 47–77.

Jiang, N. (2002). Form-meaning mapping in vocabulary acquisition in a second language. *Studies in Second Language Acquisition, 24*, 617–637.

Jiang, N. (2004a). Semantic transfer and development in adult L2 vocabulary acquisition. In P. Bogaards & B. Laufer (Eds.), *Vocabulary in a second language: Description, acquisition, and testing*. Amsterdam: Benjamins.

Jiang, N. (2004b). Semantic transfer and its implications for vocabulary teaching in a second language. *The Modern Language Journal, 88*, 416–432.

Jiang, N. (2007). Semantic representation and development in steady-state second language speakers. *Review of Applied Linguistics in China, 3*, 60–91.

Jourdenais, R., Ota, M., Stauffer, S., Boyson, B., & Doughty, C. (1995). Does textual enhancement promote noticing? A think aloud protocol analysis. In R. Schmidt (Ed.), *Attention and awareness in foreign language learning* (Tech. Rep. No. 9, pp. 183–216). Honolulu: University of Hawai'i Press.

Khoii, R., & Sharififar, S. (2013). Memorization versus semantic mapping in L2 vocabulary acquisition. *ELT Journal, 67*(2), 199–209.

Laufer, B. (1989). A factor of difficulty in vocabulary learning: Deceptive transparency. *AILA Review, 6*(1), 10–20.

Laufer, B. (1990). Ease and difficulty in vocabulary learning: Some teaching implications. *Foreign Language Annals, 23*(2), 147–155.

Laufer, B., & Girsai, N. (2008). Form-focused instruction in second language vocabulary learning: A case for contrastive analysis and translation. *Applied Linguistics, 29*(4), 694–716.

Liu, D. (2010). Is it a chief, main, major, primary, or principal concern? A corpus-based behavioral profile study of the near-synonyms. *International Journal of Corpus Linguistics, 15*(1), 56–87.

Malt, B. C., Sloman, S. A., Gennari, S., Shi, M., & Wang, Y. (1999). Knowing versus naming: Similarity and the linguistic categorization of artifacts. *Journal of Memory and Language, 40*, 230–262.

Malt, B. C., & Sloman, S. A. (2003). Linguistic diversity and object naming by nonnative speakers of English. *Bilingualism: Language and Cognition, 6*, 47–67.

Malt, B. C., Sloman, S. A., & Gennari, S. P. (2003). Universality and language specificity in object naming. *Journal of Memory and Language, 49*(1), 20–42.

Nassaji, H. (2003). L2 vocabulary learning from context: Strategies, knowledge sources, and their relationship with success in L2 lexical inferencing. *TESOL Quarterly, 37*(4), 645–670.

Olshtain, E., & Cohen, A. (1989). Speech act behavior across languages. In H. W. Dechert & M. Raupach (Eds.), *Transfer in language production* (pp. 53–67). Westport, CT: Ablex.

Paribakht, T. S. (2005). The influence of first language lexicalization on second language lexical inferencing: A study of Farsi-speaking learners of English as a foreign language. *Language Learning, 55*(4), 701–748.

Ringbom, H. (1983). Borrowing and lexical transfer. *Applied Linguistics, 4*, 207–212.

Saji, N., & Imai, M. (2013). Evolution of verb meanings in children and L2 adult learners through reorganization of an entire semantic domain: The case of Chinese carry/hold verbs. *Scientific Studies of Reading, 17*, 71–88.

Schmitt, N. (1998). Tracking the incremental acquisition of second language vocabulary: A longitudinal study. *Language Learning, 48*, 281–317.

Sharwood Smith, M. (1991). Speaking to many minds: On the relevance of different types of language information for the L2 learner. *Interlanguage Studies Bulletin (Utrecht), 7*(2), 118–132.

Sharwood Smith, M. (1993). Input enhancement in instructed SLA. *Studies in Second Language Acquisition, 15*(2), 165–179.

Storch, N., & Wigglesworth, G. (2003). Is there a role for the use of the L1 in an L2 setting? *TESOL Quarterly, 37*(4), 760–769.

Strick, G. J. (1980). A hypothesis for semantic development in a second language. *Language Learning, 30*(1), 155–176.

Turnbull, M., & Arnett, K. (2002). Teachers' uses of the target and first languages in second and foreign language classrooms. *Annual Review of Applied Linguistics, 22*, 204–218.

Yang Chao, B. (1945). *How to cook and eat in Chinese*. New York, NY: The John Day.

Zhao, T., & Macaro, E. (2016). What works better for the learning of concrete and abstract words: Teachers' L1 use or L2-only explanations? *International Journal of Applied Linguistics, 26*(1), 75–98.

Zughoul, M. R. (1991). Lexical choice: Towards writing problematic word lists. *International Review of Applied Linguistics, 29*, 45–59.

Chapter 2
Supporting Your Brain Learning Words

Ulf Schuetze, University of Victoria

Introduction

As children, we pick up between 10 and 15 new words a day without explicit instruction. This seems to come naturally to us. However, later in life as adults, learning a new language—and particularly all that new vocabulary—can feel anything but instinctive. What changes when we grow up that seems to make this linguistic acquisition more difficult?

It helps to understand how language is processed in the brain. We have to distinguish between the language network and the limbic system, as well as analyze how they are formed and interact with one another. Once we understand this, we can make recommendations about how to effectively learn words as adults, although we must keep in mind that language learning is, after all, an individual effort and much depends on the learner's background and motivation. In psycholinguistic terms, this means that if the word to be learned is not attended to properly, it cannot be acquired.

This chapter presents information about the creation and maintenance of the language network and the limbic system, followed by a discussion of attentional resources. At the end of each section, implications for learning and teaching are outlined. The concluding section provides a number of recommendations for language program directors and materials developers when structuring a vocabulary learning program.

The Language Network

It is often assumed that language processing takes place in two areas of the brain: Broca's (responsible for speech production) and Wernicke's (responsible for speech comprehension). These are the areas in which phonemes—the smallest units of sound—and lexemes—the smallest units of meaning—are processed. In learning the vocabulary of a new language, an incoming word is compared to the existing inventory of phonemes and lexemes in order to be identified. If it cannot be identified, a new record of the word is created. When a word is activated to be used in speech, lexemes and phonemes from two or more languages are called up at the same time to then be processed in Broca's area.

We now know that Broca's and Wernicke's areas are part of a larger language network called the perisylvian cortex. The cortex connects Broca's and Wernicke's areas with the primary motor cortex, which coordinates the physical aspects of speaking, as well as with the auditory cortex that processes sound. In addition, the phonological loop, which consists of two subsystems—the rehearsal component and temporary storage—is integrated into the network. Although the rehearsal takes part in Broca's area by identifying phonemes, the temporary storage subsystem is not part of Broca's area. Rather, it is on the left side of the parietal lobe, where phonemes that cannot be immediately identified are temporarily stored (Baddeley, 2007). The network is built by forming connections; the more words are acquired, the more connections are formed. The same network is used when we learn our first language (L1) as children and when we learn another language as adults. As adults, we have to form connections once again, in order to acquire the words of a second language (L2) we are learning.

In analyzing the rehearsal process in the language network, studies in cognitive psychology have shown that in order to process words into long-term memory, it works well to use spacing techniques: that is, to repeat words within a certain time frame. These techniques are used in what is labeled "rote learning," which is an effective method for beginning learners (Barcroft, 2009; van Zeeland & Schmitt, 2013). Rote learning isolates words from context. However, from a pedagogical point of view, it is desirable that a learner be able to use a word in a given context (Nation, 2001). From a psycholinguistic point of view, rote learning is efficient because repetition fosters the "subvocal rehearsal process" (Ellis, 1995). (It is beyond the scope of this chapter to go into all the details of the over 300 studies that have been carried out in this area, but for an overview see Balota, Duchek, & Logan, 2007; Roediger & Karpicke, 2010.) The idea of spacing is based on the principle of giving the brain time to process the information by providing a pause or a distraction: words are presented, a pause or a distraction is inserted, the same words are presented again, another pause or distraction is inserted, the same words are presented again, and so on. A general distinction is made between two types of intervals: uniform (pauses are consistent in length) and expanded (pauses expand in length). Initially, studies were carried out on the same day; for example, using 30-minute intervals. However, Cull (2000) argued that intervals that are spread over multiple days more accurately reflect how a language learner progresses in a language class. Therefore, he carried out a series of studies using same-day intervals (one-day learning) as well as multiple-day intervals (multiple-day learning) in order to show that in one-day and multiple-day learning, both the uniform interval and the expanded interval lead to higher retention rates compared to the massed interval (no pauses or distractions are made). His results were later confirmed by another series of studies by Carpenter and DeLosch (2005). Schuetze (2015) took this experimental design further by carrying out several retention tests to distinguish between short-term gains (test given the day after the last learning session) and long-term memory (test given four weeks after the last learning session). He showed that students (learning beginner German as an L2 at a West Coast university in North America) using the expanded interval when practicing five times in a 12-day period (practicing on days 1, 2, 4, and 8) performed better on the first test (one day after last learning session) than students who had practiced with the uniform interval in the same time period (practicing every two or three days). However, on the second test (given four weeks after the last learning session), although both groups of students did not remember as many words as they had on the first test, the ones who had used the uniform interval remembered more than those who had used the expanded interval. Another set of studies by Schuetze (2017) using a similar design showed that in order to improve retention rates, it is beneficial to increase the number of repetitions.

For instructors, educating students about efficient vocabulary learning can go a long way. This entails informing students (here referring to those who are learning another language in the context of a North American postsecondary institution where a language class has three to five contact hours per week) that spreading out vocabulary learning over several days (uniform or expanded interval) is more beneficial than cramming (massed interval). If the goal is to acquire many words quickly, an expanded interval should be used. If the goal is to acquire words so that they are consolidated into long-term memory, a uniform interval is preferred. If there is time, a combination of the two is ideal: that is, starting with an expanded interval and then continuing with a uniform interval (Schuetze, 2017).

Finally, if we come back to the function of the phonological loop, several experiments dating back to the 1960s and 1970s have shown that longer words (Baddeley, Thomson, & Buchanan, 1975) and phonologically similar words (Baddeley, 1966a, 1966b) are difficult to process. Lexical errors and word associations in tip-of-the-tongue states, which are related phonologically to the target word, also demonstrate how similar-sounding words can interfere in L2 word learning and production (Ecke, 2001, 2015). Every phoneme has a memory trace, that is, a time limit for it to be identified in the phonological loop before the loop must make room for other phonemes that need to be processed. When rehearsing the many phonemes of a longer word, there might not be enough time for processing in the loop before all the phonemes are identified, whereas rehearsing the phonemes of similar-sounding words makes it difficult to discriminate them sufficiently in the time available. The last point refers to similar-sounding words in the same language.

The implication for learning is to avoid presenting learners with too many long words or similar-sounding words at a time. In L2 acquisition, a common practice for pronunciation exercises is to present rows of similar-sounding words. Although students can practice pronouncing vowels and consonants this way, they will find it difficult to also acquire the meaning of the words that they are pronouncing. A more efficient method is to reduce the number of similar-sounding words. It is important to note that words that sound similar in two languages and have similar meanings, such as cognates, are exceptions because the new word is linked to a word that is already known in the learner's L1 (see Hall, 2002; Hall, Newbrand, Ecke, Sperr, Marchand, & Hayes, 2009).

There are other ways of learning words than rote learning. In fact, rote learning is often seen in conjunction with incidental learning. They are not mutually exclusive but are instead preferred at different levels of proficiency. Incidental learning assumes that students learn words by reading authentic texts because these texts provide a rich source of a language's vocabulary (Hulstijn, 1992). This method is often used once learners have reached an intermediate level of proficiency because it relies on the knowledge of a base vocabulary. However, the amount of reading that is required is high (Hulstijn, 2001; Schmidt, 2010; van Zeeland & Schmitt, 2013) and often beyond the scope of a second- or third-year language course. Nevertheless, students benefit from extensive reading if it can be accommodated into the curriculum. Ideally, although rote learning is an effective method at the beginner level, learners also practice some reading in first-year courses.

The Limbic System

The limbic system is another network in the brain. It connects the hippocampus (responsible for recording memories) with the amygdala (that processes emotions) and the entorhinal and perirhinal cortices that transmit information from the senses (Tranel & Damasio, 2002). The record of a word is created in the hippocampus: a protected region deep within the brain that, together with the amygdala and the two cortices, is apart of the temporal lobe. More specifically, this area is called the mesial temporal lobe. The hippocampus, the amygdala, and the cortices are represented on the left and right sides of the brain. The storage of words—more precisely, their lexemes—occurs in the nonmesial region, which is adjacent to the mesial region. This provides a safeguard: in case of damage to the hippocampus, words can still be recalled and used. However, it will be difficult to learn new words.

The amygdala plays a key role in the processing of emotions, which in turn play a role when recording information (Tranel & Damasio, 2002). If the senses are stimulated when a new word is encountered, the amygdala might tag the word in order to fast-track it (Amaral, Prince, Pitkanen, & Carmichael, 1992). Through the amygdala, a higher dose of a neurotransmitter is released, thereby processing the lexeme with heightened activation because the amygdala is connected not only to the entorhinal and perirhinal cortices that transmit sensory information but also to the basal forebrain (Amaral et al., 1992), which is connected to Broca's area. This heightened activation stimulates a memory trace—the duration of time it takes a lexeme and the phonemes of a word to be processed before they decay. Most words decay in half a second, but the trace can be prolonged to last up to two seconds. With more stimulation, the likelihood of the lexeme to be matched to the phonemes increases. This happens with emotional words. For example, the probability of processing a word such as "hot" is higher compared to a word such as "hat," even though they are only differentiated by one letter. "Hot" has many potential emotional associations such as "hot weather," "hot car," or "hot coffee." The entorhinal and perirhinal cortices connect the hippocampus with sensory information from other brain regions in order to receive visual, auditory, and olfactory information (Gluck & Myers, 2001). When a word is retrieved, these brain areas are activated again. The retrieval of a word can be triggered by emotions. If a word cannot be recalled immediately, the amygdala can be activated by stimulating the senses, which may in turn assist memory. This works well with words that are attached to an emotional situation or event. For example, imagine that you burned your tongue the first time you drank a coffee in Germany. You may then more easily recall the German word for "hot"—*heiß*!—due to the sensory and emotional experiences associated with the word.

A good strategy when learning a new language is therefore to stimulate the senses as much as possible. Because the perisylvian cortex and the limbic system interact with one another, any type of stimulation of the senses helps learning. For example, the look, feel, or taste of an object that has a name you have never heard before will assist in creating a record of the new word. Any type of situational learning is beneficial, for example, if you are learning Spanish and go to a Spanish restaurant. However, while you are there, you need to practice your Spanish and make an effort to speak the language. Otherwise, your hippocampus will not record as much as you hope.

Attention

Processing a word from first encounter to long-term memory takes place over several phases, and the phases overlap. During the first phase, the word needs to be attended to (Schmidt, 1995, 2001). Attention requires much energy and is linked to our ability to direct attention to an incoming word, to divide attention if there are several incoming words, and to switch attention if there is an unknown word (Baddeley, 2007). This is a complex process involving several areas in the frontal lobe, referred to as the central executive, that are associated with planning, organization, and decision making. Among other things, the executive control is linked to the learner's motivation and his or her familiarity or unfamiliarity with a word. If attended to, words are processed by the phonological loop that is part of the language faculty in the brain.

Our capacity to process information is limited. More attention placed on content often means that less attention is available to process form (Barcroft, 2002;

Robinson, 2003; Skehan, 2009; VanPatten, 1990, 2004). It can happen that a word is recalled quickly and is pronounced with the correct combination of a lexeme and its phonemes but with an incorrect grammatical morpheme. Skehan (2012) refers to this as a trade-off: if you focus on one aspect, the other aspects might be neglected. An example from the many language courses I have taught is that learners of German whose L1 is English often have difficulties with plural forms of nouns. When talking about movies, they recall the word *Film* (movie) and pronounce it correctly but use an incorrect plural such as *Filmen* instead of *Filme*. The reason for this has to do with the way morphemes are processed in speech production. A lexeme is recorded with morphological markers but not actual morphemes. These markers function as placeholders. They indicate what type of morpheme can be linked to the lexeme. The actual morpheme is attached to the lexeme later. By saying *Filmen* instead of *Filme*, the speech is not only inaccurate, but fluency is also compromised because the mistake has to be corrected, which takes time.

For language program directors, it would be helpful to select textbooks that have a sufficient number of activities for practicing word meaning. The type of activities should be a combination of target activities (rote learning) and reading (incidental learning). Unfortunately, in many textbooks, vocabulary is more of an afterthought; that is, words are introduced for the purpose of practicing grammar. Here lies the problem. For a learner, it can be challenging to decipher the grammatical form of a word that has just been encountered because the attentional resources are directed to either its form or its meaning. The same issue occurs when learners are asked to form a sentence with a word they have just seen or heard only once or twice. Fortunately, the past decade has seen a revived interest in vocabulary studies in research and teaching. An inspirational approach comes from Jamie Rankin at Princeton University, who developed a vocabulary-driven first-year curriculum called *der/die/das*. (See Rankin in Chapter 6).

We need to consider that the kind of trade-off being made also depends on the speaker's level of proficiency as well as his or her individual speaking preferences (Cook & Singleton, 2014; Singleton, 1995, 2007). The learner has to decide what is more important: either to get the message across by quickly recalling words even if they are not in the correct grammatical form or to assemble a perfect sentence, which may take extra time. In addition, if the concept of a word a speaker wants to use is different in the language being learned than in his or her L1, the speaker has to decide if the word chosen expresses what he or she wants to say. Since the decision has to be made quickly (a word is processed in half a second or less), the question is whether this decision-making process happens subconsciously or consciously. Likely, the answer depends on the personality of the speaker because some people like to take their time to respond or explicitly ask for assistance ("What is that word I am looking for?"), while others utter a word even though it might not be the one they had been searching for.

A question often asked is "How many words should be learned in a day, a week, or over the course of a semester?" A survey by Schmitt (2008) showed that suggestions range from 3 to 20 repetitions. This depends very much on the number of contact hours a learner has when studying a language, his or her personal motivation, and opportunities to engage in the studied language outside the classroom. Further, it also depends on the context of processing (Hulstijn, 2001; Nation, 2009; Schmitt, 2008; Schuetze, 2017; Webb, 2005), that is, if the words learned are targeted (rote learning) or are learned in context (incidental learning). So when we think about how many words we can learn at a time, ultimately there is no definitive answer. A key to success, however, is to not learn large numbers of words at a time but instead to break them down into smaller portions and repeat them.

Another good strategy is to give the brain a rest between learning sessions. We know that during rapid eye movement sleep, the dorsolateral prefrontal region rests (Muzur, Pace-Schott, & Hobson, 2002), while the main part of the limbic system is quite active. We can deduce that when the executive control is resting no new information is attended to and consequently information that entered the brain before sleep is processed again. Since the hippocampus sits deep within the limbic system, it is possible that the record of a word is reviewed to some degree. In addition to reviewing, the brain might also sort out information it receives into what is considered important and what is considered unimportant, strengthen the important information, and link it to other previously existing information. In a study on memory, participants had to learn word pairs (Wilhelm, Diekelmann, Molzow, Ayoub, Mölle, & Born, 2011). Group one was told that they would be tested on the material sometime in the future. They were divided into three subgroups: one that was allowed to sleep after the learning phase was complete (the learning phase took place in the evening and testing was done the following morning), one that was not allowed to sleep and stayed awake by playing cards and watching movies, and one that was also not allowed to sleep, but the learning phase was in the morning and the testing was in the evening of the same day. Group two was not told that there would be a test. This group was divided into the three subgroups using the same criteria as for group one. Results showed that the two subgroups that were allowed to sleep outperformed the other subgroups when they had to recall the word pairs; and of those two, the subgroup that was told that there would be a test outperformed the subgroup that was not given that information.

The implications for curricular development are to teach languages over multiple days per week in order to give the brain some rest between each teaching unit. For example, if a course has five contact hours per week, ideally it should be scheduled five days a week for one hour at a time. Research on sleep also indicates the benefits of building in review sessions before a test as well as announcing tests and exams in advance.

Conclusion

In summary, processing words is not just a matter of language faculties but also of memory and the senses. The perisylvian cortex interacts with the limbic system. Although we all have the same hardware in our brain (the language faculties, the limbic system, the central executive), it is a matter of how we use it. Some learners will form more connections within a network, as well as between networks, than others. Still, there are some general guidelines that might assist when coordinating a language program.

First, given the way the language network processes words, the factor of repetition should not be underestimated. However, if words are repeated too many times, the learner's executive control will cease to divert attentional resources to that word. One has to find a balance between introducing new words and reviewing others that have been previously introduced. There are several programs that work on the principle of flashcards, such as Quizlet, Anki, or eyeVocab.

Second, given how the language network interacts with the limbic system, stimulation should likewise not be underestimated. This stimulation can come from something as simple as providing opportunities for students to talk to native speakers or organizing field trips.

Third, a driving motivational factor for learners is to go to the country where the language they are learning is predominantly spoken. A language program should offer a summer school with a full immersion experience in that country. A question often asked is at what proficiency level it is most beneficial to participate in such a program. Although this depends on the program, if one goes abroad during the first year of foreign language studies the experience can be frustrating because the number of connections that have been formed in the brain might not be high enough to accelerate one's growth through engagement in an immersive environment. It might be more beneficial to wait until one has reached an intermediate level of proficiency. Nonetheless, language learning is an individual effort and depends very much on the individual student.

References

Amaral, D., Prince, J., Pitkanen, A., & Carmichael, S. (1992). Anatomical organization of the primate amygdaloid complex. In J. P. Aggleton (Ed.), *The Amygdala: Neurobiological aspects of emotion, memory, and mental dysfunction* (pp. 1–66). New York, NY: Wiley.

Baddeley, A. D. (1966a). Short-term memory for word sequences as a function of acoustic, semantic and formal similarity. *Quarterly Journal of Experimental Psychology, 18*, 362–365.

Baddeley, A. D. (1966b). The influence of acoustic and semantic similarity on long-term memory for word sequences. *Quarterly Journal of Experimental Psychology, 18*, 302–309.

Baddeley, A. D. (2007). *Working memory, thought, and action.* Oxford, United Kingdom: Oxford University Press.

Baddeley, A. D., Thomson, N., & Buchanan, M. (1975). Word length and the structure of short-term memory. *Journal of Verbal Learning and Verbal Behaviour, 14,* 575–589.
Balota, D., Duchek, J., & Logan, J. (2007). Is expanded retrieval practice a superior form of spaced retrieval? A critical review of the extant literature. In J. Nairne (Ed.), *The foundations of remembering* (pp. 83–105). London, UK: Psychology Press.
Barcroft, J. (2002). Semantic and structural elaboration in L2 lexical acquisition. *Language Learning, 52,* 323–363.
Barcroft, J. (2009). Effects of synonym generation on incidental and intentional vocabulary learning during second language reading. *TESOL Quarterly, 43,* 79–103.
Carpenter, S. K., & DeLosh, E. L. (2005). Application of the testing and spacing effects to name learning. *Applied Cognitive Psychology, 19,* 619–636.
Cook, V., & Singleton, D. (2014). *Key topics in second language acquisition.* Bristol, UK: Multilingual Matters.
Cull, W. (2000). Untangling the benefits of multiple study opportunities and repeated testing for cued recall. *Applied Cognitive Psychology, 14,* 215–235.
Ecke, P. (2001). Lexical retrieval in a third language: Evidence from errors and tip-of-the-tongue states. In J. Cenoz, B. Hufeisen, & U. Jessner (Eds.), *Cross-linguistic influence in third language acquisition: Psycholinguistic perspectives* (pp. 90–114). Clevedon, UK: Multilingual Matters.
Ecke, P. (2015). Was (oft lustige) Fehler und Wortfindungsprobleme über Wortschatzlern-und Verarbeitungsprozesse enthüllen. In M. Löschmann (Ed.), *Humor im Fremdsprachenunterricht* (pp. 95–111). Frankfurt am Main: Peter Lang.
Ellis, N. (1995). Vocabulary acquisition: Psychological perspectives. *The Language Teacher, 19*(2), 12–16.
Gluck, M., & Myers, C. (2001). *Gateway to memory: An introduction to neural network modeling of the hippocampus in learning and memory.* Cambridge, MA: MIT Press.
Hall, C. J. (2002). The automatic cognate form assumption: Evidence for the parasitic model of vocabulary development. *International Review of Applied Linguistics, 40,* 69–87.
Hall, C. J., Newbrand, D., Ecke, P., Sperr, U., Marchand, V., & Hayes, L. (2009). Learners' implicit assumptions about syntactic frames in new L3 words: The role of cognates, typological proximity and L2 status. *Language Learning, 59,* 153–202.
Hulstijn, J. H. (1992). Retention of inferred and given word meanings: Experiments in incidental word learning. In P. J. L. Arnaud & H. Béjoint (Eds.), *Vocabulary and applied linguistics* (pp. 113–125). London, UK: Macmillan.
Hulstijn, J. H. (2001). Intentional and incidental second-language vocabulary learning: A reappraisal of elaboration, rehearsal and automaticity. In P. Robinson (Ed.), *Cognition and second language instruction* (pp. 258–286). Cambridge, UK: Cambridge University Press.
Muzur, A., Pace-Schott, E. F., & Hobson, J. A. (2002). The prefrontal cortex in sleep. *Trends in Cognitive Sciences, 6,* 475–481.
Nation, I. S. P. (2001). *Learning vocabulary in another language.* Cambridge, UK: Cambridge University Press.
Nation, I. S. P. (2009). *Teaching vocabulary: Strategies and techniques.* Boston, MA: Heinle.
Robinson, P. (2003). Attention and memory during SLA. In C. J. Doughty & M. H. Long (Eds.), *Handbook of second language acquisition* (pp. 631–678). Oxford, UK: Blackwell.

Roediger, H. L., & Karpicke, J. D. (2010). Intricacies of spaced retrieval: A resolution. In A. S. Benjamin (Ed.), *Successful remembering and successful forgetting: Essays in honor of Robert A. Bjork* (pp. 1–36). New York, NY: Psychology Press.
Schmidt, R. (1995). Consciousness and foreign language learning: A tutorial on the role of attention and awareness in learning. In R. Schmidt (Ed.). *Attention and awareness in foreign language learning* (pp.1–64). Honolulu: University of Hawaii Press.
Schmidt, R. (2001). Attention. In P. Robinson (Ed.), *Cognition and second language instruction* (pp. 3–32). Cambridge, UK: Cambridge University Press.
Schmidt, R. (2010). Attention, awareness, and individual differences in language learning. In W. M. Chan, S. Chi, K. N. Chin, J. Istanto, M. Nagami, J. W. Sew, T. Suthiwan, & I. Walker (Eds.), *Proceedings of CLaSIC 2010* Singapore, December 2-4 (pp. 721–737), Singapore: National University of Singapore, Centre for Language Studies.
Schmitt, N. (2008). Instructed second language vocabulary learning. *Language Teaching Research, 12,* 329–363.
Schmitt, N. (2010). *Researching vocabulary.* Basingstoke, UK: Palgrave Macmillan.
Schuetze, U. (2015). Spacing techniques in second language vocabulary acquisition: Short-term gains vs. long-term memory. *Language Teaching Research, 19,* 28–42.
Schuetze, U. (2017). *Language learning and the brain: Lexical processing in second language acquisition.* Cambridge, UK: Cambridge University Press.
Singleton, D. (1995). Introduction: A critical look at the critical period hypothesis in second language acquisition research. In D. Singleton & Z. Lengyel (Eds.), *The age factor in second language acquisition: A critical look at the critical period hypothesis* (pp. 1–29). Clevedon, UK: Multilingual Matters.
Singleton, D. (2007). The critical period hypothesis: Some problems. *Interlingüística, 17,* 48–56.
Skehan, P. (2009). Modeling second language performance: Integrating complexity, accuracy, fluency, and lexis. *Applied Linguistics, 30,* 510–532.
Skehan, P. (2012). *Researching tasks: Performance, assessment, pedagogy.* Shanghai, China: Shanghai Foreign Language Education Press.
Tranel, D., & Damasio, A. R. (2002). Neurobiological foundations of human memory. In A. D. Baddeley, M. D. Koppelman, & B. A. Wilson (Eds.), *The Handbook of memory disorders* (2nd ed., pp.17–56). Chichester, UK: Wiley.
VanPatten, B. (1990). Attending to content and form in the input: An experiment in consciousness. *Studies in Second Language Acquisition, 12,* 287–301.
VanPatten, B. (2004). Input and output in establishing form-meaning connections. In B. VanPatten, J. Williams, S. Rott, & M. Overstreet (Eds.), *Form-meaning connections in second language acquisition* (pp. 31–50). Mahwah, NJ: Lawrence Erlbaum.
van Zeeland, H., & Schmitt, N. (2013). Incidental vocabulary acquisition through L2 listening. *System, 41,* 609–624.
Webb, S. (2005). Receptive and productive vocabulary learning: The effects of reading and writing on word knowledge. *Studies in Second Language Acquisition, 27,* 33–52.
Wilhelm, I., Diekelmann, S., Molzow, I., Ayoub, A., Mölle, M., & Born, J. (2011). Sleep selectively enhances memory expected to be of future relevance. *The Journal of Neuroscience, 31* (5), 1563–1569.

Chapter 3
Minor Manipulations Matter: Syntactic Position Influences the Effectiveness of Incidental Vocabulary Acquisition During L2 Reading

Maria Rogahn, Denisa Bordag, Amit Kirschenbaum, and Erwin Tschirner, University of Leipzig

Introduction

Syntactic Prominence in L1 and L2 Incidental Vocabulary Acquisition

Conveying a message involves not only the speaker's choice of which information to communicate but also how this information can be phrased in order to emphasize individual discourse entities and mark their importance. Various linguistic means can be used to express this focus, for example, syntactic structure, focus markers such as *only*, and, in speaking, also through prosody. The term "syntactic prominence" has been used to refer to the perceived importance of the constituents of a sentence based on syntactic structure (see Birch & Rayner, 1997, 2010; McKoon, Ratcliff, Ward, & Sproat, 1993). In this study, we explore whether the processing advantages observed for the prominent syntactic constituents have implications for the early stages of incidental vocabulary acquisition (IVA), that is, the acquisition of new words during reading in the first and second language (L1 and L2). This question is important for language instruction because it has practical consequences for the development of reading material. If the programmatic goal is to foster word learning through the exposure to reading materials, new lexical items should be presented, for example, in textbooks or graded readers, in such a way that the position of the new item promotes its acquisition.

Incidental Vocabulary Acquisition

A substantial portion of both L1 and L2 vocabulary is acquired incidentally, that is, as a by-product of a primary activity, such as listening or reading (Laufer, 2003). IVA through extensive reading and listening has been acknowledged as an important source of vocabulary knowledge, especially for more advanced learners (Nagy, Anderson, & Herman, 1987; Nagy, Herman, & Anderson, 1985; Sternberg, 1987).

The "default argument" (Hulstijn, 2003) behind this assumption is that the plethora of vocabulary knowledge that native and advanced speakers possess cannot have been acquired deliberately in its entirety and must therefore be due to incidental learning.

Contrary to intentional learning, where learners have a clear sense of what to learn and where to direct their attention, in an incidental acquisition setting the learner has to detect the unknown word in the context first: it must be neither overlooked nor mistaken for another, already familiar word. This crucial issue has been related to the process of "noticing" (Schmidt, 1990, 2012) the new word in the text. Noticing occurs when a subset of newly detected information becomes the focus of attention, enters short-term working memory, and is then linked with long-term memory (Robinson, 2003, p. 654). As the process of turning input into intake hinges on it, noticing has been viewed as a sine qua non prerequisite for incidental learning to take place (Ellis, 2006, 2007; Schmidt, 1990, 2012).

The frailness of the incidental "picking up" of a new word from context has been viewed as a critical issue in listening, reading while listening (Brown, Waring, & Donkaewbua, 2008), and reading (e.g., Hulstijn, Hollander, & Greidanus, 1996). Reading research has revealed large differences in the number of incidentally acquired words, both between L1 and L2 and between studies within L1 and L2 (see Waring & Nation, 2004; Waring & Takaki, 2003 for overviews). Waring and Nation (2004, p. 101) report incidental acquisition rates that vary from 4 to 25% of new words in seven L2 studies and Swanborn and De Glopper's (1999) meta-analysis of 20 L1 studies indicate that, on average, only about 15% of unknown words that were encountered during extensive reading were actually acquired. These findings resulted in questioning the reliability and effectiveness of IVA compared to intentional learning. At the same time, there are also studies demonstrating the superiority of incidental learning over intentional learning (Ahmad, 2012; Lehmann, 2007).

The differences in acquisition outcomes have led researchers to explore which factors affect incidental acquisition during reading. While some factors are rather obvious, for example, the number of occurrences of the unknown word (e.g., in L2: Hulstijn et al., 1996) or overall proportion of unknown words in the text (e.g., in L1: Nagy et al., 1987), others are more subtle.

Webb (2008) argues that IVA is crucially affected also by the quality of the context in which the unknown word appears. A number of studies have shown that context properties such as genre (e.g., Taylor & Beach, 1984; Zabrucky & Moore, 1999), topic familiarity (Pulido, 2003), and syntactic complexity (Bordag, Kirschenbaum, Opitz, & Tschirner, 2014, 2015) can indeed affect IVA and that their role can be different in L1 and L2. For example, Bordag et al. (2014) provided evidence that the L1 speakers' acquisition were not influenced by the syntactic complexity of the context, while a parallel experiment with advanced L2 learners revealed that their IVA was positively affected by syntactic complexity (Bordag et al., 2015). The authors argue that participants devoted more attention to the unknown words and to the inference of their meanings in the syntactically complex contexts because, in the more demanding context, the meaning of each individual word became crucial for building up the mental text model. Syntactic complexity in their study was manipulated along the dimensions of sentence length, number of subordinate clauses, number of embedded structures, and number of passive voice constructions and did not include a manipulation of syntactic prominence, which is the focus of the research presented here. The results of the Bordag et al. (2015) study indicate that syntactic simplifications of texts for L2 learners may have a negative effect on L2 word learning and that a sensitive and differentiated approach is needed when accommodating the syntax of texts to the proficiency level of learners.

Syntactic Prominence

The role of syntactic structure in sentence and text processing has been one of the prominent topics in the communicative approach to grammar. According to Givón (2001), "one syntactic structure is unlikely to be a 'mere' stylistic variant of another. However subtle, variant grammar entails a variant communicative effect, and thus presumably also a variant communicative goal. Subtle options of style are nothing but subtle options in the communicative use of grammar" (p. 282). Several experimental studies have supported such claims by demonstrating how seemingly small syntactic changes affect which information readers register, or fail to notice. As an example, Baker and Wagner (1987) instructed L1 readers to look for falsehoods in sentences as in the following example:

(1) (Subordinate clause): Bloodletting, generally accomplished with the aid of rats, was thought to remove "poisons" from the blood.
(2) (Main clause): Bloodletting, thought to remove "poisons" from the blood, was generally accomplished with the aid of rats. (p. 249)

The results revealed that participants were less likely to spot the occurring anomalies in subordinate clauses (although they were, of course, well aware that bloodletting does not involve rats) as in (1) than in main clauses as in (2), thus indicating that the clause type influences which information is perceived as important and is therefore instrumental for assessing truthfulness. The authors argue that syntactically less prominent concepts in subordinate clauses are more prone to result in underspecified representations, which reduces the probability that the false information or anomaly will be detected (cf. Sanford & Sturt, 2002). Sanford (2002), who also let his participants detect small changes in short texts, observed that the changes were approximately 25% more likely to be noticed if they occurred in main clauses.

Syntactic prominence has been further studied by examining constructions such as *it*-cleft sentences (e.g., in L1: Morris & Folk, 1998; in L1 and L2: Sennema-Skowronek, 2008), *wh*-questions (e.g., Birch & Rayner, 1997), and *there*-insertions (e.g., Birch & Rayner, 2010). Several authors (e.g., Birch & Rayner, 2010; McKoon et al., 1993) have argued that readers allocate more attention to syntactically prominent referents and that syntax serves as "mental processing instructions" (Givón, 1992). In their L1 study, McKoon et al. (1993) observed that syntactically prominent concepts (adjectives in predicate position, e.g., *His critical boss is demanding at times.*) were more accessible and retained longer in short-term memory than concepts presented in the less prominent position (adjectives in the prenominal position, e.g., *His demanding boss is critical at times.*). These findings, indicating that syntactic prominence influences the allocation of reader's attention (cf. noticing) and a word's retention in short-term memory, lead to the question addressed in this study, that is, whether syntactic prominence also affects IVA during reading.

With the following two research questions, we wanted to explore possible intersections of the lines of research that, on the one hand, show that IVA is affected by the syntactic context (e.g., Bordag et al., 2015) and, on the other hand, that the accessibility and retention of new words in short-term memory is affected by syntactic prominence (e.g., McKoon et al., 1993):

1. How does the syntactic prominence of a new word influence the early stages of IVA? Are new words in syntactically prominent positions (e.g., subjects in main clauses) acquired more readily than words in syntactically less prominent positions (e.g., objects in relative clauses)?
2. Do L1 and L2 learners exhibit the syntactic prominence effect to a different degree (if at all) as suggested, for example, by the results of Bordag et al. (2014, 2015)?

To our knowledge, these research topics have not been addressed so far, despite their theoretical relevance and practical implications for L2 instruction (e.g., text adaptations of graded readers or composition of learners' texts in textbooks).

Method

The present study examines syntactic prominence as a qualitative context factor that can affect incidental acquisition of lexical knowledge. Its focus is on the initial stage of word acquisition that we operationalized as the establishment of a semantic representation in the mental lexicon following meaning inference. In this respect, the study differs from most previous studies on IVA that test later acquisition stages with methods typically requiring explicit recall of the new words and/or their properties, for example, the Vocabulary Knowledge Scale (Wesche & Paribakht, 1996).

Syntactic prominence is operationalized by presenting the novel words in different syntactic contexts within short texts. Novel words with high syntactic prominence (HSP) are presented as subjects in main clauses, novel words with low syntactic prominence (LSP) as objects in subordinate clauses. Immediately after reading a short text containing the novel word (learning phase), participants completed a self-paced reading task (testing phase) in which the novel word was paired with a semantically plausible or implausible adjective in a sentential context. If an adequate meaning of the novel word has been at least temporarily stored, participants should detect the semantic violation and longer reading times should be observed in the implausible condition. The self-paced reading task has been employed in several studies (Bordag et al., 2014, 2015) to explore the initial stages of word acquisition immediately after exposure and taps into tacit knowledge (cf. Elgort & Warren, 2014).

Participants

Eighty native speakers of German, mostly students at the University of Leipzig with an average age of 23.6 years, participated in the experiment. They were paid for their participation and had normal or corrected-to-normal vision.

Sixty-four advanced L2 learners of German, mostly exchange students at the University of Leipzig with an average age of 24.2 years, participated in the experiment. Their native languages were mostly of Slavonic or Romance origin and their L2 German proficiency corresponded to level B2 or C1 of the Common European Framework of Reference for Languages (CEFR). Most participants included in the study took part in a CEFR-based test that separately measures proficiency in reading, listening, writing, and speaking as part of their admission to a German university. The minimum level required for participating in the present study was B2, and the maximum level was C1 (effective operational proficiency); C2 corresponds to mastery. Most participants reached the B2 level in one or more skills and the C1 level in the other (typically receptive) skills. Because there were four experimental lists (crossing the two two-leveled factors: Syntactic Prominence and Plausibility) and each participant was assigned to one of them, four participants created a superparticipant with a complete design (see the "Analyses" section for more detail on this method). The four individual participants that together created one superparticipant were matched for their L1: six Romance superparticipants always with one L1 (Italian, French, Portuguese, and Spanish), ten Slavonic superparticipants always with one L1 (Czech, Polish, Russian, Bulgarian, and Ukrainian). Altogether there were thus 64 participants, which equals 16 superparticipants. All participants were paid for their participation and had normal or corrected-to-normal vision.

Materials

Pseudowords.

Eighteen low-frequency, mostly concrete German nouns with the average frequency class of 17.25 were selected according to the frequency classification in the database of Wortschatz Projekt (public access available via www.wortschatz.uni-leipzig.de), which relates to the frequency of the most common word "der"—the frequency class of 17 thus means that "der" occurs 2^{17} as often than the words in this class (minimum frequency class was 15, maximum frequency class was 20, and median was 17.5).

Each low-frequency noun was later replaced by a phonologically unrelated pseudoword in the texts (see Appendix A). Pseudowords instead of existing German words were used to ensure that participants had no prior knowledge of target words. Half of the pseudowords were monosyllabic, the other half disyllabic. The pseudowords were generated with the help of the Wuggy pseudoword generator (Keuleers & Brysbaert, 2010).

Texts.

Twenty short texts (ca. 100 words each) were constructed that enabled the inference of the meaning of each low-frequency word, which was central to the text's "storyline" and was replaced by a pseudoword. Each pseudoword appeared in the text two times. The texts were written with the help of dictionary definitions of the low-frequency words and their statistical co-occurrences using the Digitales Wörterbuch der Deutschen Sprache corpus of the German language and the Wortschatz Projekt.

Two versions of each text were created, which differed in two sentences that contained the novel word (see Appendix B for example texts). In the texts in the HSP condition, these two sentences had the novel word as a subject of a main clause and therefore in nominative case. In the texts that included LSP structures, the novel words were objects in subordinate clauses.

In most of the sentences that differed between the two text versions, it was possible to use either the same verb (see the following example sentence) or a verb with the same basic meaning but different predicate–argument structure and causativity. For example, while a causative verb was used in the LSP condition (e.g., *legen*/"lay"), a corresponding inchoative or stative verb was used in the HSP condition (e.g., *liegen*/"lie").

   (3) HSP sentence (see Appendix C for a syntactic analysis)
   Nachdem die ganze Masse nun lange genug auf dem Herd stand, muss die Bräße (i.e., Pulpe/pulp (paper)) für die Weiterverarbeitung jetzt nur noch abkühlen.
   'After the whole mixture has been on the stove for long enough, the *Bräße* (i.e., *Pulpe*/pulp (paper)) only needs to cool down for further processing.'

(4) LSP sentence

Die ganze Masse stand nun lange genug auf dem Herd, sodass sie die Bräße (i.e., *Pulpe*/pulp (paper)) *für die Weiterverarbeitung jetzt nur noch abkühlen muss.*

'The whole mixture has been sitting on the stove for long enough, so that she only needs to cool down the *Bräße* (i.e., *Pulpe*/"pulp" (paper)) for further processing.'

With four exceptions (out of 40), verbs used in the HSP and corresponding LSP sentences shared the same stem. In order to construct subclauses to the corresponding main clauses, subordinating conjunctions were used in the sentences with LSP, while coordinating conjunctions, if any, were used in sentences with HSP. The novel word never appeared at the end of the text; at least five words followed. The average length of LSP and HSP texts was 99.2 and 98 words, respectively. The difference is due to the presence of an additional personal pronoun (as a subject) needed in the subordinate clause in which the novel word appeared as an object (LSP texts). Other factors affecting syntactic complexity—that is, the number of clauses per sentence, the number of passive voice constructions, and embedded structures—were kept constant between the two conditions.

In addition, seven filler texts with an existing word of medium frequency placed in two varying syntactic prominence positions were constructed, which consisted of only known high-frequency words. These filler texts helped to disguise the study's objectives.

Self-paced sentences.

Each text was followed by one to three sentences that were related to the topic of the text and which the participants read in the self-paced reading manner word by word (moving window). One of them was the critical self-paced sentence that was used for assessment. In it, the novel word was combined with an adjective that was either compatible (plausible condition) or incompatible (implausible condition) with the meaning of its corresponding low-frequency word. The adjective did not appear in the texts. A variable number of self-paced reading sentences (between one and three) was used so that participants could not create any expectations with respect to when the novel word would appear and to keep the length of the experiment as short as possible.

5. plausible

Tom stellte die wässrige Bräße (= Pulpe) auf den Herd und las ein Buch.

"Tom put the watery Bräße (= pulp (paper)) on the stove and read a book."

6. implausible

Tom stellte die elegante Bräße (= Pulpe) auf den Herd und las ein Buch.

"Tom put the elegant Bräße (= pulp (paper)) on the stove and read a book."

The novel word was preceded and followed by the same words (except for the adjective) in both conditions.

Comprehension statements.

Twenty-seven comprehension statements, each referring to the contents of one of the texts or one of the self-paced filler sentences, were created that had to be answered with a yes or no answer. The purpose of these statements was not comprehension assessment but to keep participants attentive to the texts and the self-paced sentences. None of the statements referred to the novel word itself.

Procedure

Subjects were tested individually or in pairs in an experimental room in the presence of an experimenter. They were administered written instructions on the task they would perform, mentioning that the texts they would read might contain low-frequency words, which they may not know because they come from dialects or special registers. Nevertheless, they should try to understand the texts and read them at a usual, not-too-slow speed. The experiment took on average 24 minutes for L1 speakers and 29 minutes for L2 participants.

Stimuli were presented on a 17-inch monitor using the E-Prime 2.0 (Psychology Software Tools, 2012). The experimental session started with two practice trials followed by the experimental and the filler trials. Each trial started with the presentation of a text. Participants read the text silently and pressed the space bar when they finished. The text appeared as a whole on the monitor and participants read it in a natural way.

By pressing the space bar, a plausible, an implausible, or a filler sentence appeared, with each letter masked with an X, so that each word of the sentence consisted of a row of Xs whose number corresponded with the number of the letters in the word. Each time the participant pressed the space bar, one word was disclosed, while the previous one turned into Xs again. This way, participants were able to read the whole sentence, word by word (self-paced reading with a moving window, Just & Carpenter, 1992). The reaction time of each space bar press was measured. The number of self-paced sentences following each text varied between one and three sentences, but one text was always followed by the same number of self-paced sentences in all conditions. One of the sentences was always the critical plausible or implausible sentence. The others were filler sentences.

After the presentation of the self-paced sentence(s), the statement referring to the text or a filler sentence appeared on the screen, and the participant had to agree or disagree by pressing one of the corresponding buttons: yes or no.

Each participant read each text only once, either in the syntactically high or low version, followed either by the semantically plausible or implausible sentence. That means that each participant read five texts in the HSP condition followed by a plausible sentence, five texts in the HSP condition followed by an implausible sentence, five texts in the LSP condition followed by a plausible sentence, and five texts in the LSP condition followed by a plausible sentence. Thus, there were four experimental lists and participants were always assigned to one of them. The texts and sentences in each condition rotated and were presented in a pseudorandomized fashion so that it was not possible to predict which condition would follow. For each experimental list, there were two randomizations.

Analyses

Reaction times were measured at four different positions (factor Position): at position n (the novel word itself) and the spill-over region,[1] that is, the three following words ($n + 1$, $n + 2$, and $n + 3$). The reading times of the individual words in the critical self-paced reading sentences were analyzed through 2 × 2 × 4 Analysis of Variance (ANOVAs) tests with factors Plausibility, Syntactic Prominence, and Position. The factor Plausibility had two levels (plausible vs. implausible condition), the factor Syntactic Prominence also had two (HSP and LSP), and the factor Position had four levels, that is, the positions n, $n + 1$, $n + 2$, and $n + 3$. The ANOVAs were always performed both over superparticipants (i.e., in F1) and items (i.e., F2). One superparticipant always consisted of four participants who together saw each item in each condition. Subsuming multiple participants with complementary lists under a single point (i.e., the "superparticipant") is considered a "standard procedure" (e.g., Isel, Gunter, & Friederici, 2003, p. 280) in experiments with a Latin square design.

Results

Results L1 Participants

Before statistical analyses were carried out, the reaction time data was checked for outliers. Single data points were excluded from further analyses if they deviated more than three standard deviations from the particular participant's mean. According to this procedure, 133 (2.3%) data points were removed from a dataset of 6,400 points.

Statistical tests (ANOVAs) with the factors Position (four levels), Plausibility (two levels), and Syntactic Prominence (two levels) revealed main effects for Position (F1(3, 57) = 14.6, $p < .001$, $\eta^2 = .43$; F2(3, 51) = 22.3, $p < .001$, $\eta^2 = .57$) and Plausibility (F1(1, 19) = 28.3, $p < .001$, F2(1, 17) = 4.5, $p = .048$, $\eta^2 = .21$). Participants were faster in the plausible (414.9 ms) than in the implausible (435.6 ms) condition (see Table 3.1). The interaction between Position and Syntactic Prominence was significant as well (F1(3, 57) = 3.2, $p = .03$, $\eta^2 = .14$; F2 (3, 51) = 5.5, $p = .002$, $\eta^2 = .24$).

---

[1] In the self-paced reading paradigm, effects often appear only after the presentation of the critical word; therefore, the reaction times at the spill-over regions are analyzed as well.

Table 3.1. Mean Reaction Times and Valid Values (in Percentage) for Positions n (= the Novel Word Itself), $n + 1$, $n + 2$, and $n + 3$ for the Factors Plausibility and Syntactic Prominence (L1 Participants)

		Syntactic Prominence	
Position	Plausibility	High	Low
n	Implausible	464.3 (96.7%)	450.6 (95.6%)
	Plausible	429.2 (97.2%)	430.2 (98.9%)
$n + 1$	Implausible	454.7 (96.7%)	461.3 (96.9%)
	Plausible	419.8 (99.2%)	445.7 (98.6%)
$n + 2$	Implausible	412.3 (97.2%)	412.6 (96.7%)
	Plausible	393.8 (99.2%)	390.9 (98.3%)
$n + 3$	Implausible	416.8 (97.2%)	411.9 (97.8%)
	Plausible	405.7 (97.8%)	404.2 (99.2%)

The subsequent ANOVAs over the individual positions revealed a significant Plausibility effect on the regions n (F1(1, 19) = 9.9, p = .005, η^2 = .34; F2 (1, 17) = 4.3, p = .055, η^2 = .20) and $n + 1$ (F1 (1, 19) = 19.5, p < .001, η^2 = .51; F2 (1, 17) = 6.3, p = .023, η^2 = .27) and the effect fades away at $n + 2$ (F1 (1, 19) = 5.1, p = .019, η^2 = .20; F2 (1, 17) = 4.1, p = .70, η^2 = .14), where F2 is insignificant and is absent in $n + 3$. In summary, the slower reading times in the implausible conditions at the first two positions and the absence of the corresponding interaction indicate that the novel words' meanings had been acquired by L1 speakers successfully in both Syntactic Prominence conditions.

Results L2 Participants

Statistical analyses proceeded in the same way as for the L1 participants. Two hundred and eighty eight (6.25%) data points were excluded from a dataset of 5,120 data points because they were outliers.

The ANOVAs with factors Position, Plausibility, and Syntactic Prominence revealed significant main effects for Plausibility F1 (1,15) = 12.1, p = .003, η^2 = .45, F2 (1,17) = 13.0, p = .002, η^2 = .43, Position F1 (3, 45) = 18.0, p < .001, η^2 = .56, F2 (3, 45) = 18.9, p < .001, η^2 = .52) and a tendency toward significance for Syntactic Prominence F1 (1, 15) = 3.6, p = .087, η^2 = .18, F2 (1,17) = 4.2, p = .056, η^2 = .20 (novel words that appeared in the HSP position tended to be read faster). The interaction between Position and Syntactic Prominence (F1 (3, 45) = 2.9, p = .045, η^2 = .16, F2 (3, 45) = 4.1, p = .012, η^2 = .19 as well as the triple interaction (F1 (3, 45) = 5.5, p = .003, η^2 = .27, F2 (3, 45) = 3.5, p = .064, η^2 = .15) were also significant, at least in F1.

Table 3.2. Mean Reaction Times and Valid Values (in Percentage) for Positions n (= the Novel Word Itself), $n + 1$, $n + 2$, and $n + 3$ for the Factors Plausibility and Syntactic Prominence (L2 Participants)

		Syntactic Prominence	
Position	Plausibility	High	Low
n	Implausible	530.1 (89.9%)	532.6 (85.4%)
	Plausible	495.9 (86.6%)	549.2 (90.6%)
$n + 1$	Implausible	507.2 (91.3%)	502.1 (93.8%)
	Plausible	480.2 (95.8%)	482.3 (95.5%)
$n + 2$	Implausible	457.9 (97.6%)	466.2 (95.1%)
	plausible	428.0 (96.9%)	424.7 (99.0%)
$n + 3$	Implausible	456.3 (93.4%)	467.0 (96.2%)
	Plausible	450.4 (95.8%)	466.3 (96.9%)

ANOVAs over the individual positions (see Table 3.2) revealed that, at the position n, the interaction between the factors Plausibility and Syntactic Prominence was significant in F1 (1, 15) = 10.0, p = .006, η^2 = .40, and marginally in F2 (1,17) = 3.1, p = .092, η^2 = .16, where the factor Syntactic Prominence was also significant F2 (1, 17) = 6.8, p = .019, η^2 = .30. The subsequent t-tests revealed that while the factor Plausibility was significant in the HSP condition t1(1, 15) = 3.6, p = .002, t2 (1, 17) = 1.96, p = .034, it was not significant in the LSP condition (ts < 1).

On the position n +1, only the factor Plausibility was significant F1(1, 15) = 8.8, p = .009, η^2 = .37, F2(1, 17) = 10.6, p = .005, η^2 = .38, which was also the case at the position n + 2 F1(1, 15) = 7.9, p = .013, η^2 = .34, F2 (1, 17) = 13.6, p = .002, η^2 = .44. At the position n + 3, no factors were significant. In summary, L2 learners also acquired meaning of the novel words in both conditions, but they showed an acquisition advantage for the novel words that appeared in HSP condition—as evidenced by the implausibility effect at the position n, which was significant only for the HSP words.

Comparison of the L2 and L1 results.

The results at the positions n + 1 and n + 2 indicate that both the native and non-native readers were able to infer and at least temporarily store the meanings of the novel words in both syntactic prominence conditions. There is however a crucial difference between the L1 and L2 reading behavior at the position n, the novel word itself. When the native speakers read the novel word in the self-paced reading sentence, they showed the same plausibility effect for all novel words, irrespective of the syntactic prominence condition in which they appeared. However, when the L2 learners read the novel word, the implausibility effect was observed only when the novel word appeared in the HSP condition in the previous text. The fact that the L2 implausibility effect for the HSP novel words appeared as soon as they were presented indicates a better access to their semantic representations—either through a stronger connection between form and meaning, or because of their stronger representation. These claims are supported by a joint analysis of the L1 and L2 experiments over the critical position n. In F1, two interactions were significant (Experiment × Syntactic Prominence: F1(1, 35) = 6.7, p = .014, η^2 = .16, Plausibility × Syntactic Prominence: F1(1, 35) = 5.7, p = .022, η^2 = .15) as well as (marginally) the triple interaction (Experiment, Syntactic Prominence × Plausibility): F1(1, 35) = 3.0, p = .090, η^2 = .08, which reached significance also in F2(1, 17) = 3.3, p = .037, η^2 = .19.

General Discussion

In the present study, we explored the role of syntactic prominence in L1 and L2 incidental acquisition. Our aim was to find out whether readers' ability to acquire new words during reading is influenced by the syntactic position of these words. In addition, we wanted to find out whether syntactic prominence affects L2 and L2 IVA to the same degree. These questions are relevant for authors of various types of reading materials, including texts in a text book or graded readers. Based on our results, we conclude that syntactic prominence is another factor that affects IVA in its early stages, at least in L2. In line with the previous findings, we assume that words which appear in syntactically prominent positions are perceived as more important and are processed more thoroughly which leads to their better representation in memory. Syntax, the "mental processing instructions" (Givón, 1992), might guide the reader toward paying more attention to syntactically prominent constituents and thus contribute to their noticing. According to Schmidt (1990, 2012), noticing, that is, the conscious attention paid to an instance of language, is a prerequisite for incidental acquisition and the potential to turn input into intake. In other words, specific input features, as, for example, novel words, need to attract at least a minimum of focal attention to be registered and, consequently, to be acquired. The current investigation showed that novel words with low syntactic prominence (LSP) may only barely reach this minimum to trigger noticing processes in L2 (as there was a later but still significant effect of Plausibility also in the LSP condition), while novel words with high syntactic prominence (HSP) triggered the noticing process in both groups of participants.

Another account, which might offer an explanation for the different results in the high and LSP conditions, relates to the L2 learners' possible failure to construct the overall sentence meaning, which thus might stay underspecified under some circumstances (e.g., Sanford & Sturt, 2002). A well-known example for this type of underspecification is the *Moses Illusion*. When asked: "How many animals of each kind did Moses put on the ark?," the overwhelming majority of participants in the classic study by Erickson and Matteson (1981) answered "Two" instead of noticing that it was actually Noah. In contrast, participants did notice the false information when it appeared in an *it*-cleft (Bredart & Modolo, 1988). The focus on Moses in "It was Moses who took two animals of each kind on the Ark" led to a detection of the error while "It was two animals of each kind that Moses took on the Ark" did not. A large part of representations stay underspecified or incomplete during the cumulative process of constructing the meaning of a sentence during reading. In most instances, reading can be more effective if readers process only those aspects that are relevant for their purpose. In our study, underspecification might have been promoted by the de-emphasis caused by novel word's object status and/or placement in a subordinate clause in the LSP condition. The results we obtained were, therefore, due to a negative effect of LSP on meaning construction.

An important question that arises is "Why the disadvantage of encountering a novel word in an LSP condition (i.e., as an object in a subordinate clause contrary to a subject in a main clause in the HSP condition) was observed only in L2?" One reason can be a difference in the perceived distance between the two compared constituents with respect to their syntactic prominence by the two groups of participants. For experienced L1 readers, the difference in syntactic prominence between subjects in main clauses and objects in subordinate clauses may be negligible: both types of constituents are very frequent and have been encountered innumerable times by the L1 participants. In contrast, the difference between the two clause structures might be much larger for the L2 learners, albeit advanced. Research into German interlanguage development shows that subordinate clause word order is one of the last and thus most complex structures to be acquired and used correctly, whereas L1 children typically do not display comparable difficulties (e.g., Clahsen, Meisel, & Pienemann 1983; Pienemann 1998). The gap between the syntactic prominence of subjects in the main clause and objects in the subordinate clause thus might be larger for the L2 learners than for the L1 natives, which might explain why we observe the acquisition difference for the HSP and LSP conditions with one group, but not with the other.

A difference in sensitivity to syntactic manipulation for native speakers and L2 learners has also been reported by Bordag and colleagues (Bordag et al., 2014, 2015). While syntactically complex contexts lead to better incidental acquisition of lexical knowledge (both semantic and grammatical) in L2, no difference was observed in L1. The authors argue that, while the syntactic manipulation in the experiment created two different conditions for the L2 learners, the two syntactic manipulations did not result in different processing of the texts for the experienced L1 readers: texts in the syntactically complex condition were read with almost the same ease as syntactically simple texts. For the L2 readers, reading of the syntactically complex texts was more demanding and required more attention, from which the incidental acquisition of the unknown words profited. Because more attention was necessary to construct a sentence's meaning, there was a higher potential for noticing novel words and integrating them with the constructed meaning. At the same time, there was no difference in text comprehension between the two groups, as evidenced by their responses to comprehension questions.

In the present study, syntactic complexity in the texts was kept as constant as possible between the two conditions, but LSP sentences were slightly more complex due to the subordinate sentence and the associated word order (verb final order) that differs from that of a German main clause (verb second order). However, since no advantage was observed for the acquisition of the novel words in the contexts that tended to be more complex due to the prominence manipulation, we might consider this small difference in the complexity status of the low and HSP texts negligible. Nonetheless, in future studies additional manipulations of syntactic prominence free from an alteration in syntactic complexity should be employed.

It should also be stressed that the way syntactic structures are processed depends on their properties. Results obtained for comparisons between subjects in the main clause and objects in the subordinate clause, as in our study, may not lead to the same results as comparisons between other structures. Previous studies, albeit with tasks not aiming at incidental acquisition, have shown that manipulating syntactic prominence through comparisons which involve more marked (i.e., less frequent and distinctive) structures like cleft sentences that serve to direct focus ostentatiously might well lead to advantages for processing of syntactically prominent constituents in L1. Further research is also necessary to decide which other syntactic cues are influential in L2 incidental acquisition and which individual contributions to syntactic prominence are made by the argument type and clause type, that is, the two factors that were combined in the present study.

Nevertheless, the present study is the first to indicate that IVA may benefit from syntactic prominence in L2 learning. It shows that the way information is conveyed governs the processes that are involved in the inference and acquisition of meanings of unknown words. This finding has important implications both for research of IVA in L1 and L2 and for language instruction. In L2 IVA, there are multiple factors that may contribute or hamper the acquisition of unknown words (cf. Rieder, 2002). This study indicates that there may be more subtle factors that have so far not been considered.

The study also shows that the way novel words are introduced to learners and the syntactic context in which they are placed in text books, graded readers, and reading syllabi needs to be reconsidered in light of these findings. The implication of our research is that even as nuanced factors as the syntactic position of a new word in a sentence can decide whether such word will be incidentally acquired or not. It would be advantageous for L2 learners if such findings were taken into account when preparing reading materials. Authors of textbooks are typically aware of which new words they introduce in a lesson. If they want to support the acquisition of those words, they should preferably place them in syntactically prominent positions. Similarly, when authors of graded reads consider which modifications they make, they should take into account that readers' IVA of presumably unknown words will benefit if these words are presented in syntactically prominent positions. In authentic texts, our results suggest that it will be primarily the words in syntactic prominent positions that would be expected to be picked up incidentally. Future research should focus on identifying other context factors that affect IVA, which could thus be used when constructing or adapting texts for learners of different proficiency levels to optimize their vocabulary acquisition.

Acknowledgments

We would like to thank Thomas Pechmann for his valuable comments, as well as Ricarda Theobald and Benjamin Krasselt for running the experiments. The research was part of a project grant provided to Denisa Bordag (BO-3615/2-1) and its follow-up grant (BO-3615/2-3) by Deutsche Forschungsgemeinschaft (DFG, German Research Council).

References

Ahmad, J. (2012). Intentional vs. incidental vocabulary learning. *ELT Research Journal, 1*(1), 71–79.
Baker, L., & Wagner, J. L. (1987). Evaluating information for truthfulness: The effects of logical subordination. *Memory & Cognition, 15*(3), 247–255.
Birch, S., & Rayner, K. (1997). Linguistic focus affects eye movements during reading. *Memory & Cognition, 25*(5), 653–660.
Birch, S., & Rayner, K. (2010). Effects of syntactic prominence on eye movements during reading. *Memory & Cognition, 38*(6), 740–752.
Bordag, D., Kirschenbaum, A., Opitz, A., & Tschirner, E. (2014). To store or not to store, and if so, where? An experimental study on incidental vocabulary acquisition by adult native speakers of German. In V. Torrens & L. Escobar (Eds.), *The processing of lexicon and morphosyntax* (pp.127–147). Newcastle: Cambridge Scholars Publishing.
Bordag, D., Kirschenbaum, A., Opitz, A., & Tschirner, E. (2015). Incidental acquisition of new words during reading in L2: Inference of meaning and its integration in the semantic network. *Bilingualism: Language and Cognition, 18*(3), 372–390.
Bredart, S., & Modolo, K. (1988). Moses strikes again: Focalization effect on a semantic illusion. *Acta Psychologica, 67*(2), 135–144.
Brown, R., Waring, R., & Donkaewbua, S. (2008). Incidental vocabulary acquisition from reading, reading-while-listening, and listening to stories. *Reading in a Foreign Language, 20*(2), 136–163.
Clahsen, H., Meisel, J. M., & Pienemann, M. (1983). *Deutsch als Zweitsprache: Der Spracherwerb ausländischer Arbeiter* (Vol. 3). Tübingen: Narr.

Elgort, I., & Warren, P. (2014). L2 vocabulary learning from reading: Explicit and tacit lexical knowledge and the role of learner and item variables. *Language Learning, 64*, 365–414.

Ellis, N. C. (2006). Selective attention and transfer phenomena in L2 acquisition: Contingency, cue competition, salience, interference, overshadowing, blocking, and perceptual learning. *Applied Linguistics, 27*(2), 164–194.

Ellis, N. C. (2007). The weak interface, consciousness, and form-focused instruction: Mind the doors. In S. Fotos & H. Nassaji (Eds.), *Form-focused instruction and teacher education: Studies in honour of Rod Ellis* (pp. 17–33). Oxford, UK: Oxford University Press.

Erickson, T. A., & Matteson, M. (1981). From words to meanings: A semantic illusion. *Journal of Verbal Learning and Verbal Behavior, 20*, 540–52.

Givón, T. (1992). The grammar of referential coherence as mental processing instructions. *Linguistics, 30*(1), 5–56.

Givón, T. (2001). *Syntax: An introduction*, Volume II. Amsterdam: John Benjamins Publishing Company.

Hulstijn, J. H. (2003). Incidental and intentional learning. In C. J. Doughty & M. H. Long (Eds.), *The handbook of second language acquisition* (pp. 349–381). Oxford: Blackwell.

Hulstijn, J. H., Hollander, M., & Greidanus, T. (1996). Incidental vocabulary learning by advanced foreign language students: The influence of marginal glosses, dictionary use, and reoccurrence of unknown words. *The Modern Language Journal, 80*(3), 327–339.

Isel, F., Gunter, T. C., & Friederici, A. D. (2003). Prosody-assisted head-driven access to spoken German compounds. *Journal of Experimental Psychology: Learning, Memory, and Cognition, 29*(2), 277–288.

Just, M. A., & Carpenter, P. A. (1992). A capacity theory of comprehension: Individual differences in working memory. *Psychological Review, 99*, 122–149.

Keuleers, E., & Brysbaert, M. (2010). Wuggy: A multilingual pseudoword generator. *Behaviour Research Methods, 42*(3), 627–633.

Laufer, B. (2003). Vocabulary acquisition in a second language: Do learners really acquire most vocabulary by reading? Some empirical evidence. *Canadian Modern Language Review/La revue canadienne des langues vivantes, 59*(4), 567–587.

Lehmann, M. (2007). Is intentional or incidental vocabulary learning more effective? *International Journal of Foreign Language Teaching, 3*(1), 23–28.

McKoon, G., Ratcliff, R., Ward, G., & Sproat, R. (1993). Syntactic prominence effects on discourse processes. *Journal of Memory and Language, 32*(5), 593–607.

Morris, R. K., & Folk, J. R. (1998). Focus as a contextual priming mechanism in reading. *Memory & Cognition, 26*(6), 1313–1322.

Nagy, W. E., Anderson, R. C., & Herman, P. A. (1987). Learning word meanings from context during normal reading. *American Educational Research Journal, 24*(2), 237–270.

Nagy, W. E., Herman, P. A., & Anderson, R. C. (1985). Learning words from context. *Reading Research Quarterly, 20*(2), 233–253.

Pienemann, M. (1998). Developmental dynamics in L1 and L2 acquisition: Processability Theory and generative entrenchment. *Bilingualism: Language and Cognition, 1*(1), 1–20.

Psychology Software Tools, Inc. (2012). E-Prime (Version 2.0). Sharpsburg, PA, USA.

Pulido, D. (2003). Modelling the role of second language proficiency and topic familiarity in second language incidental vocabulary acquisition through reading. *Language Learning, 53*(2), 233–284.

Rieder, A. (2002). *Beiläufiger Vokabelerwerb: Theoretische Modelle und empirische Untersuchungen*. Doctoral dissertation, Universität Tübingen. Retrieved June 2, 2017, from http://w210.ub.uni-tuebingen.de/volltexte/2002/646/

Robinson, P. J. (2003). Attention and memory during SLA. In C. M. Doughty & M. H. Long (Eds.), *The handbook of second language acquisition* (pp. 631–678). Oxford: Blackwell.

Sanford, A. J. (2002). Context, attention and depth of processing during interpretation. *Mind & Language, 17*(1–2), 188–206.

Sanford, A. J., & Sturt, P. (2002). Depth of processing in language comprehension: Not noticing the evidence. *Trends in Cognitive Sciences, 6*(9), 382–386.

Schmidt, R. (1990). The role of consciousness in second language learning. *Applied Linguistics, 11*(2), 129–158.

Schmidt, R. (2012). Attention, awareness, and individual differences in language learning. In W. M. Chan, K. N. Chin, S. Bhatt, & I. Walker (Eds.), *Perspectives on individual characteristics and foreign language education*. (Vol. 6, pp. 27–50). Boston De Gruyter Mouton.

Sennema-Skowronek, A. (2008). *The use of focus markers in second language word processing* (Doctoral dissertation). Retrieved from Institutional Repository of the University of Potsdam: https://publishup.uni-potsdam.de/opus4-ubp/frontdoor/index/index/docId/3087.

Sternberg, R. J. (1987). Most vocabulary is learned from context. In M. G. McKeown & M. E. Curtis (Eds.), *The nature of vocabulary acquisition* (pp. 89–105). Hillsdale, NJ: Lawrence Erlbaum.

Swanborn, M. S., & De Glopper, K. (1999). Incidental word learning while reading: A meta-analysis. *Review of Educational Research, 69*(3), 261–285.

Taylor, B. M., & Beach, R. W. (1984). The effects of text structure instruction on middle-grade students' comprehension and production of expository text. *Reading Research Quarterly, 19*(2), 134–146.

Waring, R., & Nation, I. S. P. (2004). Second language reading and incidental vocabulary learning. In D. Albrechtsen, K. Haastrup, & B. Henriksen (Eds.) *Angles on the English speaking world 4: Writing and vocabulary in foreign language acquisition* (pp. 97–110) Copenhagen, Denmark: Museum Tusculanum Press.

Waring, R., & Takaki, M. (2003). At what rate do learners learn and retain new vocabulary from reading a graded reader? *Reading in a Foreign Language, 15*(2), 130–163.

Webb, S. (2008). The effects of context on incidental vocabulary learning. *Reading in a Foreign Language, 20*(2), 232–245.

Wesche, M., & Paribakht, T. S. (1996). Assessing second language vocabulary knowledge: Depth versus breadth. *Canadian Modern Language Review, 53*(1), 13–40.

Zabrucky, K., & Moore, D. (1999). Influence of text genre on adults' monitoring of understanding and recall. *Educational Gerontology, 25*(8), 691–710.

Appendix

Appendix A: German Low-Frequency Words, Pseudowords, and Their English Translations

German Low-Frequency Word	Pseudoword Used	English Translation
Warze	Zolm	wart
Haube	Resch	bonnet
Jojo	Driebott	yo-yo
Zwirn	Wück	twine
Zwille	Pünz	slingshot
Lid	Schrilbe	eyelid
Schnorchel	Frahl	snorkel
Furt	Schöffzark	ford
Narkose	Bontur	anesthesia
Straßenwalze	Nausel	road roller
Pipette	Gindel	pipette
Sternschnuppe	Flozett	shooting star
Schuldschein	Jonk	IOU (borrower's note)
Schleppe	Leuk	train (clothing)
Zuber/Bütte	Treb	trough (washing)
Rain (Feld)	Spaut	field margin
Pulpe	Bräße	pulp (paper)
Gugelhupf	Kälit	Gugelhupf/Bundt cake
Zunder	Reulick	tinder
Smaragd	Heif	emerald

Appendix B: Example Texts

High Syntactic Prominence Example Text for "Bräße," i.e., "*Pulpe*"/*paper pulp*
(critical sentences are underlined)

Katja findet es sehr schade, dass jedes Jahr so viel Zeitungspapier in den Müll geworfen wird. Deshalb hat sie sich überlegt, aus dem ganzen Altpapier neues Papier herzustellen. Zuerst zerreißt sie dafür die Zeitung in kleine Stücke, mischt sie mit Wasser, und dann kocht die Bräße in einem großen Topf etwa zwei

Stunden. Als Katja bemerkt, dass der Brei aus Wasser und Papier noch zu dick ist, schüttet sie etwas mehr Wasser hinzu, damit er wieder etwas flüssiger wird. <u>Nachdem die ganze Masse nun lange genug auf dem Herd stand, muss die Bräße für die Weiterverarbeitung jetzt nur noch abkühlen.</u>

English Translation High Syntactic Prominence Example Text for "Bräße", i.e., "Pulpe"/*paper pulp*

(critical sentences are underlined)

Katja thinks it is a shame that so much newspaper is thrown into the rubbish bins every year. She has therefore decided to make new paper from the waste paper. <u>First, she rips the newspaper into little pieces, mixes them with water and then the Bräße boils in a pot for around two hours.</u> When Katja notices that the mash of water and paper is still too thick she pours more water into it so that it becomes more fluid. <u>After the whole mixture has been on the stove for long enough, the Bräße only needs to cool down for further processing.</u>

Low Syntactic Prominence Example Text for "Bräße," i.e., "Pulpe"/*paper pulp*

(critical sentences are underlined)

Katja findet es sehr schade, dass jedes Jahr so viel Zeitungspapier in den Müll geworfen wird. Deshalb hat sie sich überlegt, aus dem ganzen Altpapier neues Papier herzustellen. <u>Zuerst zerreißt sie dafür die Zeitung in kleine Stücke und mischt sie mit Wasser, damit sie dann die Bräße in einem großen Topf etwa zwei Stunden kochen kann.</u> Als Katja bemerkt, dass der Brei aus Wasser und Papier noch zu dick ist, schüttet sie etwas mehr Wasser hinzu, damit er wieder etwas flüssiger wird. <u>Die ganze Masse stand nun lange genug auf dem Herd, sodass sie die Bräße für die Weiterverarbeitung jetzt nur noch abkühlen muss.</u>

English Translation Low Syntactic Prominence Example Text for "Bräße," i.e., "Pulpe"/*paper pulp*

(critical sentences are underlined)

Katja thinks it is a shame that so much newspaper is thrown into the rubbish bins every year. She has therefore decided to make new paper from the waste paper. <u>First, she rips the newspaper into little pieces and mixes them with water so that she can boil the Bräße in a pot for around two hours.</u> When Katja notices that the mash of water and paper is still too thick she pours more water into it so that it becomes more fluid. <u>The whole mixture has been on the stove for long enough, so that she only needs to cool down the Bräße for further processing.</u>

Appendix C: Syntactic Analysis of Example Sentences 3 and 4

Syntactic Prominence		First Field	Left Bracket	Central Field	Right Bracket
Low	Main clause	*Die ganze Masse*_{antecedent} The whole mixture_{antecedent}	*stand* sat/stood	*nun lange genug auf dem Herd* now long enough on the stove	
	Subordinate clause		*sodass* so that	*sie* [subject] *die Bräße* [object]_{postcedent} *für die Weiterverarbeitung jetzt nur noch* she [subject] the *Bräße* [object]_{postcedent} (i.e., *Pulpe* / pulp (paper) for further processing now only	*abkühlen muss.* cool down must.
High	Main clause		*muss* must	*die Bräße* [subject]_{postcedent} (i.e., *Pulpe* / pulp (paper)) *für die Weiterverarbeitung jetzt nur noch* the *Bräße* [subject]_{postcedent} (i.e., *Pulpe* / pulp (paper)) for further processing now only	*abkühlen.* cool down.
	Subordinate clause	*Nachdem die ganze Masse*_{antecedent} *nun lange genug auf dem Herd stand* After the whole mixture_{antecedent} now long enough on the stove sat/stood			

Chapter 4
The Relationship Between Reading Proficiency and Vocabulary Size: An Empirical Investigation

Erwin Tschirner, Universität Leipzig
Jane Hacking, Fernando Rubio, University of Utah

Introduction

Reading proficiency is arguably the most important modality for academic achievement. Students need to be able to read and understand large quantities of academic texts such as introductory college textbooks, newspaper articles, scholarly articles, and reports of all kinds, including technical reports. Students of second languages (L2) also need to read literary texts such as novels, short stories, and poetry. Research on L2 reading is extensive and varied, addressing such questions as the role of L1 literacy (e.g., Bernhardt, 2010; Garrison-Fletcher, 2012; Sparks, Patton, Ganshow, & Humbach, 2012), grammatical knowledge (e.g., Berkemeyer, 1994; Koda, 1993), or vocabulary knowledge (e.g., Schmitt, 2008; Schmitt, Jiang, & Grabe, 2011) in the development of L2 reading proficiency. Bernhardt (2010) argues for a model of L2 reading that captures the contribution and interaction of many variables (e.g., L1 literacy, background knowledge, and processing strategies) to be able to move beyond partial explanations of the variance in L2 reading performance. Citing Brisbois (1995) Bernhardt notes, for example, that vocabulary knowledge accounts for 27% of this variance. We concur that a comprehensive model is important, but we also see the need for further understanding the role of specific variables such as vocabulary knowledge, especially in the L2 learning of languages other than English.

The role of vocabulary size as a predictor of reading proficiency has traditionally been conceived in terms of lexical frequency studies of texts, which examine the percentages of high- and low-frequency words the text contains. The emphasis on lexical frequency has at times led to daunting claims about how large one's vocabulary needs to be. For reading purposes, the figure most often cited is 8,000 to 9,000 word families consisting of approximately 24,000 individual lexical items, the knowledge which allows readers of English to read a broad range of texts (e.g., Nation, 2006). Hazenberg and Hulstijn (1996) estimated the minimum vocabulary size needed to manage university study in Dutch as an L2 to be 10,000 base words (for a discussion of terminology, see below). They also found that the average vocabulary size of Dutch native speakers entering college in the Netherlands was 18,800 base words. Although figures of around 17,000 base words or word families are common assumptions regarding the vocabulary size of beginning college students (D'Anna, Zechmeister, & Hall, 1991; Goulden, Nation, & Read, 1990), a more recent study found that first-year British university students had an average vocabulary size of 10,000 word families (Milton & Treffers-Daller, 2013).

Vocabulary researchers use the terms "base words" (e.g., Hazenberg & Hulstijn, 1996) or "root forms" (e.g., Schmitt, 2010) to refer to the primary word forms to which inflectional and derivational affixes are added. The term "word family" includes the base/root form (e.g., work), its inflections (works, worked, working), and transparent derivations (worker). In addition, researchers try to measure two dimensions of vocabulary knowledge: *size/breadth* and *depth*. Measurements of vocabulary size typically seek to count the number of words a learner knows in a basic form–meaning way, whereas measurements of depth attempt to capture a learner's grasp of such things as a word's grammatical features, how it is used in sentences, its collocations, its associations, and constraints on its use.

Vocabulary size is clearly linked to the acquisition of competence in reading and to success in school learning in early childhood (Bornstein & Haynes, 1998; Ouellette, 2006). Milton and Treffers-Daller (2013) estimated that children learn approximately 500 new word families (in their L1) per year during their school years and that college students add about the same number of word families per year of study. They also noted that the resulting 10,000 base words at the beginning of college study still made it hard for these students to read introductory college textbooks and scholarly articles and suggested that student achievement may be explained as much by vocabulary size as by academic ability. Nation (2006) estimated that 8,000–9,000 word families are needed to reach the 98% text coverage of a wide range of nonacademic texts (novels, newspapers), which he suggested was necessary for reading efficiently and with adequate comprehension. In addition, Nation (2006) showed that the most frequent 1,000 word families in English average six types per word family. He therefore estimated that a vocabulary of 8,000 word families involves knowing approximately 34,000 individual word forms or types. For languages such as French or German, which have a much greater range of inflected word forms, a vocabulary of 6,500 base words may entail about 41,000 types (Kusseling & Lonsdale, 2013, p. 444). This finding is certainly relevant to the current study, which deals with three such highly inflected languages.

A major strand of both L1 and L2 vocabulary research concerns lexical thresholds, or how much vocabulary knowledge is required to achieve particular goals. For reading proficiency, this line of inquiry is commonly conceptualized in terms of text coverage, that is, how many individual words are typically included in certain kinds of texts such as novels and newspapers. Having established that a reader needs to understand between 95% and 98% of the tokens of a particular text in order to understand it (Carver, 1994; Hu & Nation, 2000; Schmitt, 2008; Schmitt, Jiang, & Grabe, 2011), the question, then, was how many words one needs to know on average in order to understand the 95% or 98% of the tokens of similar texts. Corpus-based research showed, for example, that the most frequent 9,000 word families provided coverage of 98% of the tokens in a wide range of texts in English (Nation, 2006). The assumption, of course, is that a reader needs to understand 98% of the tokens to gain adequate understanding of a text. Schmitt, Schmitt, and Clapham (2001), however, did not find any threshold percentage, that is, a percentage at which comprehension dramatically improved, but rather a linear relationship between vocabulary knowledge and reading comprehension. Comprehension was measured using two instruments: a multiple-choice test "with an emphasis on items that required some inferencing skills in using information from the text" and a graphic organizer completion task, which "requires readers to recognize the organizational pattern of the text and see clear, logical relationships among already-filled-in information and the information sought through the blanks" (p. 31). Although text coverage of 95% was adequate for 60% comprehension and text coverage of 98% was adequate for 70% comprehension, they also found that text coverage of 90% still allowed a comprehension rate of 50% (Schmitt, et al., 2011, p. 35).

Another line of inquiry has attempted to correlate vocabulary size directly to reading proficiency by looking at the relationship between vocabulary breadth and the comprehension rate for a particular text. Reading proficiency and vocabulary size typically correlated strongly, between $r = 0.5$ and $r = 0.82$ (Laufer, 1992; Qian, 1999, 2002). Despite the fact that there were strong correlations between vocabulary size and reading comprehension, there was also a wide variation in the strengths of the correlations. On the one hand, this variation was probably due to the notion of "adequate comprehension" and the kinds of texts learners had to read, while on the other hand it may also have been due to the vocabulary size test used.

The two measures most commonly used in vocabulary size research are Nation's Vocabulary Levels Test (VLT) and Meara's XLex vocabulary test (Meara & Milton, 2003). Xing and Fulcher (2007) showed that two VLTs created using the same guidelines do not necessarily exhibit precisely the same level of difficulty. One reason for this discrepancy presumably has to do with the fact that target words are randomly selected from the thousand words that constitute a particular frequency band and may cluster more around the more frequent half of the band for one test than for the other.

There are several different mastery criteria used in vocabulary size studies, that is, the number of words the test taker needs to identify correctly in order to be considered to have mastered a particular band. The two most common percentages used are 80% (e.g., Xing & Fulcher, 2007) and 85% (e.g., Schmitt, Schmitt, & Clapham, 2001). Because test difficulty may vary, the mastery criteria should probably be empirically established for each test separately. We suggest correlating the results of several mastery criteria (e.g., 75%, 80%, and 85%) with the overall raw score of the test and to select the mastery criteria that best correlates with the overall score.

To date, there is little empirical evidence relating vocabulary size to established frameworks of reference such as the Common European Framework of Reference for Languages (CEFR) or the American Council on the Teachers of Foreign Languages (ACTFL) Proficiency Guidelines. A handful of studies focusing on the CEFR suggested that the receptive knowledge of the most frequent 3,000 lexemes of a language is related to the CEFR B1 level, whereas knowledge of the most frequent 5,000 lexemes is related to the C1 level (Huhta, Alderson, Nieminen, & Ullakonoja, 2011; Meara & Milton, 2003; Milton, 2010).

Frameworks and Vocabulary Size

Although the ACTFL Reading Proficiency Guidelines (ACTFL, 2012) do not contain any explicit references to vocabulary size or content other than some very general descriptors such as "broad vocabulary" (Superior), "precise, often specialized vocabulary" (Superior), "high-frequency vocabulary" (Intermediate), "cognates and formulaic phrases" (Novice), there are published vocabulary lists, called vocabulary profiles, associated with the CEFR for many European languages. These lists are often staggering in size. For French, for example, the A1 level is associated with 975 base words, A2 with 1,645 words, B1 with 3,388 words, and B2 with 6,407 words (Kusseling & Lonsdale, 2013, p. 444). For Spanish, the Instituto Cervantes includes 1,146 words and phrasal words in its recommendations for A1, 2,730 words for A2, 6,066 words for B1, 11,830 words for B2, 14,910 words for C1, and 23,343 words for C2 (Hacking, Tschirner, & Rubio, in press). The lexical minimums for receptive purposes established by the Test of Russian as a Foreign Language are 2,300 for Level 1, which is thought to be equivalent to the CEFR level B1, 10,000 for Level 2 (= B2), 12,000 for Level 3 (= C1), and 20,000 for Level 4 (= C2) (Hacking & Tschirner, 2017). The *English Profile* established the following vocabulary sizes for the CEFR levels A1 to C2: 785 (A1), 2,382 (A2), 5,327 (B1), 9,502 (B2), 11,908 (C1), and 15,715 (C2) (Lahti, 2015). The Goethe Institute has published German word lists only for levels A1 to B1. The A1 list contains 650 words (Perlmann-Balme, n.d.) and the A2 list contains 1,300 words (Glaboniat, Perlmann-Balme, & Studer, 2016). The revised word list for the CEFR level B1 for German contains approximately 3,500 words (Glaboniat et al., 2016). For B2, the Goethe Institute refers to the word lists contained in *Profile Deutsch* (Glaboniat, Müller, Rusch, Schmitz, & Wertenschlag, 2005), which contains a total of 6,053 lexical items (excluding the multiword units that Profile Deutsch calls *Sprechhandlungen* [functions], which consist of phrases and short clauses). There are no suggestions for C1 and C2. Table 4.1 summarizes these assumptions for the languages discussed above.

Table 4.1. Vocabulary Size Assumptions for Various CEFR Levels by European National Test Institutes

	French	Spanish	Russian	English	German
A1	975	1,146	N/A	785	650
A2	1,645	2,730	N/A	2,382	1,300
B1	3,388	6,066	2,300	5,327	3,500
B2	6,407	11,830	10,000	9,502	6,053
C1	N/A	14,910	12,000	11,908	N/A
C2	N/A	23,343	20,000	15,715	N/A

These numbers are considerably different from language to language and appear to be very high at the higher levels, with B2 approaching or surpassing the 10,000 mark established by Hazenberg and Hulstijn (1996) for university study for several languages. The C2 level requirements for these languages, in fact, approach or surpass even native speaker's estimates of beginning college students. One reason for this wide disparity in vocabulary size assumptions may be the fact that the above lists were commonly not based on frequency studies but instead consisted of older lists, often from the 1970s, which were revised mostly on the basis of expert opinion. A comparison of the German B1 list with a frequency dictionary, for example, showed that the overlap between the two lists was only 60%—that is, 40% of the 3,500 words of the German B1 list did not belong to the most frequent 3,500 words of German, and 40% of the most frequent words of German were not included in the vocabulary list (Tschirner, 2017). Further, the CEFR vocabulary range descriptors focus mainly on production—predominantly oral production—in everyday language use, particularly at levels A1 to B2. For example, at the A2 level a learner "has a sufficient vocabulary for the expression of basic communicative needs," while at the B2 level he or she "has a good range of vocabulary for matters connected to his/her field and most general topics" and "can vary formulation to avoid frequent repetition, but lexical gaps can still cause hesitation and circumlocution" (Council of Europe, 2001, p. 112). This focus on production stems from the fact that the precursor of the CEFR, the Threshold Level project of the 1970s and 1980s, had a firm foundation in speech act theory, and it therefore conceived foreign language learning primarily as the acquisition of notions and (speech) functions. Tschirner (2017) argued that the CEFR approach focusing on production and speech functions is radically different from the receptive and frequency-based approaches common to vocabulary size studies in English as a second or foreign language (ESL/EFL). This difference affects how basic vocabularies are conceptualized, what words are considered important at what CEFR level, and how they are selected, and it produces vocabulary lists that are rather different from each other.

Research Questions

The focus of this inquiry is to establish vocabulary sizes required for various reading proficiency levels. The discrepancy between the results of the few existing empirical studies and the numbers established by corpus linguistic evidence is staggering. Because more and more researchers and curriculum specialists argue that vocabulary should be learned directly as well as indirectly, the question is how many words and what words. To provide evidence of the relationship between reading proficiency levels as defined by ACTFL and vocabulary size in German, Russian, and Spanish, the following research questions were addressed:

1. How well does reading proficiency as defined by ACTFL predict vocabulary size measured as the receptive knowledge of various bands of the most frequent 5,000 words in German, Russian, and Spanish?
2. What vocabulary sizes are predicted by what ACTFL reading proficiency levels in these languages?
3. What are the differences, if any, between German, Russian, and Spanish with respect to the relationship between reading proficiency level and vocabulary size?

Methods

Participants

Participants in this study were college students of German, Russian, and Spanish enrolled at two U.S. universities and at one university in Germany. There were 48 students of Russian and 52 students of Spanish enrolled at one of the two U.S. universities. There were 197 students of German. Ninety-seven of them were enrolled at the other U.S. institution, while one hundred students were enrolled at the German university. All U.S. students had American English as their first language (L1). Of the students in Germany, 75 spoke Arabic, 12 spoke Dutch, 11 spoke Thai, and two spoke Brazilian Portuguese as their L1. All participants took both the ACTFL Reading Proficiency Test (RPT) and the VLT. The Russian and Spanish tests were administered between September 2015 and January 2017, and the German tests were administered between June 2016 and June 2017.

Instruments

The ACTFL RPT is a standardized test for the global assessment of reading ability in a language (ACTFL, 2013). The test measures how well a person spontaneously reads texts when presented with texts and tasks as described in the 2012 ACTFL Proficiency Guidelines. The test formats used in this study consisted of 10 to 25 texts, depending on a participant's proficiency level. There were five sublevels: Intermediate Low (IL), Intermediate Mid (IM), Advanced Low (AL), Advanced

Mid (AM), and Superior (S). Each sublevel consisted of five texts accompanied by three tasks (items) with four multiple-choice responses, only one of which was correct. Test specifications included genre, content area, rhetorical organization, reader purpose, and vocabulary (ACTFL, 2013). Texts and tasks aligned at each level; for example, an Intermediate task required understanding information that was contained in one sentence, whereas Advanced tasks required the ability to understand information that was spread out over several sentences or paragraphs. Tasks and multiple-choice responses were in the target language and the test was web based.

The RPT is a timed test with a total test time of 25 minutes per sublevel. Two sublevels are scored together: either the two levels taken or, if more than two levels are taken, the two highest levels that can be scored according to the specific algorithm of the test. Because there are no Novice texts or tasks, the Novice levels are determined according to how close the test taker is to the Intermediate level. Test takers whose scores are below 33.3% of the maximum Intermediate score possible are rated NL, test takers whose score is between 33.3% and 50% are rated NM, and test takers whose scores are between 50% and 66.6% are rated NH. The test is Internet administered and computer scored (ACTFL, 2013).

The VLT consists of a receptive and a productive test (Institute for Test Research and Test Development, n.d.). It is modeled after the English VLT pioneered by Paul Nation (Nation, 1990). The VLT measures how many of the most frequent 5,000 words of German, Russian, and Spanish are known. It consists of five bands: the most frequent 1,000 words, 1,001 to 2,000 words, 2,001 to 3,000 words, 3,001 to 4,000 words, and 4,001 to 5,000 words. The receptive test, which was used in the present study, consisted of 10 clusters of six words each for each of these five bands. Each band was thus represented by 60 words. These words consisted of 30 nouns, 18 verbs, and 12 adjectives and were chosen at random from the 1,000 words of a band. Each cluster focused on one part of speech (e.g., nouns). Three words of a cluster were targets, which needed to be defined by choosing from a list of synonyms and paraphrases. The other three words were distractors. The maximum score per band was 30, that is, three points per cluster. Figure 4.1 provides an example of a cluster of the receptive VLT in English. Test takers are requested to select the word from column 2 that best matches the explanation in column 4.

1	business	A	part of a house
2	clock	B	animal with four legs
3	shoe	C	something used for writing
4	wall		
5	pencil		
6	horse		

Figure 4.1. Sample receptive Vocabulary Levels Test cluster

The definition of receptive mastery of a particular band varies slightly in the literature. The two most common percentages used are 80% (e.g., Xing & Fulcher 2007) and 85% (e.g., Schmitt, et al. 2001). In addition to the mastery criteria of 80% and 85%, we added 75% to this study in order to determine which of the three percentages shows the strongest internal consistency and reliability of the vocabulary tests. Hacking and Tschirner (2017) argued that the mastery criteria should be established individually for each test, and they proposed to use the percentage that best correlates with the composite score consisting of the summed individual band scores. The maximum composite score for the five bands was 150, that is, five times 30.

Analysis

To examine the internal consistency and reliability of each VLT, Cronbach's alpha was computed with the individual band scores as input. If Cronbach's alpha was above 0.70, the VLT was considered to be internally consistent.

To determine the best mastery criteria for each VLT, that is, 75%, 80%, or 85%, the vocabulary levels of each student were calculated using these mastery criteria. First, raw scores were turned into percentages. These percentages were then used to provide a vocabulary level for each test taker. If a test taker, for example, scored 90% on the first band, 90% on the second band, 75% on the third band, 70% on the fourth band, and 40% on the fifth band, his or her vocabulary level was 3,000 if the mastery criterion was 75%, and it was 2,000 if the mastery criterion was 80% or 85%. The highest band that crossed the 75%, 80%, or 85% threshold was considered to be the respective vocabulary level of the test taker.

Spearman's rho was calculated in order to assess the relationship between students' composite vocabulary scores, consisting of all correct answers of all bands, and the vocabulary levels established for them by each mastery criteria. The mastery criteria correlating most highly with the composite score was used as the mastery criteria for that particular test.

To answer research question 1, separate linear regression analyses were conducted with ACTFL reading proficiency level as the predictor variable and vocabulary levels as the response variable for each language. The results of the regression equation for each ACTFL level were used to answer research questions 2 and 3.

Results

Reading Proficiency

The German and Spanish RPT were scored according to the ACTFL scale. The Russian RPT was originally scored according to the ILR scale and was rescored for this study using the algorithm used for ACTFL proficiency levels. Following Rifkin (2005) and others, ACTFL levels were coded numerically as follows: NL = 1, NM = 2, NH = 3, IL = 4, IM = 5, IH = 6, AL = 7, AM = 8, AH = 9, and S = 10. Figure 4.2 shows the distribution of the scores for the three languages.

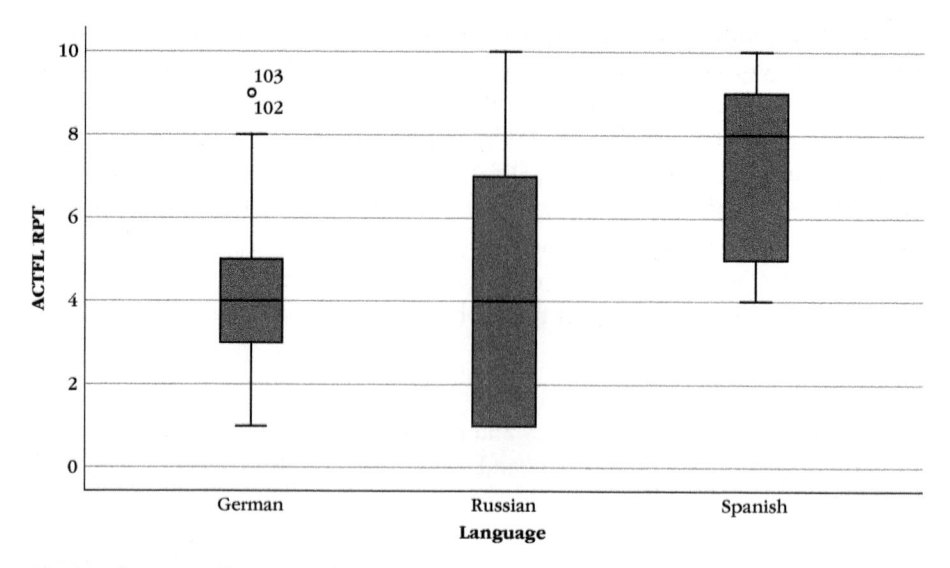

Figure 4.2. Distribution of ACTFL reading proficiency scores for German, Russian, and Spanish

Figure 4.2 shows that there were a few deviations from the normal distribution for each language. The distribution of German scores was leptokurtic, as can be seen by the interquartile range (box), which is relatively small: the central 50% of the scores varied from 3 (NH) to 5 (IM). In addition, there were two outliers at 9 (AH). The distribution of Russian scores was platykurtic. The central 50% of the scores varied from 1 (NL) to 7 (AL). In addition, it was positively skewed, that is, scores were bunched at the lower end of the scale (the NL level). Finally, the distribution of Spanish scores was negatively skewed; that is, the scores were bunched at the upper end of the scale (S). In general, however, the distributions are close enough to a normal distribution to make statistical inferences. The median (the line in the box) for German and Russian was similar (4 = IL), while it was considerably higher for Spanish (8 = AM), indicating that the Spanish students were, on average, much more proficient than the German and Russian students. The central 50% of the scores varied from 5 (IM) to 9 (AH). All three distributions, however, provided sufficient information, with data points ranging from 1 (NL) to 9 (AH) for German, 1 (NL) to 10 (S) for Russian, and 4 (IL) to 10 (S) for Spanish.

Vocabulary Size

Cronbach's alpha was computed with the individual band scores as input in order to determine the internal consistency of the three VLTs and to provide an overall reliability estimate. Cronbach's alpha is a measure of the internal consistency of the test, and it provides an estimate of the relationship between items and the interaction between subjects and items. In this case, each band was considered an item. Cronbach's alpha examines how closely related these bands are and whether they could be considered to measure the same construct. In this sense, Cronbach's alpha may be deemed a measure of scale reliability. Cronbach's alpha levels above 0.70 are considered acceptable levels. Table 4.2 provides Cronbach's alpha for the three languages. Table 4.2 also provides the correlations between each mastery criteria—75%, 80%, and 85% correct—and the composite score consisting of the summed individual band scores in order to determine the mastery criterion that best correlates with the composite score.

Table 4.2. Cronbach's Alpha Coefficient of Reliability Computed between Bands ($p < 0.05$) and Pearson's r Correlations Between Composite Vocabulary Score of the Vocabulary Levels Test and Three Mastery Criteria: 75%, 80%, and 85%

	N	Alpha	75%	80%	85%
German	197	0.939*	0.905**	0.891**	0.853**
Russian	48	0.951*	0.960**	0.959**	0.923**
Spanish	52	0.951*	0.956**	0.956**	0.937**

*$p < .05$. **$p < .01$.

Table 4.2 shows that Cronbach's alpha was statistically significant ($p < 0.05$) and very high for all three languages, indicating high internal consistency and reliability for the three vocabulary tests. Table 4.2 also shows that the mastery criterion best correlating with the composite score was 75% for German and Russian. For Spanish, the best correlation was tied between 75% and 80%. In the following, therefore, the mastery criteria of 75% will be used.

Reading Proficiency and Vocabulary Size

To provide an overview of the results, Tables 4.3–4.5 show cross tabulations of participants' ACTFL reading proficiency levels and vocabulary size for the three languages in question. Vocabulary sizes are indicated as follows: 0 = less than 1,000, 1 = 1,000, 2 = 2,000, 3 = 3,000, 4 = 4,000, and 5 = 5,000.

Table 4.3 shows that most test takers scored below the 1,000-vocabulary threshold for German. Most IL readers ($N = 61$, i.e., 79.2% of 77) scored below 1,000, while 18 (50% of 36) of the IM readers scored at 1,000 and above. All IH readers scored at 4,000 and above. It should be noted, however, that there were only three data points. All AL readers scored at 1,000 and above, and the majority of them ($N = 8$, i.e., 62% of 13) were at the 5,000 level. All AM and AH readers had a vocabulary size of at least 5,000.

Table 4.4 shows that approximately half of the test takers scored below the 1,000-vocabulary threshold in Russian. Half of the IL readers (3 of 6) scored below 1,000, the other half at 1,000. Fifty percent of the IM readers (3 of 6) scored above 1,000. AL and AM readers had vocabulary sizes of at least 3,000, and S readers had sizes of at least 4,000 words. Again, for some levels, there were very few data points.

Table 4.3. Cross Tabulation of Reading Proficiency Ratings and Vocabulary Levels for German

		\multicolumn{10}{c}{RPT}	
		NL	NM	NH	IL	IM	IH	AL	AM	AH	S	Total
Vocabulary Band	0	5	19	32	61	18	0	0	0	0	0	135
	1	0	0	2	12	2	0	2	0	0	0	18
	2	0	0	1	2	5	0	3	0	0	0	11
	3	0	0	0	2	4	0	0	0	0	0	6
	4	0	0	0	0	1	2	0	0	0	0	3
	5	0	0	0	0	6	1	8	2	2	0	24
Total		5	19	35	77	36	3	13	7	2	0	197

Note: NL = Novice Low, NM = Novice Mid, NH = Novice High, IL = Intermediate Low, IM = Intermediate Mid, IH = Intermediate High, AL = Advanced Low, AM = Advanced Mid, AH = Advanced High, S = Superior

Table 4.4. Cross Tabulation of Reading Proficiency Ratings and Vocabulary Levels for Russian

		NL	NM	NH	IL	IM	IH	AL	AM	AH	S	Total
Vocabulary	0	13	2	4	3	3	0	0	0	0	0	25
	1	0	0	0	3	0	2	0	0	0	0	5
	2	0	0	0	0	2	0	0	0	0	0	2
	3	0	0	0	0	1	0	2	1	0	0	4
	4	0	0	0	0	0	1	2	0	0	2	5
	5	0	0	0	0	0	0	1	1	0	5	7
Total		13	2	4	6	6	3	5	2	0	7	48

Table 4.5. Cross Tabulation of Reading Proficiency Ratings and Vocabulary Levels for Spanish

		NL	NM	NH	IL	IM	IH	AL	AM	AH	S	Total
Vocabulary	0	0	0	0	6	8	2	0	0	0	0	16
	2	0	0	0	1	0	0	0	0	0	0	1
	3	0	0	0	0	0	0	1	0	1	1	3
	4	0	0	0	0	0	0	5	3	5	3	16
	5	0	0	0	0	0	0	2	3	6	5	16
Total		0	0	0	7	8	2	8	6	12	9	52

Table 4.5 shows that most Spanish students ($N = 35$, i.e., 67.3% of 52) had vocabulary sizes of at least 3,000 words. Apart from one IL test taker, all Intermediate readers had vocabulary sizes of less than 1,000 words. Most of the Advanced readers had vocabulary sizes of at least 4,000 words, and most of the Superior readers had vocabulary sizes of at least 5,000 words.

In general, the Intermediate range seemed to be associated with a threshold vocabulary size of 1,000 words, while the Advanced range was associated with at least 3,000 or 4,000 words. The reason why German Advanced RPT levels seem to be associated with the 5,000 range may be due to the fact that most of the German students who had reached this vocabulary range were Dutch. The close relationship between Dutch and German may have given them an advantage with respect to vocabulary, but not necessarily with respect to reading. For Spanish, there seemed to be a gap between Intermediate and Advanced readers. Readers who were at the Advanced stage may have been able to take advantage of the vast shared vocabulary between English and Spanish, which may be particularly extensive at the 4,000 and 5,000 bands.

To determine the strength of the relationship between reading proficiency and vocabulary size and the predictive power of reading proficiency on vocabulary size, three separate linear regression analyses were conducted.

The simple linear regression analysis with reading proficiency as the predictor and vocabulary size as the response variable yielded a significant and large effect for all three languages. For German, it was as follows: $N = 197$, $R^2 = 0.531$, $p < 0.01$, intercept (α): -2.375, slope (β): 0.803. The model thus explained 53.1% of the vocabulary results, which is a large effect.

For Russian, the effect was also significant and even larger: $N = 48$, $R^2 = 0.796$, $p < 0.01$, intercept (α): -1.031, slope (β): 0.565. The model thus explained 79.6% of the vocabulary results.

For Spanish, the effect was also significant and also very large: $N = 52$, $R^2 = 0.736$, $p < 0.01$, intercept (α): -3.31, slope (β): 0.865. The model explained 73.6% of the vocabulary results.

To summarize for all three languages, the answer to research question 1 was that ACTFL reading proficiency strongly predicted vocabulary size, explaining between 53.1% (German), 73.4% (Spanish), and 79.6% (Russian) of the VLT results.

To answer the question of what vocabulary sizes are predicted by various reading proficiency levels (research question 2) and what differences there are between languages (research question 3), regression equations based on the above linear regression analyses were used to predict vocabulary sizes from ACTFL reading proficiency levels. For example, for Spanish the regression equation was $y = -1.031$ (intercept) $+ x * 0.565$ (slope), with y representing vocabulary size and x reading proficiency. Table 4.6 shows the vocabulary predictions by language and

ACTFL level. Because the ACTFL Novice level is characterized by understanding only isolated words and phrases, that is, it does not require any textual comprehension, the following table only includes ACTFL Intermediate, Advanced, and Superior levels.

Table 4.6. Vocabulary Size Predictions by ACTFL Reading Proficiency Levels

ACTFL Rating		IL	IM	IH	AL	AM	AH	S
Vocabulary Size	German	0.837	1.640	2.443	3.246	4.049	4.852	5.655
	Russian	1.229	1.794	2.359	2.924	3.489	4.054	4.619
	Spanish	0.114	0.970	1.826	2.682	3.538	4.394	5.250

Note: IL = Intermediate Low, IM = Intermediate Mid, IH = Intermediate High, AL = Advanced Low, AM = Advanced Mid, AH = Advanced High, S = Superior

Table 4.6 shows some clear patterns emerging for all three languages. Note that the figures provided represent the vocabulary ranges. For example, German IL = 0.837 indicates that IL predicts a vocabulary size of 83.7% of the 1,000 band, while IM = 1.640 indicates that IM predicts mastery of the 1,000 band plus 64% of the 2,000 band. Although there were some differences between the three languages at the IL and IM levels, IH seemed to be associated with the 2,000-word level, AL with the 3,000-word level, AM with the 3,000- and 4,000-word level, AH with the 4,000- and 5,000-word level, and S with the 5,000-word level. Although Russian started higher at IL and ended lower at S and Spanish started very low at IL, the general pattern of the regression analysis provides additional support for the postulation that the Intermediate level is associated with vocabulary sizes between 1,000 and 2,000 words and the Advanced level is associated with vocabulary sizes between 3,000 and 4,000 words.

Examining both the cross tabulation and regression results in response to RQ 2, the following seems to hold for all three languages: Intermediate Mid (IM) appears to be the threshold for the 1,000 band, while Advanced Low (AL) readers control the 3,000 band; Advanced Mid (AM) appears to be the threshold for the 4,000 band, while Superior (S) readers control, at least, the most frequent 5,000 words.

Discussion

Our study aimed at establishing the relationship between vocabulary knowledge and reading proficiency of L2 German, Russian, and Spanish learners. According to the 2012 ACTFL Proficiency Guidelines, readers with an ACTFL Advanced Mid (AM) reading proficiency are able to understand authentic narrative and descriptive texts such as "expanded descriptions of persons, places, and things and narrations about past, present, and future events." They understand the "main ideas, facts, and many supporting details." They even "may derive some meaning from texts that are structurally and/or conceptually more complex." At the Advanced High (AH) level, they "begin to recognize author-intended inferences" and they have gained an "emerging awareness of the aesthetic properties of language and of its literary styles," which permits them to comprehend "a wide variety of texts" (ACTFL, 2012, p. 22). These descriptors seem to come close to what Schmitt (2008, p. 332) and others call "adequate comprehension" of "a wide variety of texts." Vocabulary researchers commonly associate this level of reading proficiency with a receptive vocabulary size of 8,000 to 9,000 words based on corpus linguistic studies. The few empirical studies relating vocabulary size with reading proficiency suggest that far fewer lexical items may be needed to gain adequate comprehension of a wide variety of texts. The results of the present study support these suggestions.

If we take the AM/AH levels to be indicative of the ability to achieve adequate comprehension of a wide variety of texts, then a vocabulary size of 4,000 to 5,000 words may be sufficient for German, Russian, and Spanish. Reading proficiencies of AM and AH predicted a knowledge of the most frequent 4,000 to 5,000 words in all three languages. It is important to note, however, that the German data are based on students with very different L1 backgrounds (Arabic and Thai as well as English and Dutch), which resulted in correlations that were much lower than the ones for Russian and Spanish. This may indicate that language distance is a variable that should be controlled in future studies.

Milton and Treffers-Daller (2013) suggested that children and young adults add approximately 500 base words to their L1 mental vocabulary per year in a largely intentional and explicit way. They question the explanations of vocabulary growth that primarily rely on implicit learning and argue that intentionally learning one to two new words per day is a thoroughly achievable task. Although L2 learners do not have the same amount of time as native speakers to grow their vocabularies, their task also seems a doable one. They probably need to learn 1,000 base words per year. And again, intentionally learning three to four new words per day appears to be a thoroughly achievable task. In addition, a more intentional approach to reading instruction that matches reading difficulty levels with the vocabulary size at a student's disposal may be required. In what follows, we examine some curricular implications suggested by both the results of our study and the literature review contained in this chapter.

Implications for Language Program Directors: An Intentional Approach toward Vocabulary Building and Reading Instruction

As mentioned in the introductory section, a common goal of language programs is the ability to read and analyze a variety of authentic texts, which typically requires an Advanced level of proficiency in the ACTFL scale. Tschirner (2016) found that mean reading proficiency levels of college students were IH and AL in languages such as French, German, and Spanish in their fourth year of foreign language instruction, while the top 15% of students were AM, AH, and Superior. Reading may, in fact, be the only skill in which classroom L2 learners without extensive immersion experience may be able to reach the Advanced level. If, as we claim, there is a strong correlation between vocabulary knowledge and reading proficiency, it is imperative that language programs provide the necessary conditions to encourage and facilitate the acquisition of sufficient vocabulary to make the Advanced level an attainable goal of every language student. The most effective way to achieve that goal is to guarantee a clear articulation of vocabulary objectives across levels of instruction. Since this level of coordination is not common in most programs, language program directors (LPDs), in their position as overseers of the language curriculum, should play an active role in providing a well-articulated sequence of vocabulary learning objectives from beginning- to intermediate-, to advanced-level courses.

If we agree that reaching the 4,000 to 5,000 bands of vocabulary knowledge in the process of completing an undergraduate degree is a desirable goal, then approximately 1,000 words would need to be learned and retained per year. As Nation (2014) argues, a frequency approach will go a long way toward achieving the vocabulary sizes needed for effective reading proficiency—that is, the words studied in the first year should include the most frequent 1,000 of a language, the words studied in the second year should include the words from 1,001 to 2,000, and so on. The LPD, often the only expert in language acquisition in his/her program, can play a crucial role in helping faculty identify the vocabulary coverage needed to meet the objectives of each level in a language sequence and also in selecting appropriate materials that match the students' breadth of vocabulary. This process can begin with a basic assessment of students' vocabulary size, for example, by means of the VLT used in our study followed by an assessment of the appropriateness of the materials selected for each course. Cobb (2009) provides a number of suggestions that will help instructors become more aware of how vocabulary can determine the appropriateness of texts for learners and what vocabulary will be most useful to teach (see Cobb, 2009, for additional recommendations).

In addition to *what* vocabulary to teach, the LPD should also provide guidance and expertise on *how* to teach it. Research shows that becoming proficient at reading cannot be the result of exposure to input alone and that a combination of extensive reading and explicit vocabulary instruction may be the most effective recipe for success (Mondria, 2003; Schmitt, 2007). Although vocabulary depth—that is, the knowledge of how words are used, which includes knowledge about grammar, collocations, connotations, register, and style—still largely needs to be acquired experientially (i.e., while reading, writing, listening, and speaking), vocabulary breadth—that is, understanding the dictionary meaning of words—may be learned by studying words directly using well-established activities that commit words to memory (Khoii & Sharififar, 2013). Grabe (2009) argues that in order to learn vocabulary, students need a combination of "vocabulary instruction, vocabulary-learning strategies, extensive reading and word learning from context, heightened student awareness of new words, and motivation to use and collect words" (p. 283). Nation (2013) maintains that a successful vocabulary learning program consists of 25% direct learning, 25% input-oriented learning (listening and reading), 25% output-oriented indirect learning (speaking and writing), and 25% fluency training. In other words, such a program requires the use of known vocabulary in differing contexts and under increased comprehension strain due, for example, to the time pressure of the communication situation. Nation also argues that graded readers rather than authentic materials help students acquire new vocabulary more effectively and efficiently, especially at the lower levels of language acquisition (Nation & Wang, 1999).

Although L2 teaching pedagogy has emphasized the importance of learning new words in context and doing extensive reading for vocabulary acquisition, the specific word-level learning strategies that, for example, Grabe (2009) mentions have been largely absent from most current, communicative-oriented language classrooms. The extensive body of research associated with vocabulary learning clearly suggests that direct vocabulary learning is not only beneficial but is also efficient, because it reduces the number of encounters needed with a new vocabulary item from 12 to perhaps three (Nation, 2014). The present study indicates that although the number of words one needs to know in order to read and understand most nonacademic texts, including literary texts, is still large, it is not as daunting as the corpus linguistic research seems to suggest. Rather than 8,000 to 9,000 words—as, for example, Nation (2014) postulates for reading newspapers and novels with sufficient ease and speed—4,000 to 5,000 words may be just as adequate, if the newspaper-and-novel level can be equated with ACTFL Advanced Mid or Advanced High.

As Nation and others have argued, studying words directly must be accompanied by activities in which words are used—in the present case, used in reading. Because it may be impossible to reach even 90% text coverage in reading passages with 1,000 or fewer words, an extensive reading approach based on controlled vocabulary materials, such as graded readers, would still be required. While there has been a renaissance in the production of graded readers in a number of languages over the past 10 years, these readers have usually not been developed based on word frequency studies but instead with a focus on short sentences, simple words, and simple syntax. However, there is a strong possibility that such texts will include high-frequency vocabulary. Highlighting these high-frequency items would provide students with the experiential lexical encounters they need in order to solidify their knowledge of the meaning of these words and begin their long-term acquisition of word depth. Graded readers are available in the three languages studied here.

The German Bookshop[1] provides a number of options for all levels and ages, some with accompanying audio materials. In Spanish, European Schoolbooks Limited[2] offers a variety of graded readers of different levels and genres, from comic books to literary classics. The same company also offers a number of options in Russian.[3]

When graded readers are not available or are inadequate for the learner's level of proficiency, we suggest taking advantage of technology in order to determine the degree of lexical complexity of a text and thereby its appropriateness based on the learners' vocabulary size. Cobb (2009) provides a complete overview of ways in which computational tools can facilitate vocabulary learning and the development of reading proficiency in general, mainly by matching learners' level of vocabulary knowledge to texts that are slightly above that level. The CALPER Corpus Portal developed by the Center for Advanced Language Proficiency Education and Research at Penn State University also provides a useful resource that describes in detail how to build a corpus and then use it for instructional purposes including vocabulary instruction.[4]

Matching texts to learners' vocabulary levels is an example of the type of lexical learning that Nation calls fluency training. Another approach toward achieving the text coverage needed for text comprehension and lexical learning is reading the same text several times, while focusing on different parts of its vocabulary load and focusing on it in various ways. While high-frequency vocabulary may be pretaught and be the explicit focus of vocabulary exercises associated with the reading passage, less frequent vocabulary necessary for understanding the passage and for achieving 90% text coverage may simply be glossed using a variety of techniques. Distinguishing between these two kinds of lexical items while reading, that is, words needed for text comprehension and words to be learned, allows learners to gain explicit knowledge of high frequency words in context while achieving the satisfaction of understanding a reading passage.

In sum, the guidance and expertise provided by the LPD are crucial for leading discussions about how the teaching and learning of vocabulary should progress between levels of instruction. Understanding the complex processes involved in L2 reading and the critical role of vocabulary knowledge in those processes is essential for providing an effective approach to vocabulary building and reading instruction.

Conclusion

Overwhelming evidence shows that there is a close relationship between the size of one's vocabulary and the ease with which different kinds of texts may be read.

---

[1] https://www.germanbookshop.co.uk/germanbooks/section/m4/c21
[2] https://www.eurobooks.co.uk/languagebooks/subject/SPA/m4/c21/6
[3] https://www.eurobooks.co.uk/languagebooks/subject/RUS/m4
[4] http://calper.la.psu.edu/content/corpus-portal

The question continues to be how large of a vocabulary learners need for various purposes and how it can be learned. While figures derived from corpus linguistic research have been rather daunting, consisting of 8,000 to 9,000 lexical units, the few existing empirical studies linking vocabulary size to reading proficiency seemed to question this conclusion. In addition, almost all studies looking at vocabulary sizes and what they allow people to do focused on English. The present study therefore took as its starting point languages other than English, in this case German, Russian, and Spanish, and it asked what vocabulary sizes are predicted by various reading proficiency levels. The present study provided additional strong evidence to support the argument that vocabulary size is a very strong predictor of reading proficiency, and it provided preliminary answers to what kinds of vocabulary sizes may be needed for various reading proficiency levels as measured by the ACTFL Proficiency Guidelines. For all three languages, the predictions were very similar, ranging from 1,000 to 2,000 words for the Intermediate levels to 3,000 to 4,000 words for the Advanced level and 5,000 words for the Superior level. We also argued that the best mix for quickly building up a sufficiently large vocabulary for reading purposes includes studying vocabulary directly while solidifying form–meaning comprehension and gaining vocabulary breadth knowledge through extensive reading (Day & Bamford, 1998). Among the most crucial aspects of a vocabulary program are the selection of the vocabulary and the selection of the reading texts used to solidify and expand the learning of words. The selection of vocabulary should be informed by frequency studies, while the selection of texts should be informed by the vocabulary load of the text, which calls for the use of graded readers at reading proficiency levels below the Advanced level.

References

ACTFL (2012). *ACTFL proficiency guidelines* [Electronic document]. Retrieved from http://www.actfl.org/sites/default/files/pdfs/ACTFLProficiencyGuidelines2012_FINAL.pdf

ACTFL (2013). *ACTFL reading proficiency test (RPT): Familiarization manual and ACTFL proficiency guidelines 2012—reading* [Electronic document]. Retrieved from https://www.languagetesting.com/pub/media/wysiwyg/ACTFL_FamManual_Reading_2015.pdf

Berkemeyer, V. (1994). Anaphoric resolution and text comprehension for readers of German. *Die Unterrichtspraxis, 27*(2), 15–22.

Bernhardt, E. B. (2010). *Understanding advanced second-language reading.* New York, NY: Routledge.

Bornstein, M., & Haynes, O. M. (1998). Vocabulary competence in early childhood: Measurement, latent construct, and predictive validity. *Child Development, 69,* 654–671.

Brisbois, J. E. (1995). Connections between first- and second-language reading. *Journal of Reading Behavior, 27,* 565–584.

Carver, R. P. (1994). Percentage of unknown vocabulary words in text as a function of the relative difficulty of the text: Implications for instruction. *Journal of Reading Behavior, 26,* 413–437.

Cobb, T. (2009). Necessary or nice: Computers in second language reading. In Z. Han & N. J. Anderson (Eds.), *Second language reading research and instruction: Crossing the boundaries* (pp. 144–172). Ann Arbor, MI: University of Michigan Press.

Council of Europe (2001). *Common framework of reference for languages.* Cambridge, UK: Cambridge University Press.

D'Anna, C. A., Zechmeister, E. B., & Hall, J. W. (1991). Toward a meaningful definition of vocabulary size. *Journal of Reading Behavior, 23,* 109–122.

Day, R. R., & Bamford, J. (1998). *Extensive reading in the second language classroom.* Cambridge, UK: Cambridge University Press.

Garrison-Fletcher, L. (2012). *The acquisition of L2 reading comprehension: The relative contribution of linguistic knowledge and existing reading ability* (Doctoral Dissertation). Retrieved from ProQuest Dissertations and Theses Database. (UMI No. 3499239).

Glaboniat, M., Müller, M., Rusch, P., Schmitz, H., & Wertenschlag, L. (2005). *Profile Deutsch.* Berlin, Germany: Langenscheidt.

Glaboniat, M., Perlmann-Balme, M., & Studer, T. (2016). *Goethe-Zertifikat B1: Deutschprüfung für Jugendliche und Erwachsene, Wortliste.* Munich, Germany: Goethe-Institut.

Goulden, R., Nation, I. S. P., & Read, J. (1990). How large can a receptive vocabulary be? *Applied Linguistics, 11,* 341–363.

Grabe, W. (2009). *Reading in a second language: Moving from theory to practice.* New York, NY: Cambridge University Press.

Hacking, J. F., & Tschirner, E. (2017). The contribution of vocabulary knowledge to reading proficiency: The case of college Russian. *Foreign Language Annals, 50,* 500–518.

Hacking, J. F., Tschirner, E., & Rubio, F. (in press). Vocabulary size, reading proficiency and curricular design: The case of college Chinese, Russian and Spanish. In S. Gass & P. Winke (Eds.), *Foreign language proficiency in higher education.* Cham, Switzerland: Springer.

Hazenberg, S., & Hulstijn, J. (1996). Defining a minimal receptive second language vocabulary for non-native university students: An empirical investigation. *Applied Linguistics, 17,* 145–163.

Hu, M., & Nation, I. S. P. (2000). Unknown vocabulary density and reading comprehension. *Reading in a Foreign Language, 13,* 403–430.

Huhta, A., Alderson, J. C., Nieminen, L., & Ullakonoja, R. (2011, August). Diagnosing reading in L2: Predictors and vocabulary profiles. Paper presented at the ACTFL CEFR Conference, Provo, UT.

Institute for Test Research and Test Development (n.d.). *Vocabulary Tests.* Retrieved from http://www.itt-leipzig.de/static/startseite.html.

Khoii, R., & Sharififar, S. (2013). Memorization versus semantic mapping in L2 vocabulary acquisition. *ELT Journal, 67,* 199–209.

Koda, K. (1993). Transferred L1 strategies and L2 syntactic structure in L2 sentence comprehension. *Modern Language Journal, 77,* 490–500.

Kusseling, F., & Lonsdale, D. (2013). A corpus-based assessment of French CEFR lexical content. *Canadian Modern Language Review, 69,* 436–461.

Lahti, L. (2015). Supplement to Lauri Lahti's conference article "Educational framework for adoption of vocabulary based on Wikipedia linkage and spaced learning." Retrieved from https://aaltodoc.aalto.fi/bitstream/handle/123456789/15382/J__lahti_lauri_2015.pdf?sequence=1&isAllowed=y

Laufer, B. (1992). How much lexis is necessary for reading comprehension? In P. J. L. Arnaud & H. Béjoint (Eds.), *Vocabulary and applied linguistics* (pp. 126–132). London, UK: Macmillan.

Meara, P., & Milton, J. (2003). *The Swansea levels test.* Newbury, United Kingdom: Express.

Milton, J. (2010). The development of vocabulary breadth across the CEFR levels. In I. Bartning, M. Martin, & I. Vedder (Eds.), *Communicative proficiency and linguistic development: Intersections between SLA and language testing research, Eurosla Monographs* (Vol. 1) (pp. 211–232). N. P.: Eurosla. Retrieved from http://eurosla.org/monographs/EM01/EM01tot.pdf

Milton, J., & Treffers-Daller, J. (2013). Vocabulary size revisited: The link between vocabulary size and academic achievement. *Applied Linguistics Review, 4,* 151–172.

Mondria, J.-A. (2003). The effects of inferring, verifying, and memorizing on the retention of L2 word meanings. *Studies in Second Language Acquisition, 25,* 473–499.

Nation, I. S. P. (1990). *Teaching and learning vocabulary.* New York, NY: Newbury House.

Nation, I. S. P. (2006). How large a vocabulary is needed for reading and listening? *Canadian Modern Language Review, 63,* 59–82.

Nation, I. S. P. (2013). *Learning vocabulary in another language* (2nd ed.). Cambridge, UK: Cambridge University Press.

Nation, I. S. P. (2014). How much input do you need to learn the most frequent 9,000 words? *Reading in a Foreign Language, 26*(2), 1–16.

Nation, I. S. P., & Wang, K. (1999). Graded readers and vocabulary. *Reading in a Foreign Language, 12,* 355–380.

Ouellette, G. (2006). What's meaning got to do with it: The role of vocabulary in word reading and reading comprehension. *The Journal of Educational Psychology, 98,* 554–566.

Perlmann-Balme, M. (n.d.). *Goethe-Zertifikat A1: Start Deutsch 1, Wortliste.* Retrieved from https://www.goethe.de/pro/relaunch/prf/et/A1_SD1_Wortliste_02.pdf

Rifkin, B. (2005). A ceiling effect in traditional classroom foreign language instruction: Data from Russian. *Modern Language Journal, 89,* 3–18.

Schmitt, N. (2007). Current perspectives on vocabulary learning and teaching. In J. Cummins & C. Davison (Eds.), *International handbook of English language teaching.* New York, NY: Springer, 827–841.

Schmitt, N. (2008). Review article: Instructed second language vocabulary learning. *Language Teaching Research, 12,* 329–363.

Schmitt, N. (2010). *Researching vocabulary: A vocabulary research manual.* London, UK: Palgrave Macmillan.

Schmitt, N., Schmitt, D., & Clapham, C. (2001). Developing and exploring the behavior of two new versions of the vocabulary levels test. *Language Testing, 18,* 55–88.

Schmitt, N., & Schmitt, D. (2014). A reassessment of frequency and vocabulary size in L2 vocabulary teaching. *Language Teaching, 47,* 484–503.

Schmitt, N., Jiang, X., & Grabe, W. (2011). The percentage of words known in a text and reading comprehension. *The Modern Language Journal, 95,* 26–43.

Sparks, R. L., Patton, J., Ganschow, L., & Humbach, N. (2012). Do L1 reading achievement and L1 print exposure contribute to the prediction of L2 proficiency? *Language Learning, 62,* 473–505.

Tschirner, E. (2016). Listening and reading proficiency levels of college students. *Foreign Language Annals, 49,* 201–223.

Tschirner, E. (2017). Wortschatzwissen als Grundlage zweitsprachlicher Kompetenzen. In M. Clalüna & B. Tscharner (Eds.), *Bausteine des Spracherwerbs DaF/DaZ: Wortschatz—Chunks—Grammatik: Akten der Sechsten Gesamtschweizerischen Tagung für Deutschlehrerinnen und Deutschlehrer,* 17. und 18. Juni 2016 (pp. 11–21). Bern, Switzerland: AKDaF.

Xing, P., & Fulcher, G. (2007). Reliability assessment for two versions of vocabulary levels tests. *System, 35,* 181–191.

Chapter 5
Vocabulary Coverage and Lexical Characteristics in L2 Spanish Textbooks

Claudia Sánchez-Gutiérrez, University of California, Davis
Nausica Marcos Miguel, Denison University
Michael K. Olsen, Tennessee Technological University

Introduction

Textbooks are part of most educational settings and often guide the design of curricular content (Marcos Miguel, 2015; McDonough, Shaw, & Masuhara, 2013; McGrath, 2013). In the case of second language (L2) teaching, textbooks inform teachers' and Language Program Directors' (LPDs') choices regarding the vocabulary items to target in instruction (Allen, 2008). However, little is known about the characteristics of vocabulary in textbooks at the university level and how these characteristics might affect word learnability.

Previous literature has analyzed the extent to which textbooks follow a frequency criterion, as identified by frequency lists, when selecting vocabulary (Davies & Face, 2006; Lipinski, 2010). While this is a good starting point for research, it fails to account for lexical characteristics that might influence word learnability (Milton, 2009). For example, research shows that short words with concrete meanings are learned more quickly than long words with abstract meanings (Alsaif & Milton, 2012). Yet few studies have questioned the lexical characteristics of the words included in textbooks (e.g., Alsaif & Milton, 2012).

This study will include both a lexical frequency analysis and an investigation into the lexical characteristics of the words in the textbooks. Concretely, it will explore two lexical characteristics that affect word learnability, namely, word length and concreteness of meaning. Moreover, the evolution of word length and concreteness from elementary textbooks (ETs) to intermediate textbooks (ITs) will be investigated. This information is relevant for language teachers and LPDs, as it may help them select more learnable and useful lexical items for their curricula, make informed decisions on textbook adoptions, and better train their students to cope with lexical characteristics that increase the learning burden of a word (Laufer, 1990, 2012).

Lexical Frequency

While many vocabulary selection criteria for L2 classrooms could be proposed, lexical frequency has been one of the most used in the L2 acquisition literature (Horst, 2013; Nation, 2006; Schmitt & Schmitt, 2014). For example, Barcroft's (2012) input-based incremental vocabulary instruction approach suggests that vocabulary learning should not be reduced to incidental learning, but should rather be the result of a vocabulary plan based on a needs analysis or on frequency lists for the target language. For English, Barcroft points to the Academic Word List as well as more specific frequency lists for health or banking as useful resources for LPDs and other language teaching practitioners. Similar resources exist for other languages (see Appendix I).

Several authors have argued that learning the most frequent words in an L2 provides significant coverage of the linguistic input to which speakers of that language are exposed. Webb and Rodgers (2009a, 2009b) show that knowing the 3,000 most frequent words in English allows learners to understand over 95% of the words in TV shows and movies. Davies (2005) presents similar results in Spanish, noting that the 3,000 most frequent words in Spanish offer 94% coverage in oral texts. The level of coverage offered by these 3,000 words is smaller for written texts. For instance, Davies (2005) calculated that, in Spanish, the 3,000 most frequent words cover approximately 90% of words in written texts.

Schmitt, Jiang, and Grabe (2011) demonstrated that learners who know 95% to 98% of the words in a text are likely to understand it at 60%–68%.[1] Van Zeeland and Schmitt (2012) found that 95% of lexical coverage ensures a comprehension of about 75%. While knowledge of the 3,000 most frequent words in an L2 does not ensure complete comprehension of written and oral texts, compelling reasons nevertheless exist for prioritizing these words in the L2 classroom.

First, the frequency distribution of vocabulary in any given language is extremely skewed, with a few words being very frequent and covering most of the vocabulary. Meanwhile, a substantial number of words is rarely repeated, offering insignificant overall lexical coverage. As evidenced in Figure 5.1, the 1,000 most frequent words offer extremely broad coverage, while each of the next 1,000 words quickly becomes insignificant in terms of coverage. This explains why learning the first 1,000 words is so vital for L2 learners. However, a lexicon of merely 1,000 words is not sufficient to even approximate the coverage needed to facilitate text comprehension, and words in the next two bands of 1,000 words still offer an additional coverage of 3%–8% each. Frequency bands after the 3,000-word threshold, conversely, do not even reach 1% of coverage.

Additionally, Schmitt and Schmitt (2014) note that learner dictionaries of English generally comprise around 3,000 words, 90% of which are amongst the

---

[1] This number was based on the results of a reading comprehension questionnaire completed immediately after the reading took place.

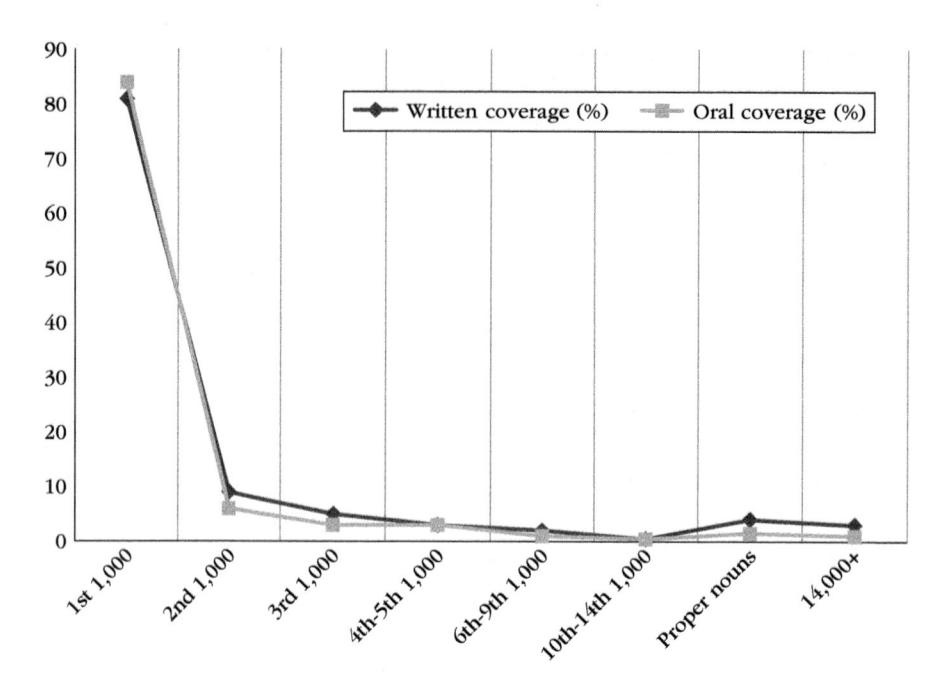

Figure 5.1. Percentages of text coverage by frequency (Nation, 2006, p. 79)

3,000 most frequent words. The authors argue that this finding demonstrates how word frequency and word usefulness, as judged by lexicographers, are not at odds, but actually tend to cohere. If the words chosen by lexicographers to be part of learner dictionaries correspond, for the most part, with the 3,000 most frequent words in the language, it seems obvious that those words should be given priority in the classroom. Finally, the authors show that most L2 English graded readers[2] contain around 3,000 different words, suggesting that the acquisition of 3,000 words is a reasonable goal for learners who wish to be equipped for reading non-adapted L2 texts. All these arguments indicate that teachers should prioritize the most frequent 3,000 words, as these words provide a solid lexical base for understanding most English L2 texts that students will encounter. These arguments might be applied to other L2s. For instance, Davies' (2005) study shows similar percentages of coverage at each frequency level for Spanish.

In the context of American universities, where language courses are generally taught for two years, after which students are expected to enroll in target-language literature, culture or linguistics classes, the 3,000 most frequent words should be taught during those first two years to the extent possible. Gairns and Redman (1986), reported by Milton (2009), "suggest an average of 8 to 12 productive items

---

[2] These are addressed mostly to elementary and intermediate learners, as more advanced learners are expected to read unmodified texts.

per class as representing reasonable input, which might lead to over 1000 items being presented in 125 hours of tuition" (p. 196). Therefore, in a semester of 14 weeks with three hours of instruction per week, a teacher could present 336–504 words per semester, 672–1,008 per year,[3] and 1,344–2,016 in two years.

Thus, while time constraints may prevent students from learning all 3,000 words, the concept of frequency and the goal of 3,000 words can nevertheless serve as guiding principles for vocabulary selection. It is not a matter of teaching all 3,000 words, but of ensuring that most words taught belong to the list of most frequent words.

Impact of Lexical Characteristics in Learning and Processing Burden

Although frequency represents a useful measure for selecting vocabulary, it does not provide information on the learning burden of those words. Indeed, the most frequent words are not necessarily the easiest to learn and, conversely, infrequent words could potentially be extremely easy. For this reason, Laufer (1990) suggests that word learnability should also be taken into account when selecting vocabulary for the L2 classroom. She states that:

> When words are easy to learn, they should be taught even if, on the basis of the frequency/range principles, they would not be considered useful. Cognates, words related structurally to already familiar words, and words with exact L1 equivalents all may require little learning effort and at the same time increase the communicative ability of the learner considerably. (p. 150).

LPDs, textbook authors, and language instructors should thus reflect on their criteria for selecting target vocabulary: frequency is important, but learner characteristics and word learnability must be considered as well. Of the many factors affecting word learnability, similarities between the L1 and the L2 (e.g., cognateness and L1 equivalency) may seem like the best complement to frequency when selecting target vocabulary. Yet this selection criterion cannot be the main or the only one. If we take English as the L1 by default, and thus assume that students will learn Spanish–English cognates faster than noncognates, we might favor L1 English students over learners with different linguistic backgrounds (see Szubko-Sitarek, 2011). Given the increasingly diverse population of students in American universities (Institute of International Education, 2015), a vocabulary list based only on frequency and L1/L2 similarities may disadvantage certain multilingual learners. Thus, when selecting vocabulary, it is important to also consider learnability characteristics that are not related to the learner's L1.

---

[3] These numbers would include instances of both explicit teaching and incidental learning, given that several words, as articles or classroom management words will be repeated class after class and might not require as much explicit attention.

Several authors have investigated such characteristics (Alsaif & Milton, 2012; Masrai & Milton, 2015; Willis & Ohashi, 2012) and have found an increased learning burden for words that are long, as opposed to short (Alsaif & Milton, 2012; Peters, 2016; Willis & Ohashi, 2012), and abstract, as opposed to concrete (Alsaif & Milton, 2012; De Groot & Keijzer, 2000; Ellis & Beaton, 1993). Thus, the longer and more abstract a word is, the more difficult it is to retain, whereas the shorter and more concrete it is, the easier it is to retain. The form *dog* will be more easily remembered than *institutionalization*.

However, the difficulty of long and abstract words can be tackled with two simple strategies. On the one hand, while words in Spanish tend to be longer than their English counterparts (Cantos & Sanchez, 2011), this is mostly due to the reliance of the Spanish language on suffixation as a means of creating new words (Lang, 2009). Thus, training the students in the recognition and use of productive affixes and word formation rules in Spanish could go a long way in addressing the difficulties that word length might represent (Morin, 2003, 2006). On the other hand, words with abstract meanings are more difficult to learn because they cannot be directly associated with images or sensorial experiences. Indeed, abstract vocabulary is so difficult to learn that a popular vocabulary-acquisition strategy, the keyword technique (see Hulstijn, 1997; Ecke, 1999, 2004 for a review), encourages learners to visualize a concrete object that they can link to an abstract concept. For example, a Spanish speaker learning the word *canny* in English could choose to associate it with the similar-sounding *can*, which is a Spanish word for *dog*. Then, he could elaborate the image of a dog with a pipe looking like a detective, which would be easy to connect to the meaning of *canny* as "clever." In this way, the abstract word *canny* is now attached to an image that bridges in a more concrete way the newly encountered word in the L2 with the L1.

Textbook Analyses of Frequency, Concreteness, and Length

Word frequency in L2 English textbooks is relatively well researched (Alcaraz Mármol, 2009; Criado & Sánchez, 2009; Donzelli, 2007; Milton, 2009). Most of these studies determine the extent to which textbooks include vocabulary items from the first 2,000–3,000 most frequent English words and above.[4] For example, Donzelli (2007) analyzed a textbook utilized in a primary school for Italian-speaking children who were learning English. The textbook included half of the items from the 1,000-word band, 17.80% of the items from the 2,000-word band, and 30% from the 2,500–3,000-word band. The presence of low-frequency words (over the

---

[4] The program Range (Nation, n.d.) is widely used for the purpose of determining what percentage of words in a text is drawn from which band of the word list. The New General Service List, the Academic Word List, and the British National Corpus (BNC) or the Corpus of Contemporary American English (COCA) are the main tools for measuring frequencies in English as an L2. For more information, visit: https://www.victoria.ac.nz/lals/about/staff/paul-nation

2,500 mark, in this case) led Donzelli to conclude that the book offered a rich lexical input where word frequency was not the leading criterion in vocabulary selection. Some examples of "unusual words" in the textbook were *basketball, soccer, homework, chicken,* and *geese*. Although these are not high frequency in the wordlists utilized, they are pertinent words for students that age, according to the author.

Similarly, Alcaraz Mármol (2009) found 50% of words from the 1,000-word band, 16% of words from the 2,000-word band, and 40% of words from the 2,000–3,000-word band in a primary textbook utilized for Spanish-speaking children learning English in Spain. She also separately analyzed each textbook chapter and found different percentages by chapter. Nevertheless, words in the 1,000 band were consistently the most frequent, representing between 53% and 80% of the words in each chapter. As was the case with Donzelli's (2007) findings, the words above the 2,000-band referred to specific content targeting young learners, such as *hamster, schoolbag, spider, pumpkin,* or *zoo*.

Compared to English, there are fewer studies on frequency in Spanish L2 textbooks (Davies & Face, 2006; Godev, 2009; López Jiménez, 2014). Two previous studies analyzing frequencies in adult L2 Spanish textbooks are Davies and Face (2006) and Godev (2009).[5] Davies and Face explored the vocabulary chapter lists (i.e., the list of explicit targets at the end of each chapter) of six Spanish textbooks: three first-year and three second-year textbooks used in American universities. These textbooks included 10%–50% of the 2,000 most frequent Spanish words. As was the case in other studies (e.g., Lipinski, 2010; see Milton, 2009), vocabulary selection varied by book. For example, a book such as "Dos Mundos" had 3,217 words, of which only 50% belonged to the 1,000–3,000 band, whereas only 28% of the 1,689 words in "Mundo 21" were in the 1–1,689 band. Thus, textbook authors seemingly disregard frequency when selecting target items and cover only a relatively small percentage of the most frequent Spanish words. These results were confirmed in Godev's (2009) study, which also suggested that frequency played little to no role in the selection of vocabulary for five first-year college Spanish textbooks published in the United States.

This situation is not exclusive of Spanish and English L2 textbooks, as Lipinski (2010) also found that 50% to 60% of the words in the 1,000 band were included in three German L2 textbooks for first- and second-year programs. Words from the 2,000- and 3,000-word bands were represented only minimally in these textbooks, at approximately 30% and 15%–20%, respectively. These results are disheartening, given the importance of focusing on those 3,000 most frequent words in the L2 classroom (see Horst, 2013; Schmitt & Schmitt,

---

[5] In most studies on Spanish L2, Davies' (2006) *Frequency Dictionary* is used for frequency assessments of textbook vocabulary, as it presents the 5,000 most frequent words of the Spanish language, calculated from a version of the *Corpus del Español*, which contains 20 million words (Davies, 2002).

2014). Moreover, low-frequency words are common in L2 textbooks because vocabulary selection is generally based on semantic clusters (e.g., food, family, and free time) rather than frequency (Davies & Face, 2006; López Jiménez, 2014).

While the role of frequency in selecting textbook vocabulary items has been studied often, it is rarely studied in combination with the concreteness and length of target items. Indeed, to the best of our knowledge, only one such study has been conducted that pointed in that direction. Alsaif and Milton (2012) analyzed 22 English L2 textbooks, from beginner to advanced levels, used in Saudi Arabia primary and secondary schools. When the included vocabulary items were added together as a sum, all 22 textbooks covered "just over 80% of the 2000 most frequent words" and "half of the most frequent 5000 words" (p. 26) in seven years of English courses. Additionally, Alsaif and Milton noticed that little new vocabulary was added in higher proficiency textbooks that was not already present in lower proficiency books. This insufficient inclusion of appropriate vocabulary at increasing proficiency levels might explain the stagnating vocabulary level observed by Alsaif (2011) in students of English in Saudi Arabia. Finally, the authors reported that shorter and more concrete words in the textbooks were learned better by the students. Alsaif and Milton (2012) interpret this finding as an argument in favor of introducing not only high-frequency words in the textbooks but also words that are short and concrete, whenever these fit into a communicative context that is relevant for the course.

Objectives and Research Questions

This study aims to complement previous research in two ways. First, it will analyze word frequency, concreteness, and word length in a larger corpus of textbooks than any previous studies and will be the first to look at these three variables in Spanish L2 textbooks. Additionally, it will explore the extent to which words in ET and IT textbooks differ from one another in terms of these three characteristics. While Alsaif and Milton (2012) have already looked at the percentage of words from different frequency bands added to textbooks as proficiency levels increase, no study to date has analyzed the evolution of word concreteness and length at different proficiency levels.

Accordingly, this study addresses the following research questions (RQs):

1. To what extent do elementary and intermediate Spanish textbooks cover the 3,000 most frequent words in Spanish?
2. Is there an increase in the number of less frequent words from elementary to intermediate textbooks?
3. Are words in intermediate Spanish textbooks more abstract and longer than words in elementary Spanish textbooks?

Methods

Textbooks

Sixteen textbooks used in American Universities were selected for this study. Eight textbooks were ETs, designed for students with novice proficiency levels, and eight were ITs, designed for students at novice-high and intermediate levels of proficiency on the ACTFL proficiency scale. ETs are generally used during the first year of university-level Spanish courses, whereas ITs are used during the second year of Spanish instruction. Table 5.1 lists the specific books included in each proficiency level.

Processing of the Textbook Glossaries

The glossary at the end of each of the 16 textbooks was scanned and saved in plain text format. Additionally, the list of the 20,000 most frequent words in Spanish was downloaded[6] from the website of the *Corpus del Español* (Davies, 2002) and divided into four frequency bands: band 1 was composed of the first 1,000 most frequent words in Spanish, band 2 contained the next 1,000 most frequent words, band 3 contained the next 1,000 most frequent words, and the low-frequency band included all the words that were not among the 3,000 most frequent words in the corpus. AntWordProfiler (Anthony, 2014) was used to perform the frequency analyses: each glossary was entered in the software as a User File and the lists of

Table 5.1. Textbooks Analyzed in this Study

Elementary Textbooks	Intermediate Textbooks
Adelante, 2nd ed. (2015), Vista Higher Learning	*Anda*, 2nd ed. (2013), Pearson *(EC)*
Arriba, 6th ed. (2015), Pearson	*(AC) Atando Cabos*, 4th ed. (2012), Pearson
(CB) Con Brío, 3rd ed. (2013), Wiley	*Conexiones*, 5th ed. (2014), Pearson
(DyH) Dicho y Hecho, 10th ed. (2015), Wiley	*En Comunidad* (2008), McGraw-Hill
(DM) Dos mundos, 6th ed. (2006), McGraw-Hill	*Enfoques*, 4th ed. (2016), Vista Higher Learning
Nexos, 3rd ed. (2013), Cengage	*Fusión* (2010), Pearson
(PV) Pura Vida (2014), Wiley	*Imagina*, 3rd ed. (2015), Vista Higher Learning
Vistas, 4th ed. (2012), Vista Higher Learning	*(PyA) Punto y Aparte*, 5th ed. (2015), McGraw-Hill

---

[6] This is not a free service, but the list of the first 5,000 most frequent words in Spanish will soon be available in the second edition of the *Frequency Dictionary of Spanish* (Davies & Davies, 2018). The second edition will represent a significant improvement compared with the first one (Davies, 2006), as frequency data are obtained from a corpus of two billion words, extracted from websites and blogs from all over the Spanish-speaking world. Additionally, data were gathered during 2013–2014, which ensures that frequency counts are based on the current state of the language.

words from each frequency band were entered as Levels lists.[7] Using these data, the program sorted the words from each glossary into the appropriate frequency list and tallied the number of words from each glossary belonging to each band.

Additionally, the concreteness and word length data were obtained from EsPal (Duchon, Perea, Sebastián-Gallés, Martí, & Carreiras, 2013), an online repository of lexicometric information (e.g., length, frequency, concreteness, and familiarity) calculated from a corpus of over 700 million words in Spanish. Length was computed as the number of letters in a word, while concreteness data were obtained by asking native speakers of Spanish to rate the concreteness of words on a scale from 1 (extremely abstract) to 7 (extremely concrete).

Results

Lexical Frequency in Textbooks

Two aspects of the frequency of words in ETs and ITs were studied to answer RQ1: (1) the distribution of words in each textbook by frequency bands (i.e., 1, 2, 3, and low frequency) and (2) the percentage of words from each band in each textbook. These are complementary ways of looking at the data, as the former gives an insight into the coverage offered by words from each band in each textbook, while the latter indicates a distributional proportion of words from each band.

This distinction is relevant because the first measure is dependent on the length of the glossary. For example, if a textbook with a glossary of 4,500 words includes 900 of the 1,000 most frequent words, these will barely represent 20% of the total glossary. This result might give the false impression that the book includes few words from band 1. Conversely, if those same 900 words are part of a glossary that contains 1,200 words, the proportion will be 75%. Thus, while the level of coverage offered by words in a specific frequency band provides important information, such data should be analyzed in the light of a second result: the number of words at each frequency band included in the textbook. Ideally, a textbook that focuses on the 3,000 most frequent words in Spanish should follow these two premises: (1) words from bands 1 to 3 offer a high level of coverage in the glossary, and (2) most words from those frequency bands are included. ETs should include most of the words from band 1 and around 50% of those in band 2, while ITs should include the other 50% of words in band 2 and most words from band 3. Table 5.2 describes the number and percentage of coverage of words in each frequency band in ETs.

As can be observed in Table 5.2, words from bands 1 to 3 represent over 50% of the words in all ETs, with four books reaching a coverage of over 60% for those words: *Adelante*, *Con Brío*, *Dicho y Hecho*, and *Vistas*. However, Figure 5.2 shows

---

[7] For more information on the program, see http://www.laurenceanthony.net/software/antwordprofiler/

Table 5.2. Total of Words and Distribution of Words by Frequency Band in Elementary Texts

	Adelante		Arriba		CB		DyH		DM		Nexos		PV		Vistas	
	N	%	N	%	N	%	N	%	N	%	N	%	N	%	N	%
1	576	33.4	729	24.8	381	32.3	408	32.7	832	21.6	534	28.9	379	33.2	438	33.8
2	303	17.6	535	18.2	222	18.8	223	17.9	638	16.6	316	17.1	181	15.9	222	17.1
3	197	11.4	387	13.1	133	11.3	131	10.5	481	12.5	228	12.4	125	11	149	11.5
1–3	1,076	62.4	1,651	56.1	736	62.3	762	61	1,951	50.6	1,078	58.4	685	60	809	62.4
> 3	647	37.6	1,292	43.9	445	37.7	487	39	1,902	49.4	768	41.6	456	40	488	37.6
Total	1,723		2,943		1,181		1,249		3,853		1,846		1,141		1,297	

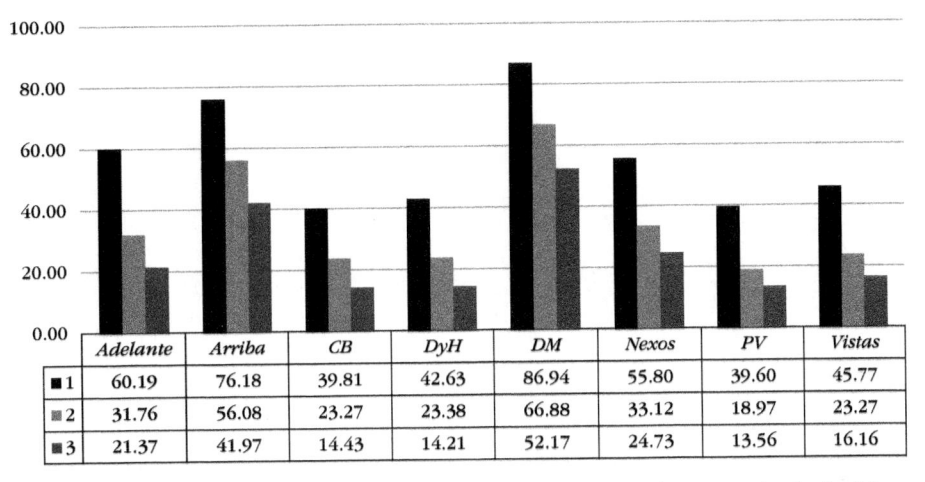

	Adelante	Arriba	CB	DyH	DM	Nexos	PV	Vistas
■ 1	60.19	76.18	39.81	42.63	86.94	55.80	39.60	45.77
■ 2	31.76	56.08	23.27	23.38	66.88	33.12	18.97	23.27
■ 3	21.37	41.97	14.43	14.21	52.17	24.73	13.56	16.16

Figure 5.2. Percentages of words from frequency bands 1 to 3 included in elementary texts

that only *Adelante* includes more than 50% of the words in band 1. Thus, none of the books meet our two criteria: namely, they do not include most of the words in band 1 nor approximately half of those in band 2, and bands 1 to 3 do not offer a maximal coverage of the vocabulary in the textbooks.

Other textbooks, such as *Dos Mundos* or *Arriba*, include a broader selection of words from bands 1 to 3 than *Adelante*. However, in these cases, the presence of a high number of words from a specific frequency band probably does not result from a clear selection criterion but rather from the length of the glossaries. Therefore, more words from all bands, independent of frequency, are included.

Among the ITs, (Table 5.3) only *Anda* presents a coverage of over 60% for words in bands 1 to 3. However, due to its short glossary (1,007 words), the actual number of words included from band 1 is so low that it does not even cover 40% of the 1,000 most frequent words in Spanish, as can be observed in Figure 5.3. The situation for words in bands 2 and 3 is no better, with a proportion of 19.71% and 11.39%, respectively.

Table 5.3. Total of Words and Distribution of Words by Frequency Band in Intermediate Texts

	Anda		AC		Conexiones		EC		Enfoques		Fusión		Imagina		PyA	
	N	%	N	%	N	%	N	%	N	%	N	%	N	%	N	%
1	349	34.7	350	29	350	21.6	833	22.6	434	23.1	237	19.2	629	27.6	870	20.5
2	188	18.7	195	16.2	261	16.1	620	16.8	322	17.2	185	15	410	18	693	16.3
3	105	10.4	143	11.9	205	12.7	468	12.5	248	13.2	128	10.4	288	12.6	575	13.6
1–3	642	63.8	688	57	816	50.4	1,921	52.1	1,004	53.5	550	44.5	1327	58.1	2,138	50.4
>3	365	36.2	518	43	802	49.6	1,768	47.9	872	46.5	685	55.5	956	41.9	2,104	49.6
Total	1,007		1,206		1,618		3,689		1,876		1,235		2,283		4,242	

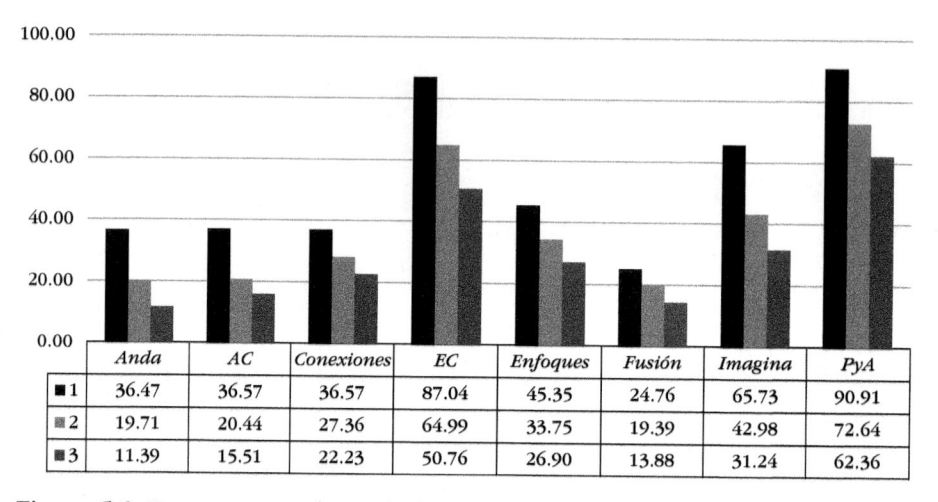

	Anda	AC	Conexiones	EC	Enfoques	Fusión	Imagina	PyA
■ 1	36.47	36.57	36.57	87.04	45.35	24.76	65.73	90.91
■ 2	19.71	20.44	27.36	64.99	33.75	19.39	42.98	72.64
■ 3	11.39	15.51	22.23	50.76	26.90	13.88	31.24	62.36

Figure 5.3. Percentages of words from frequency bands 1 to 3 included in intermediate texts

Thus, while this textbook seemingly offers good coverage, this perception was due only to the limited length of the glossary, not to a clear frequency-based criterion for vocabulary selection. Unlike *Anda*, *Imagina* includes over 65% of the words in band 1, almost 43% of those in band 2, and 31% of those in band 3. The book, thus, offers a balance between decent coverage and the inclusion of a high number of words among the first 3,000. Again, other textbooks, such as *En Comunidad* or *Punto y Aparte*, include more words from those first three bands, but this is only because they include more words in total, at all frequency bands.

In order to get a general idea of the number of words from each of the first three frequency bands that will be encountered by students using any of these textbooks in the first two years of college-level Spanish, a comparative analysis was carried out for the words that are shared between ETs and ITs and those that are specific to each type of book. Only the words that appeared in over half the glossaries in each category were selected for analysis. Thus, only words that appeared in at least five of the eight ETs were included in the analyses, as were those that appeared in at least five of the eight ITs. This criterion ensures that the included words appear in most textbooks and, thus, will be encountered by most L2 Spanish students learning Spanish in American universities. Table 5.4 presents the results of this analysis.

The increase in words from the ETs to the ITs is not very high, as only 270 new words are added within the first three bands.[8] After two years of language study, learners have been exposed to 59% of the words in band 1 and less than 33% of the words in band 2. This is not consistent with Schmitt and Schmitt's (2014) suggestion that the 3,000 most frequent words should be prioritized in language programs, as none of the first three frequency bands was completely covered in these glossaries targeting the first two years of instruction. However, the total number of words (1,619) presented in the ITs and ETs that we analyzed does approach the 2,000 words that can be learned by L2 students in two years, according to Gairns and Redman's (1986) suggestion of teaching 8–12 words per class.

Concreteness and Length in Textbooks

The unique words in ETs and ITs displayed in Table 5.4 were further analyzed to explore whether length (measured in number of letters) and concreteness (ranked from 1 to 7 by native speakers) vary by proficiency level. Table 5.5 shows the *t*-test analyses indicating that words in ITs were significantly longer and less concrete than words in ETs, thus adding to the learning burden of those new words. Length increases not only across proficiency levels but also by bands, as words in band 1 are the shortest, and low-frequency words are the longest. The trend is exactly the opposite when it comes to concreteness, with words in higher frequency bands being more concrete than those in lower bands.

Table 5.4. Unique and Shared Words per Frequency Band across all Elementary Texts and Intermediate Texts

	Unique ETs	Shared	Unique ITs	Total	Percentage of Band(s)
Band 1	182	302	106	590	59
Band 2	123	101	109	333	33.3
Band 3	89	52	55	196	19.6
Total bands 1–3	394	455	270	1,119	37.3
Low frequency	270	124	106	500	2.9*
Total	664	579	376	1,619	

* This percentage was calculated from the remaining 17,000 words in the Davies corpus.

---

[8] This claim is based on the analysis of all the words that appeared in at least five of the textbooks. If a word appeared in one, two, three, or four of the textbooks, but not in five of them, it was not included in the analysis.

Table 5.5. Lexicometric Characteristics of Words per Frequency Band in Elementary and Intermediate Texts

	Length Unique ETs	Length Unique ITs	t-test length	Concreteness Unique ETs	Concreteness Unique ITs	t-test concreteness
Band 1	5.92 (1.82)	6.71 (1.84)	3.48*	4.9 (0.99)	3.73 (0.87)	9.03**
Band 2	6.63 (2.04)	7.28 (2.26)	2.31*	5.26 (0.91)	4.23 (0.76)	8.42**
Band 3	6.57 (1.69)	7.36 (2.07)	2.51*	5.2 (0.88)	4.41 (.87)	4.5**
Low frequency	7.16 (2.22)	7.87 (2.53)	2.65*	5.67 (0.79)	4.54 (.96)	8.08**

Note: ** = $p < .001$, * = $p < .05$

Discussion

Following Schmitt and Schmitt (2014), the 3,000 most frequent words should be a main vocabulary-acquisition goal for students enrolled in a language course. In American universities, this would mean that 3,000 words should be learned during the first two years of language instruction. However, Gairns and Redman (1986) calculated that approximately 10 words could be taught per class, which amounts to 1,000 in a year and 2,000 in two years. Of course, that all these words can be taught does not mean that students will learn all of them. Thus, learning 3,000 words in two years might not be feasible in most instructional settings. In all cases, the final selection of words to include in a language course, be it 1,000, 2,000, or 3,000, should be drawn to the extent possible from the 3,000 most frequent words.

According to the results of this study, textbook authors do not seem to prioritize those 3,000 words when selecting the vocabulary to be included in their glossaries. Less than half of the 3,000 most frequent words of Spanish are generally included in ETs and ITs, and words that are among those 3,000 represent approximately 50%–64% of words in the glossaries. The other 35% of words in the textbooks are low-frequency words that may not be as useful. These results echo those obtained in previous analyses of word frequency in L2 textbooks (Davies & Face, 2006; Godev, 2009; Lipinski, 2010), which also concluded that textbook authors do not seem to base their vocabulary selection on a clear frequency criterion.

The only textbooks that included a higher number of high-frequency words were those that contained more than 3,000 words in their glossaries. This implied that they also presented more low-frequency words than the shorter glossaries and that they included more vocabulary items than those that can be expected to be learned in two years of language instruction.

Additionally, the number of words among the 3,000 most frequent increased by only 270 words from ETs to ITs, which is consistent with Alsaif and Milton's (2012) observation that L2 English textbooks at higher levels of proficiency do not add much vocabulary to that already presented in lower proficiency levels. Interestingly, the number of low-frequency words even decreased in ITs and many infrequent words were shared between ETs and ITs. This might be due to the fact that infrequent words deal with classroom topics (e.g., pizarra [blackboard] and rotulador [marker]) or contents related to grammar and metalinguistic terms (e.g., sustantivo [noun], adjetivo [adjective], oración [clause], subjuntivo [subjunctive], and gerundio [gerund]), which are used both in the first and second year of language instruction.

Overall, the situation depicted by these results might have negative implications for students, as the first 3,000 most frequent words in Spanish cover up to 94% of the words in an oral context and almost 90% of them in written texts (Davies, 2005). Limited or no exposure to these frequent words might decrease students' chances of understanding authentic written and oral texts, and learn new words from them, undermining instructors' efforts to help them become independent learners. This is even more problematic in a context where students are expected to be ready to enroll in content courses in their L2 after two years of language instruction, which would require enough vocabulary knowledge to be able to read literature texts.

Given these circumstances, it is advisable that textbook authors and publishers reevaluate the criteria they use to select vocabulary in ETs and ITs. However, instructors and LPDs cannot wait until textbooks change; they need immediate solutions. These solutions can take one or both of the following forms: (1) selecting frequent words over infrequent ones when textbooks offer long lists of words for a specific topic (e.g., targeting only the most frequent words from long lists of food items in a chapter about the supermarket) and (2) complementing classroom vocabulary exercises with homework that specifically focuses on the 3,000 most frequent words.

These solutions can be implemented easily with the aid of a frequency dictionary for the target language. For Spanish, Davies' (2006) frequency dictionary offers a helpful vocabulary list of the 5,000 most frequent words in Spanish,[9] and similar frequency lists are available for a variety of languages (Appendix I). Additionally, the book includes lists of words, organized by frequency, for some of the most studied semantic clusters introduced in ETs and ITs, such as the vocabulary of clothing or food. Thus, an LDP could establish a clear list of vocabulary for the chapter that introduces clothing by using Davies' (2006) list of clothes to select only those items of clothing whose names are among the 3,000 most frequent words. By tailoring word lists in this way, more in-class time can be devoted to

---

[9] The second edition of the *Frequency Dictionary of Spanish* (Davies & Davies, 2018) has been recently published.

those words that will be most useful for students. Without such tailoring, classroom time may be spent inefficiently in the superficial presentation of a long list of words, many of which are not used often in real-life contexts.

The vocabulary practiced in the classroom can also be supplemented with online flashcards that target words from the frequency dictionary that are not contained in the textbook. LPDs could use programs such as Quizlet, Memrise, Cerego, or Anki to develop sets of online flashcards and incorporate the study of those words into course assignments. Learners should be made aware of the goals of these learning activities and receive specific information on the importance of learning the most frequent words of their L2.

With respect to the analyses of concreteness and length, it is clear that, overall, the learning burden of words increases in ITs (see Table 5.5). Indeed, words are significantly longer and more abstract in ITs than in ETs. Interestingly, length increases incrementally with each frequency band. This offers an additional justification for focusing on the most frequent words, which are also the shortest.

Cantos and Sanchez (2011) show that the distribution of word lengths in English and Spanish is quite similar, except for 10-letter words, which appear significantly more often in Spanish than in English texts. Thus, words that are 10 letters long or more are expected to be more challenging for English speakers who learn Spanish. One exception might be the words that are 10 letters or longer but include a base that is easily identifiable by learners. For example, *pescadería (fish store)* has 10 letters, but students might be able to recognize *pescado (fish)* in it. As such, this word would not present as much of a burden as a 10-letter words such as *patrocinar*, which does not include high-frequency morphological bases. This would also be the case for long words that are cognates between Spanish and English, such as *discriminación*. Cognates would presumably not require much acquisition effort, even if this advantage is more evident for L2 learners than for L3 learners (Szubko-Sitarek, 2011). Table 5.6 presents all of the low-frequency words specific to ETs or ITs that are longer than 10 letters, specifying whether each word contains a recognizable base and whether it could be considered a cognate (i.e., either the whole word or the base resembles the English equivalent in form and meaning). The bolded words are the ones that might be more difficult to learn.

Most of the 61 low-frequency words that are 10 letters long or longer should be easy to learn, due either to their cognateness or to their recognizable base. Only eight of them (bolded in Table 5.6) would present some degree of difficulty because they are not built on frequent and transparent bases or because the semantic interpretation of their morphemic base might be confusing. For example, depending on the context, *dependiente [salesperson, dependent]* might not have a transparent meaning, if interpreted as a derivation of *depender [to depend]*.

As was demonstrated above, students' ability to recognize morphemes might solve some of the issues that arise from encountering long words. Thus, it is

Table 5.6. Words 10 or more letters long in Elementary and Intermediate Texts

ETs	Cognate	Base	ITs	Cognate	Base
estacionamiento		X	*discriminación*	X	
puertorriqueño		X	*extraterrestre*	X	
contabilidad	X	X	*entendimiento*		X
nacionalidad	X	X	*deforestación*	X	
refrigerador	X		*supermercado*		X
antibiótico	X		*controversia*	X	
apartamento	X		*autorretrato*		X
dependiente	+/−	+/−	**invernadero**		
despertador		X	*desigualdad*		X
electrónica	X		*ascendencia*	X	
estudiantil		X	*emocionante*	X	X
hamburguesa	X		*entretenido*	X	X
hermanastro		X	*equilibrado*		X
impermeable	X		*impresionar*	X	X
informática	X		*medicamento*	X	X
mantequilla			*inundación*		X
radiografía	X		*campamento*		X
reproductor	X	X	*documental*	X	X
restaurante	X		*intermedio*	X	X
anaranjado		X	*analfabeto*	X	
antipático	X		*apasionado*	X	X
baloncesto			*autoestima*	X	
canadiense		X	*disponible*		X
carpintero	X		*entretener*	X	
cumpleaños		X	*inesperado*		X
dominicano		X	**patrocinar**		
escritorio		X			
estornudar					
improbable		X			
medianoche		X			
microondas		X			
psicología	X				
servilleta					
sociología	X				
sustantivo					

important to reflect on derivational affixation in the classroom (Sánchez-Gutiérrez, Marcos Miguel, & Robles García, in press). However, textbooks lack activities that facilitate the learning of derivation (Robles García & Sánchez-Gutiérrez, 2016; Sánchez-Gutiérrez, 2014; Neary-Sundquist, 2015). One recommendation is to identify productive affixes in the L2 and tailor activities toward them. For example, in Spanish, when teaching the vocabulary of the professions, the instructor could discuss how most words that refer to athletes or to musicians end in *-ista*. This initial presentation could trigger review activities in which the instructor starts class by asking students to recall, in one minute, as many words ending in *-ista* as they can. In such an activity, the suffix would serve as a memory retrieval cue.

For the concreteness factor, even though words in ITs are less concrete[10] than those in ETs, the average concreteness rates are still high. Given that this variable is rated from 1 (extremely abstract) to 7 (extremely concrete), an average of 4–5 means that few words are extremely abstract. As such, these words do not present an added difficulty. The relative ease of learning these words can be clearly illustrated with words from Table 5.6 such as *estacionamiento, supermercado*, or *autorretrato*, which are low-frequency and long, but do not present the additional burden of being abstract. However, some words, even among the 3,000 most frequent, do present low rates of concreteness. Overall, verbs are rated as more abstract than nouns; thus, it would be helpful to apply a pedagogical treatment that makes verbs more imageable for the students. To this end, instructors could train students in using the keyword technique for navigating abstract vocabulary.

Conclusion

This study aimed at analyzing the frequency, length, and concreteness of the vocabulary included in Elementary Textbooks (ETs) and Intermediate Textbooks (ITs) in college-level Spanish instruction in the United States. The findings can be summarized in three points: (1) frequency is not the main factor in vocabulary selection for L2 Spanish textbooks, (2) vocabulary additions in ITs are not driven by the need to cover a certain number of frequent words, and (3) words that are exclusively presented in ITs are longer and less concrete than those that are specific to ETs. Therefore, while we clearly advocate for the more systematic inclusion of the 3,000 most frequent words in textbooks, we are aware that this change might take some time. In the meanwhile, we invite teachers and LPDs to supplement their materials so that students get the best exposure possible to those words. Several apps and programs can easily be used for this purpose, and the information about word frequency is already available for most commonly taught languages (see Appendix I). Additionally, some techniques, which previous

---

[10] It needs to be reminded here that no function words were included in these analyses, so the difference cannot be simply due to the presence of more function words on one level over the other.

research has proven to be effective, are proposed here to address the difficulty of learning long and abstract words. Concretely, we suggest that a more systematic approach to the study of L2 words' morphological structure could be beneficial, given that it allows to interpret longer words based on morphemes that students may already recognize. We also propose that the keyword technique could be often used in class in order to address the specific challenges that abstract words present for the students. By training students in the recognition of morphological patterns and in the keyword technique at elementary levels of proficiency, we believe that instructors can contribute to lowering the burden of learning long and abstract words while also helping students to develop useful strategies that they can use on their own in more advanced levels.

References

Alcaraz Mármol, G. (2009). Vocabulary in EFL textbooks: Frequency levels. In P. Cantos Gómez & A. Sánchez Pérez (Eds.) *A survey on corpus based studies*. Available online at http://www.um.es/lacell/aelinco/contenido/index.html

Allen, H. W. (2008). Textbooks materials and foreign language teaching: Perspectives from the classroom. *NECTFL Review*, *62*, 5–28.

Alsaif, A. (2011). *Investigating Vocabulary Input and Explaining Vocabulary Uptake among EFL Learners in Saudi Arabia*. PhD dissertation, Swansea University, Swansea, UK.

Alsaif, A., & Milton, J. (2012). Vocabulary input from school textbooks as a potential contributor to the small vocabulary uptake gained by English as a foreign language learners in Saudi Arabia. *The Language Learning Journal*, *40*(1), 21–33.

Anthony, L. (2014). AntWordProfiler (Version 1.4.1) [Computer Software]. Tokyo, Japan: Waseda University. Available online at http://www.laurenceanthony.net/

Barcroft, J. (2012). *Input-Based Incremental Vocabulary Instruction*. Alexandria, VA: TESOL International Association.

Cantos, P., & Sánchez, A. (2011). El inglés y el español desde una perspectiva cuantitativa y distributiva: equivalencias y contrastes. *Estudios Ingleses de la Universidad Complutense*, *19*, 15–44.

Criado, R., & Sánchez, A. (2009). Vocabulary in EFL textbooks: A contrastive analysis against three corpus-based word ranges. In P. Cantos Gómez & A. Sánchez Pérez (Eds.), *A survey on corpus based studies*. Available online at http://www.um.es/lacell/aelinco/contenido/index.html

Davies, M. (2002) *Corpus del Español: 100 million words, 1200s–1900s*. Available online at http://www.corpusdelespanol.org

Davies, M. (2005). Vocabulary range and text coverage: Insights from the forthcoming Routledge frequency dictionary of Spanish. In D. Eddington (Ed.). *Selected Proceedings of the 7th Hispanic Linguistics Symposium* (pp. 106–115). Somerville, MA: Cascadilla.

Davies, M. (2006). *A frequency dictionary of Spanish. Core vocabulary for learners*. New York, NY: Routledge.

Davies, M., & Davies, H. (2018). *A frequency dictionary of Spanish. Core vocabulary for learners* (2nd ed.). New York, NY: Routledge.

Davies, M., & Face, T. L. (2006). Vocabulary coverage in Spanish textbooks: How representative is it? In N. Sagarra & A. J. Toribio (Eds.), *Selected Proceedings of the 9th Hispanic Linguistics Symposium* (pp. 132–143). Somerville, MA: Cascadilla.

De Groot, A., & Keijzer, R. (2000). What is hard to learn is easy to forget: The roles of word concreteness, cognate status, and word frequency in foreign language vocabulary learning and forgetting. *Language Learning, 50*(1), 1–56.

Donzelli, G. (2007). Foreign language learners: Words they hear and words they learn: A case study. *Estudios de Lingüística Inglesa Aplicada, 7*, 103–125.

Duchon, A., Perea, M., Sebastián-Gallés, N., Martí, A., & Carreiras, M. (2013). EsPal: One-stop shopping for Spanish word properties. *Behavior Research Methods, 45*(4), 1246–58.

Ecke, P. (1999). Resumen práctico de mnemotécnicas para la enseñanza de lenguas extranjeras *Estudios de Lingüística Aplicada, 29*, 55–70.

Ecke, P. (2004). Die Schlüsselwort-Mnemonik für den fremdsprachigen Wortschatzerwerb: Zum Stand der Forschung. *Fremdsprachen Lehren und Lernen, 33*, 213–230.

Ellis, N. C., & Beaton, A. (1993). Psycholinguistic determinants of foreign language vocabulary learning. *Language Learning, 43*(4), 559–617.

Gairns, R., & Redman, S. (1986). *Working with words. A guide to teaching and learning vocabulary*. Cambridge: Cambridge University Press.

Godev, C. B. (2009). Word-frequency and vocabulary acquisition: An analysis of elementary Spanish college textbooks in the USA. *Revista de Lingüística Teórica y Aplicada, 47*(2), 51–68.

Horst, M. (2013). Mainstreaming second language vocabulary acquisition. *The Canadian Journal of Applied Linguistics, 16*(1), 171–188.

Hulstijn, J. H. (1997). Mnemonic methods in foreign language vocabulary learning: Theoretical considerations and pedagogical implications. In J. Coady & T. Huckin (Eds.), *Vocabulary acquisition: A rationale for pedagogy* (pp. 203–224). Cambridge, Cambridge University Press.

Institute of International Education. (2015). *Open Doors Report*. IIE Books. Available online at https://www.iie.org/en/Research-and-Insights/Open-Doors

Karpicke, J. D., & Roediger, H. L. (2008). The critical importance of retrieval for learning. *Science, 319*(5865), 966–968.

Lang, M. F. (2009). *Formación de palabras en español. Morfología derivativa productiva en el léxico moderno*. Madrid: Cátedra.

Laufer, B. (2012). Word difficulty. In C. A. Chapelle (Ed.), *Encyclopedia of Applied Linguistics*, Oxford: Wiley-Blackwell.

Laufer, B. (1990). Why are some words more difficult than others? Some intralexical factors that affect the learning of words. *IRAL-International Review of Applied Linguistics in Language Teaching, 28*(4), 293–308.

Lipinski, S. (2010). A frequency analysis of vocabulary in three first-year textbooks of German. *Die Unterrichtspraxis/Teaching German, 43*(2), 167–174.

López Jiménez, M. D. (2014). A critical analysis of the vocabulary in L2 Spanish textbooks. *Porta Linguarum, 21*, 163–181.

Marcos Miguel, N. (2015). Textbook consumption in the classroom: Analyzing a classroom corpus. *Procedia Social and Behavioral Sciences, 198*, 309–319.

Masrai, A., & Milton, J. (2015). Investigating the relationship between the morphological processing of regular and irregular words and L2 vocabulary acquisition. *International Journal of Applied Linguistics and English Literature, 4*(4), 192–199.

McGrath, I. (2013). *Teaching materials and the roles of EFL/ESL Teachers*. London: Bloomsbury.

McDonough, J., Shaw, C., & Masuhara, H. (2013). *Materials and methods in ELT. A teacher's guide*. Oxford: Wiley-Blackwell.

Milton, J. (2009). *Measuring second language vocabulary acquisition*. Bristol: Multilingual Matters.

Morin, R. (2003). Derivational morphological analysis as a strategy for vocabulary acquisition in Spanish. *The Modern Language Journal, 87*(2), 200–221.

Morin, R. (2006). Building depth of Spanish L2 vocabulary by building and using word families. *Hispania, 89*(1), 170–182.

Nation, I. S. P. (2001). *Learning vocabulary in another language.* Cambridge: Cambridge University Press.

Nation, I. S. P. (2006). How large a vocabulary is needed for reading and listening? *Canadian Modern Language Review, 63*(1), 59–82.

Heatley, A., & Nation, I. S. P. (1994). RANGE [Computer Software]. University of Wellington, Victoria. Available online at https://www.victoria.ac.nz/lals/about/staff/paul-nation

Neary-Sundquist, C. (2015). Aspects of vocabulary knowledge in German textbooks. *Foreign Language Annals, 48*(1), 68–81.

Peters, E. (2016). The learning burden of collocations: The role of interlexical and intralexical factors. *Language Teaching Research, 20*(1), 113–138.

Robles García, P., & Sánchez-Gutiérrez, C. (2016). La morfología derivativa en los manuales de español elemental estadounidenses: un estudio exploratorio. *Revista Electrónica de Lingüística Aplicada, 15*(1), 70–86.

Sánchez-Gutiérrez, C. (2014). Morfología derivativa y manuales de E/LE: un análisis crítico. *Anexos de la Revista Española de Lexicografía, 22,* 163–178.

Sánchez-Gutiérrez, C., Marcos Miguel, N., & Robles García, P. (in press). What derivational suffixes should we teach in Spanish as a second language courses? *Issues in Hispanic and Lusophone Linguistics, 16.*

Schmitt, N., Jiang, X., & Grabe, W. (2011). The percentage of words known in a text and reading comprehension. *The Modern Language Journal, 95*(1), 26–43.

Schmitt, N., & Schmitt, D. (2014). A reassessment of frequency and vocabulary size in L2 vocabulary teaching. *Language Teaching, 47*(4), 484–503.

Szubko-Sitarek, W. (2011). Cognate facilitation effects in trilingual word recognition. *Studies in Second Language Learning and Teaching, 1*(2), 189–208.

Van Zeeland, H., & Schmitt, N. (2012). Lexical coverage and L2 listening comprehension: How much does vocabulary knowledge contribute to understanding spoken language? *Applied Linguistics, 34*(4) 457–479.

Webb, S., & Rodgers, M. P. (2009a). Vocabulary demands of television programs. *Language Learning, 59*(2), 335–366.

Webb, S., & Rodgers, M. P. (2009b). The lexical coverage of movies. *Applied Linguistics, 30*(3), 407–427.

Willis, M., & Ohashi, Y. (2012). A model of L2 vocabulary learning and retention. *The Language Learning Journal, 40*(1), 125–137.

Appendix I. Resources to Find Word Frequencies

Routledge has frequency dictionaries for Spanish, Persian, Turkish, Korean, Japanese, Dutch, Russian, Arabic, Czech, French, German, Mandarin Chinese, and Portuguese.

Other corpora and frequency lists can be found online:

ARABIC

http://arabicorpus.byu.edu/

ENGLISH

https://www.victoria.ac.nz/lals/resources
https://www.lextutor.ca/
https://www.wordandphrase.info/

GERMAN

http://wortschatz.uni-leipzig.de/en

PORTUGUESE

http://www.corpusdoportugues.org/

SPANISH

http://www.bcbl.eu/databases/espal/index.php
http://www.corpusdelespanol.org/
https://www.wordandphrase.info/span/

Chapter 6
der | die | das: Integrating Vocabulary Acquisition Research into an L2 German Curriculum

Jamie Rankin, Princeton University

Introduction

There is ample anecdotal evidence that novice foreign language (second language or L2) learners are frustrated not so much by syntax, pronunciation, or sociocultural ambiguity as by the sheer amount of vocabulary to be learned. Even if they can form this or that tense, produce new sounds, and navigate unfamiliar cultural perspectives, they consistently cite vocabulary and the monumental task of learning it as a central problem—perhaps *the* central problem (Barcroft, 2004; Folse, 2004, 2008; Green & Meara, 1995; Nation, 2006)—in their pursuit of L2 competence.

And no wonder: researchers in L2 vocabulary acquisition have long argued that L2 reading fluency requires a substantial amount of vocabulary knowledge. In an early study, Laufer (1992) suggested attaining a vocabulary of some 3,000 word families,[1] or around 5,000 individual words, corresponding to 95% coverage of most texts, as a kind of threshold for basic comprehension. Hu and Nation (2000), Nation (2006), and Schmitt (2008) have subsequently argued that 95% coverage is in fact insufficient, calling instead for 98%–99% text coverage, which in turn would require 8,000–9,000 word families. Yet even these daunting numbers may not be sufficient, with Schmitt, Jiang, and Grabe (2011) speculating in a more recent study that "they probably underestimate the lexis required" (p. 27), based on a straightforward linear relationship between vocabulary knowledge and text comprehension, with no "threshold" interrupting the upward line. They summarize their findings by suggesting, along with Nation, that learners "need to know something on the order of 8,000–9,000 word families to be able to read widely in English without vocabulary being a problem" (p. 39). Instructors who embrace

---
[1] Analyses of vocabulary distinguish between *lemmas* and *word families*. The lemma of the verb *to play* comprises all forms of that word: *play, plays, playing, played*. The word family of *play*, on the other hand, includes those forms as well as all lemmas derived from them—*playground(s), playpen(s), player(s), playful(ly), outplayed*, and so forth. In the following discussion, *word families* are identified as such, while *word* is used for ease of comprehension to refer to a *lemma*.

the goal of L2 literacy that exhibits both depth and breadth will share Schmitt et al.'s (2011) view that "it is worth doing everything possible to increase learners' vocabulary knowledge" (p. 39).

It follows, then, that vocabulary learning should play a central role in L2 instruction, particularly in college-level courses that focus on developing literacy skills, and that teachers and textbooks should focus from the very outset on "increasing the size of the learners' recognition vocabulary" (Nation, 1993, p. 118) by fostering deliberate, intentional vocabulary study (Elgort, 2011; Ellis, 2005). Yet this is arguably not the case, either in terms of the vocabulary items offered in textbooks or the pedagogical model driving their presentation. Regarding the choice of vocabulary offered, consider the German introductory textbook *Kontakte* (Tschirner, & Nikolai, 2017). Its chapter on "living" and "home," for example, ends with an active vocabulary list that learners are presumably expected to learn for classroom use and assessment, which includes *Rasenmäher* (lawn mower), *Frühjahrsputz* (spring cleaning), *Staub saugen* (to vacuum), and *Skihütte* (ski lodge). All quite interesting, no doubt, but not words that learners might expect to encounter frequently in spoken or written discourse, given their rare appearance in major text corpora.[2] This is merely anecdotal, of course, but teachers (and students) familiar with this and similar textbooks will probably agree that the vocabulary choices appear to be dictated more by the preferences of the textbook authors than by the frequency of the vocabulary across discourse genres and texts.

Regarding the presentation and pedagogical application of vocabulary, one finds minimal evidence in current textbooks of any systematic, explicit engagement across chapters with previously learned vocabulary. Beyond the chapter-level presentation of new words, which involves (in some textbooks at least) a handful of exercises for recognition or production, there is little if any intentional, targeted review of these vocabulary items in subsequent chapters. A detailed analysis of current textbooks along these lines is beyond the scope of this chapter; suffice it to say that an early assessment by Green and Meara (1995) and Meara (1980) of the disjunction between what L2 learners feel they need to know, that is, vocabulary, and what instructors and textbooks choose to focus on, still holds true today.

The project described in this chapter is based on the conviction that we must rethink our pedagogy of vocabulary for beginning L2 instruction with respect to the two issues outlined above: (1) which words to introduce and (2) how to embed and deploy these words throughout the curriculum in ways that maximize student learning. The discussion begins with a brief review of the research touching on both issues. This is followed by a description of an online curriculum for

---

[2] These words do not appear at all in the Jones and Tschirner (2006) list of the most frequently used 4,000 words in German, and a search through multiple corpora via the *Digitales Wörterbuch der Deutschen Sprache* (DWDS; *Digital Dictionary of the German Language*) (https://www.dwds.de) confirms their relative obscurity, with only a handful of appearances in millions of words of running text.

beginning German that seeks to integrate this research into a fully developed textbook. It concludes with student feedback regarding the results, and suggestions for how instructors might incorporate some of its insights into their classroom teaching.

Which Words?

In choosing vocabulary items for beginning-level textbooks, most authors have favored a hybrid approach that combines words based on topical choices (family, travel, university life, food, the environment, etc.) with words that cluster around grammatical structures (prepositions, limiting words, conjunctions). Researchers in L2 vocabulary acquisition, in contrast, advocate an entirely different approach, one that prioritizes high-frequency L2 vocabulary (Laufer, 1992, Laufer & Nation, 1995; Nation, 1993, 2001, 2006; and many others) and recommend that L2 instruction should initially focus on building a foundation of the most frequently used 2,000–3,000 word families. Since most readers of this chapter will already be familiar with the former, I will begin by looking more closely at the rationale behind the latter.

Arguments for organizing vocabulary instruction around high-frequency lexis are based on the unique relationship between the upper end of frequency lists and the amount of text these words cover. To understand this relationship, consider a list of L2 vocabulary items, ranked according to how frequently they appear in corpora of written and/or transcribed spoken discourse. In English, for example, this could be some (updated) version of the General Service List (West, 1953), such as Browne, Culligan, and Phillips, 2013, or an altogether different list such as Davies and Gardner (2010) or Kucera and Francis (1967). These lists contain upward of 5,000 words in ranked order of frequency, usually with a numerical indication of how often a word appears per 1,000,000 words of running text. L2 vocabulary studies using these lists often refer to frequency "bands," the first consisting of the most frequent 1,000 words, the second band of the next 1,000 items (1,001–2,000), the third band of items 2,001–3,000, and so on. What is remarkable about these bands is the percentage of text coverage they represent—remarkable not only for the consistency one finds across analyses of various text corpora but also for the startling disparity in text coverage between the first band (1–1,000) and all the rest.

Two examples, cited in Nation (2001, pp. 14–15), illustrate this phenomenon for English. The Brown Corpus (Kucera & Francis, 1967; one of the earliest analyses of its kind) is a collection of 500 texts, representing 15 text genres and totaling just over 1,000,000 running words. Using a ranked frequency list of the words in the corpus, one finds that the first band of words (i.e., the most frequently used 1,000 words across all 500 texts) covers 72% of the texts, the second band covers 5.7%, and the third band covers 4.3%. A later study by Carroll, Davies, and Richman

(1971) analyzing a significantly larger text corpus of some 288,000,000 running words yields very similar results. The first frequency band accounts for 74.1% of the texts, the second band covers 7.2%, and the third band covers 3.9%, with each additional band providing less and less coverage. Notice the extraordinary power of that first band: if you know these words in English, you can read upward of 70% of a very wide array of authentic texts. Admittedly, this cannot be considered *fluent* reading, since every fourth word, on average, will still be unfamiliar. And there are obvious caveats about which kinds of texts this array might include (a sonnet or an online blog? Faulkner or J. K. Rowling?) and which of the available frequency lists may be more or less accurate. Yet considered from the perspective of L2 acquisition, the research leaves little room for doubt regarding the strategic advantage of learning the most frequently used vocabulary. To quote Nation and Waring (1997):

> The significance of this information is that although there are well over 54,000 word families in English, and although educated adult native speakers know around 20,000 of these word families, a much smaller number of words, say, between 3–5,000 word families is needed to provide a basis for comprehension. (p. 10)

Similar results have been found for texts in German (Jones, 2004, 2006). Frequency lists for German vocabulary span more than a century, from Kaeding's *Häufigkeitswörterbuch der deutschen Sprache* (1897) to a recent compilation by Quasthoff, Fiedler, and Hallsteinsdottir (2011) of openly available Internet texts. Some of these lists focus on specialist domains, such as newsprint (Rosengren, 1972), while others simply compare the vocabulary used in German textbooks (Tussing & Zimmermann, 1977, 1980). The most widely known (and arguably the most balanced and user-friendly) compilation is Jones and Tschirner, (2006, hereafter referred to as J–T), a ranked compilation of the 4,000 most frequently used words in German. The J–T list is based in equal parts on transcriptions of spoken German, newspaper articles, literary texts, and academic texts (i.e., academic journals from the sciences and the humanities) from a corpus of 4,000,000 words of running text and supplemented with a smaller corpus (200,000 words of running text), comprising what J–T refer to as "instructional" texts, for example, product information and rental contracts.

Jones (2006) claims that the most frequently used 1,000 words in German cover approximately 73% of most German texts. If this is true—and one would be hard-pressed to disagree, given its consistency with similar results for English—it stands to reason that all of these words should be presented and reviewed in beginning-level textbooks. Further, if Jones (2006) is correct that additional text coverage plummets to 6% and then to 3.7% with the introduction of the second and third frequency bands, respectively, then one assumes that words in these secondary and tertiary bands (and others even further down the frequency list) should receive less attention.

Lipinski (2010) demonstrates conclusively that on both counts this is far from the case. Her analysis compares the first 1,000 words in J–T with the active vocabulary lists in three of the top-selling German college-level textbooks at that time: *Kontakte* (Tschirner, Nikolai, & Terrell, 2009), *Deutsch heute* (Moeller, Hoecherl-Alden, Adolph, & Berger, 2009), and *Neue Horizonte* (Dollenmayer & Hansen, 2008). The results should have come as something of a shock to instructors, textbook authors, and publishers alike—not to mention the L2 German learners who rely on (and pay dearly for) such books. Of the top 1,000 words in J–T, *Deutsch heute* introduces 637, *Neue Horizonte* introduces 605, and *Kontakte* introduces 530. Conversely, Lipinski shows that these textbooks introduce a significant number of words as active vocabulary that lie beyond the four bands of vocabulary (4,000 words) in J–T. *Deutsch heute* features 561 such words, *Neue Horizonte* has 482, and fully 44% of the total active vocabulary items in *Kontakte* (953 words) lie beyond the J–T list, which is to say that students using this text are expected to learn almost 1,000 words that they will rarely encounter in either spoken or written discourse, and therefore will be far less likely to retain. Figure 6.1 (Lipinski, 2010, p. 171) shows the numbers for all four bands in J–T from the three textbooks in question.

Not only does Lipinski (2010) document the degree to which such textbooks fail to provide learners with many of the words they will most likely hear and read, she notes as well that words are introduced more or less randomly from chapter to chapter throughout the book with no relation to their relative frequency of use (p. 173). In short, she reveals a serious shortcoming in current textbooks regarding the words that students should learn in order to become effective readers of the target language.

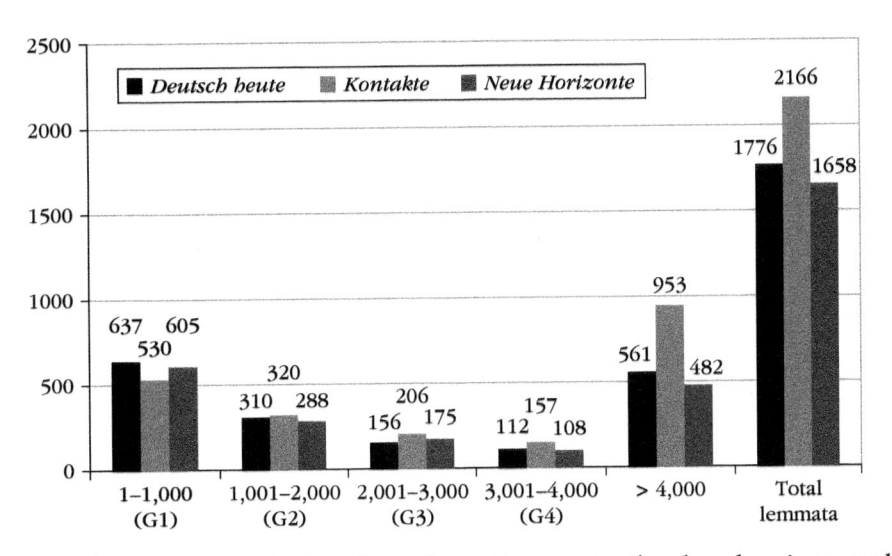

Figure 6.1. Active vocabulary from three German textbooks, showing word counts from the four frequency bands in Jones and Tschirner (2006); from Lipinski (2010, p. 171); *used with permission of the publisher, John Wiley and Sons.*

It was the Lipinski (2010) study in particular that served as the impetus for developing a new vocabulary-focused curriculum for our two-semester beginning German sequence—one that could take advantage of the exponentially powerful text coverage afforded by the 1,000 or so most-frequently-used words and that could incorporate the findings of L2 vocabulary research in the design of its presentation and review structure. We (a small team of colleagues and graduate student Teaching Assistants) decided to see whether this approach could be woven into a full-fledged introductory German program using the top 1,200[3] words in the J–T list. A working title was needed, and the top entry was the very first item in the J-T list: *der|die|das*, the cluster of definite articles in German.

First we had to face the feasibility question: Would it actually be possible to create a viable program using these specific lexical choices, that is, by starting with vocabulary rather than content? Forty hours, 1,200 individual Post-it notes, and a great deal of puzzling and shuffling later, it appeared that we could, as a seminar room became something of a laboratory for considering possible intersections of cultural topics, grammar features, and vocabulary Figure 6.2.

In the process, the question emerged of how strictly the curriculum should adhere to the list. My own first impression of J–T, to be honest, was that it had

Figure 6.2. Seminar room converted into a laboratory for distributing vocabulary across cultural and grammatical topics.

---

[3] The choice of 1,200 was arbitrary, but based on several practical considerations. Given the structure of our academic year, we wanted 16 chapters and felt that 80 words per chapter (on average) was a reasonable amount.

some serious credibility issues. How could the most frequently used 1,200 words in German not include items of clothing—a staple feature in almost all introductory textbooks? And where were all the words for ordering food in a restaurant or buying a train ticket? Equally surprising was the appearance of words in the top 1,200 that are not normally learned until (much) later, if at all, in most L2 German curricula: *mittlerweile* (meanwhile), *Ansatz* (initial approach to a topic or an argument), *ebenfalls* (likewise, also), *GmbH* (Limited Liability Company). I wanted more proof that it "worked," that is, that the top 1,200 words would in fact provide the kind of substantial coverage that the research promised, and in texts that students might want to read online, such as www.spiegel.de or www.zeit.de. Using online media texts, several randomly selected probes convinced me. For the sake of this chapter, I tested the list again on the first five paragraphs of a text picked at random—you'll have to trust me here—from *Die Zeit*, a well-known German media source: *Braunschweig: Der perfekte* Plan B (Raether, 2017). Written for a German audience by a well-known journalist, the article describes with nuance and wit the aesthetic pleasures the author unexpectedly discovers as an avowed "big city person" in the decidedly smallish city of Braunschweig. That is to say, the text is neither overly abstract nor patronizingly simplistic. Including the title, the lead-in paragraph, and the byline information, the text excerpt contains 410 word tokens (i.e., it has a word count of 410). Excluding proper names (*Barcelona, Frank Sinatra, New York*) and cognates (*Panorama, Rekord, Spiritualität*), only 48 of these word tokens are not included in the top 1,200 words of J–T. In other words, someone familiar with the top 1,200 words in J–T should be able to recognize 88% of the words in the text.

Persuaded that incorporating the J–T list into the curriculum would serve our students well, but that they would want additional vocabulary, we decided on a dual approach. Regarding the core vocabulary—the words to be emphasized, learned, systematically reviewed, and tested—we would follow the J–T list scrupulously, with no additions or deletions. But we would also include additional vocabulary in domains that would be of potential interest to students, based on prior classroom experience. (An anecdote: several students from the pilot class recounted later that they had been dubious about *GmbH* as a high-frequency word, but that upon landing at the Munich airport for a subsequent summer program they saw it literally dozens of times within their first hour in Germany, on the way from the airport into the city, on billboards and commercial trucks. Who knew?)

Distribution and Presentation of Vocabulary

Distributing vocabulary in a pedagogically meaningful way across 16 chapters is somewhat akin to solving a three-dimensional puzzle. Ideally, the vocabulary should be presented from higher frequency to lower frequency in linear sequence from start to finish. But certain cultural topics call for specific words, which leads to violating the sequence of the list. An early chapter entitled *Autobahn*, for example, was a natural venue for items such as *Auto*, *Straße* (street), and *fahren* (to drive, ride), all of which appear high on the J–T list. But we also wanted to offer cultural content relating to German engineering and pre-1989 East/West transit issues so that it made sense to include words such as *Modell* (model), *herstellen* (to produce, manufacture), *Technik* (technology), *der Osten* (the East), and *damals* (back then, at that time), which necessitated pulling words from further down the list.

And then there were grammar-related choices. Like other inflected languages, German has many high-frequency words that require an understanding of certain grammatical and syntactic rules, such as case-sensitive prepositions and subordinating conjunctions. Do you introduce the (extremely) frequently used preposition *in* (in, into; 4 on the J–T list) before explaining the accusative case and the dative case, and how *in* can take either, depending on context? Do you have students learn the subordinating conjunction *dass* (that; 22 on the J–T list) before they can cope with some of German's more intricate word order rules? There were no easy answers here. Some words on the list were sufficiently cognate with English and could appear in texts before being formally introduced. In other cases, the words required either a delayed presentation or (in order to offer a complete set of prepositions when that grammatical point came up) an earlier presentation than the J–T sequence would dictate. The resulting distribution of words from chapter to chapter involved numerous compromises, yet we were careful to ensure that the top 400 words would all be included in the first eight chapters of the curriculum, that is, the chapters covered during the first of two semesters.

Once the distribution of words from chapter to chapter was settled, we had to decide how users would see and interact with the vocabulary in its initial presentation. These decisions were driven by consideration of two branches of L2 vocabulary research: (1) studies showing the benefits of list-based "paired associates" and the more explicit and intentional vocabulary instruction that these entail (Cobb, 2007; Ellis, 2005; De Groot & Keijzer, 2000; Elgort, 2011; Folse, 2008, chapter 4; De Groot & Keijzer, 2000, Griffin & Harley, 1996; Laufer & Girsai, 2008; Prince, 1996); and (2) studies promoting incidental vocabulary learning through reading (Coady, 1997; Dupuy & Krashen, 1993; Horst, Cobb & Meara, 1998; Krashen, 1989; McQuillan, 2016; Rott, 1999). Since the research supports both pedagogical approaches, we decided to include both. Vocabulary would be available in list format, which mirrors the design of most textbooks; but it would also be embedded in meaning-based contexts, and would take advantage of our decision to present the curriculum in an online format (https://www.dddgerman.org[4]) that includes text, audio, and video components.

To illustrate this approach, the following section presents both modes of vocabulary presentation from a subsection of Chapter 9 ("Mallorca"), which explores various layers of meaning and identity associated with this island

---

[4] To comply with copyright laws, the site is password protected. Readers interested in viewing it are welcome to request access by emailing the author at jrankin@princeton.edu.

in German culture. First, the list of core vocabulary—split into two sections (Figures 6.3 and 6.4) here for the sake of the printing format, but one continuous page on the website—in the familiar "paired associates" format:

WORTSCHATZ **KAPITEL 9: THEMA 1**
andererseits on the other hand
die Angabe [Angaben] statement, information
der Anspruch [Ansprüche] claim, demand, right [Anspruch + auf [acc.] claim, right to
die Aufnahme [Aufnahmen] recording; admission (into an institution)
bereit ready
der Betried [Betriebe] business, firm, enterprise
bezahlen [bezahlte	bezahlt] to pay (for)
der Druck [Drücke] pressure
einerseits on the one hand
endlich finally
jedoch however, though

Figure 6.3. Vocabulary list (Part 1) from *der | die | das*, Chapter 9 Thema 1.

krank sick
die Luft [Lüfte] air
das Meer [Meere] sea, ocean
der Monat [Monate] month
rechnen [rechnete	gerechnet] to reckon, calculate
die Regel [Regeln] rule
das Schiff [Schiffe] ship
selbstverständlich of course, obvious(ly)
der Staat [Staaten] state, nation
der Urlaub [Urlaube] vaction
die Verantwortung [normally used in sing.] responsibility
überlegen [überlegte	überlegt] to consider, reflect

Figure 6.4. Vocabulary list (Part 2) from *der | die | das*, Chapter 9, Thema 1

Second, a series of screenshots show how the same words are embedded in the cultural content of the chapter using interactive tasks to be completed by learners as individual homework assignments. The print format here prevents showing the tasks in full, with all of the embedded words; suffice it to say that all of the words on the "paired associate" list above are incorporated into the interactive tasks. In Figure 6.5 (Interaktion 9.1) one can see that all core words are highlighted using the same color for both formats; a mouse-over on a highlighted word in either format triggers a tool-tip field with an English gloss,[5] and clicking on a highlighted word activates an audio rendition of the word. This mixture of visual and auditory modalities is designed to focus learners' attention on these vocabulary items in different ways, reflecting Mayer's cognitive theory of multimedia learning (Mayer, 2009), which acknowledges the separate but complementary functions of auditory and visual channels in perception and learning.

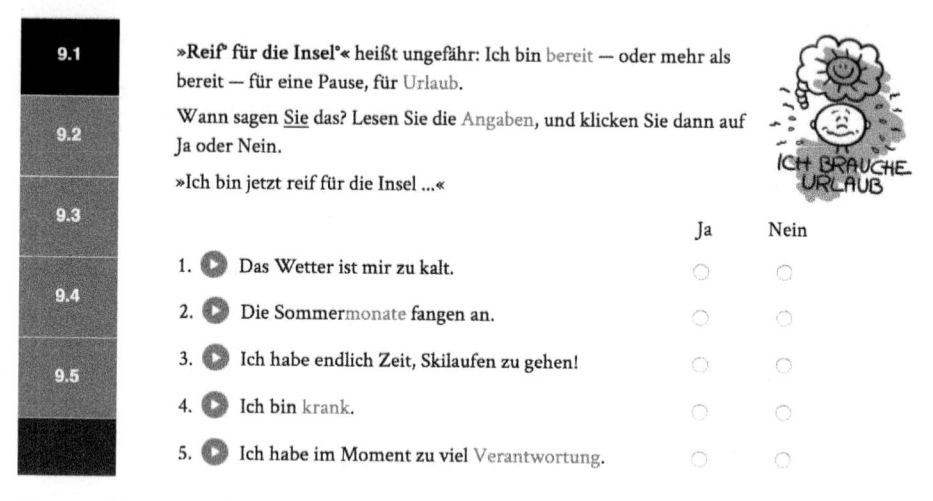

9.1	»Reif° für die Insel°« heißt ungefähr: Ich bin bereit — oder mehr als bereit — für eine Pause, für Urlaub.		
9.2	Wann sagen Sie das? Lesen Sie die Angaben, und klicken Sie dann auf Ja oder Nein.		
	»Ich bin jetzt reif für die Insel ...«		
9.3		Ja	Nein
	1. ▶ Das Wetter ist mir zu kalt.	○	○
9.4	2. ▶ Die Sommermonate fangen an.	○	○
9.5	3. ▶ Ich habe endlich Zeit, Skilaufen zu gehen!	○	○
	4. ▶ Ich bin krank.	○	○
	5. ▶ Ich habe im Moment zu viel Verantwortung.	○	○

Figure 6.5. *Interaktion* 9.1.

The statements describe when one might feel ready for a vacation (*Reif für die Insel*, literally *ripe for the island* = ready for a vacation). Clicking on the audio play icon triggers an audio file of the sentence that follows, recorded by native speakers with various regional accents. In Interaktion 9.2 (Figure 6.6) users are instructed to read the introductory text, listen to the audio while reading along, and indicate in a radio box whether or not they agree with the statements.

Audio files describing five speakers' vacation plans, followed by two written statements, only one of which correctly paraphrases the information in the audio file. Users listen and click on the correct paraphrase.

---

[5] Words appearing in the cultural content that are not included in the core vocabulary are marked with a "degree" symbol [°], and also respond to a mouse-over with a tool-tip field showing an English gloss.

DER | DIE | DAS

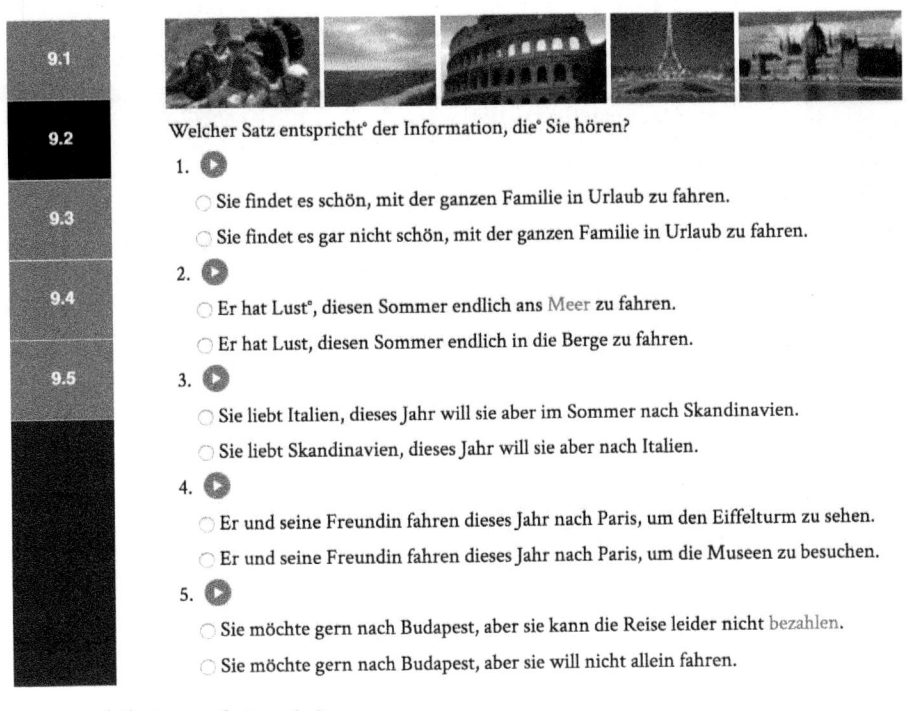

9.1	
9.2	Welcher Satz entspricht° der Information, die° Sie hören? 1. ▶ ○ Sie findet es schön, mit der ganzen Familie in Urlaub zu fahren. ○ Sie findet es gar nicht schön, mit der ganzen Familie in Urlaub zu fahren.
9.3	2. ▶ ○ Er hat Lust°, diesen Sommer endlich ans Meer zu fahren. ○ Er hat Lust, diesen Sommer endlich in die Berge zu fahren.
9.4	3. ▶ ○ Sie liebt Italien, dieses Jahr will sie aber im Sommer nach Skandinavien. ○ Sie liebt Skandinavien, dieses Jahr will sie aber nach Italien.
9.5	4. ▶ ○ Er und seine Freundin fahren dieses Jahr nach Paris, um den Eiffelturm zu sehen. ○ Er und seine Freundin fahren dieses Jahr nach Paris, um die Museen zu besuchen. 5. ▶ ○ Sie möchte gern nach Budapest, aber sie kann die Reise leider nicht bezahlen. ○ Sie möchte gern nach Budapest, aber sie will nicht allein fahren.

Figure 6.6. *Interaktion* 9.2.

Below the YouTube link shown here Figure 6.7 (Interaktion 9.3) is the text of the first two verses of the song, which feature core vocabulary items. At the end of the song, users are asked to identify which words or phrases from the song indicate whether it is meant to be humorous or melancholy—or both—and to type these words or phrases into a text box.

Interaktion 9.4 (Figure 6.8) presents an authentic text from an Austrian government website, describing how much vacation time Austrians are entitled to by law. A text box below the text includes five core vocabulary words, all of which appear in the text. In the questions that follow, users' attention is directed to specific collocations of nouns and prepositions in the text, with answers to be typed into the small field.

In the final activity (Figure 6.9) students see a cartoon from which the caption has been deleted. Students are asked to choose which of the suggested captions they like best, all of which include embedded core vocabulary words, or to create their own caption by typing it into a text box.

The examples of embedded vocabulary shown above (Figures 6.5–6.9 illustrate our decision to organize the core vocabulary in nonsemantic sets (Erten & Tekin, 2008; Folse, 2008, chapter 3; Tinkham, 1993, 1997; Waring, 1997) in an intentional break from the more or less ubiquitous use of semantic sets in L2 introductory

> Vor mehr als 30 Jahren hat Peter Cornelius, ein österreichischer Sänger, ein bekanntes Lied° geschrieben: *Reif für die Insel.* Vor ein paar Jahren hat er eine neue Aufnahme davon gemacht.
>
> Unten finden Sie den Text zum Lied und einen Link zum YouTube-Video. (Er singt das Lied mit österreichischem Akzent — also haben wir für Sie den Text in Standard-Deutsch gegeben.)
>
> Lesen Sie den Text gut durch und hören Sie sich das Lied an:
>
> [Peter Cornelius - Reif für die Insel [Live]]
>
> Oder klicken Sie hier.

Figure 6.7. *Interaktion* 9.3.

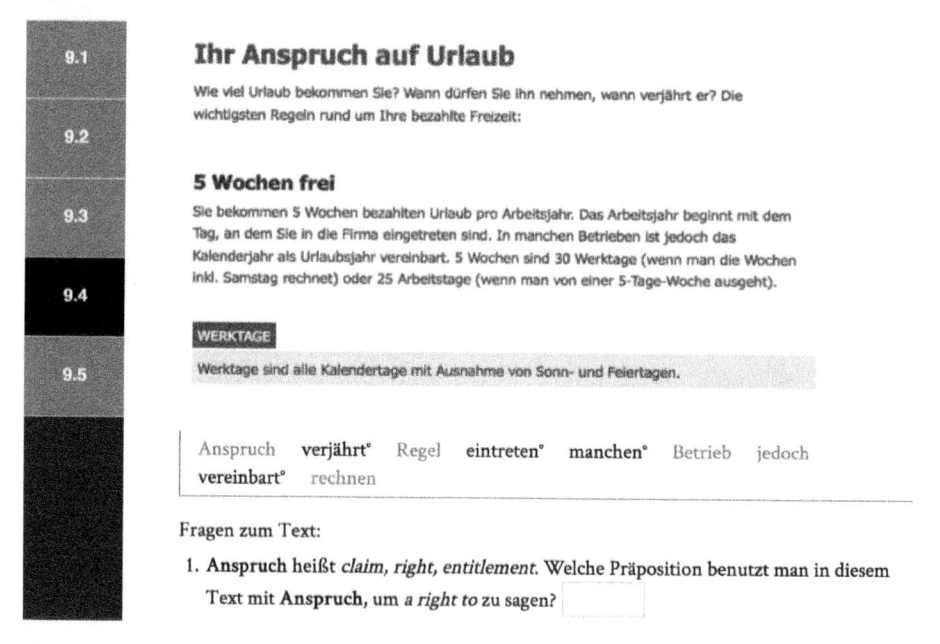

> ## Ihr Anspruch auf Urlaub
>
> Wie viel Urlaub bekommen Sie? Wann dürfen Sie ihn nehmen, wann verjährt er? Die wichtigsten Regeln rund um Ihre bezahlte Freizeit:
>
> ### 5 Wochen frei
>
> Sie bekommen 5 Wochen bezahlten Urlaub pro Arbeitsjahr. Das Arbeitsjahr beginnt mit dem Tag, an dem Sie in die Firma eingetreten sind. In manchen Betrieben ist jedoch das Kalenderjahr als Urlaubsjahr vereinbart. 5 Wochen sind 30 Werktage (wenn man die Wochen inkl. Samstag rechnet) oder 25 Arbeitstage (wenn man von einer 5-Tage-Woche ausgeht).
>
> **WERKTAGE**
> Werktage sind alle Kalendertage mit Ausnahme von Sonn- und Feiertagen.
>
> Anspruch **verjährt°** Regel **eintreten°** **manchen°** Betrieb jedoch **vereinbart°** rechnen
>
> Fragen zum Text:
>
> 1. **Anspruch** heißt *claim, right, entitlement.* Welche Präposition benutzt man in diesem Text mit **Anspruch**, um *a right to* zu sagen? ▢

Figure 6.8. *Interaktion* 9.4.

textbooks. Semantic sets consist of elements that are related by an overarching rubric such as *colors, family members,* or *buildings in a city.* While such sets are popular among instructors and learners alike, no doubt because it is believed that

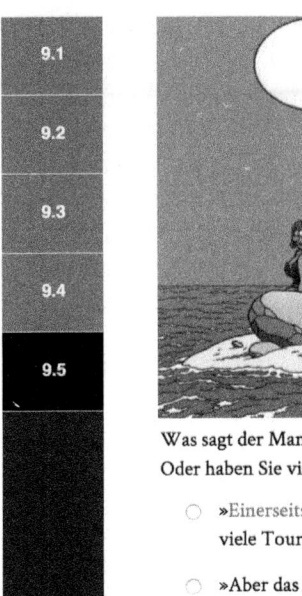

Was sagt der Mann auf diesem Cartoon? Klicken Sie auf den besten Text für dieses Bild. Oder haben Sie vielleicht eine bessere Idee?

- »Einerseits haben wir nichts zu essen und trinken, aber andererseits gibt es nicht zu viele Touristen, und die Luft ist ganz frisch, nicht wahr?«
- »Aber das Hotel hat uns gesagt, ein Schiff kommt jede Stunde hier vorbei°!«
- »Du hast doch immer gesagt, du würdest° gern auf einer Privatinsel Urlaub machen.«

Figure 6.9. *Interaktion* 9.5.

this kind of grouping facilitates learning, the research suggests otherwise: "Contrary to frequent practice in many course books, presenting new vocabulary that belongs to the same semantic set together may cause interference due to cross-association and may even hinder vocabulary learning" (Erten & Tekin, 2008, p. 407). Nonsemantic sets, on the other hand, consist of words that can be used to discuss a theme or topic, and can include all parts of speech. Consider the core vocabulary words from Chapter 9 that are shown in Figure 6.4 above:

>*krank* sick
>*Luft* air
>*Meer* sea, ocean
>*Monat* month
>*rechnen* to reckon, calculate
>*Regel* rule
>*Schiff* ship
>*selbstverständlich* of course, obvious(ly)
>*Staat* state, nation
>*Urlaub* vacation
>*Verantwortung* responsibility
>*überlegen* to consider, reflect

While several of these (*Meer, Schiff, Urlaub*) might cluster around the rubric of "*vacation*", the list as a whole does not form a semantic set. Yet as the *Interaktionen* show, these words can be used in meaning-based contexts to illustrate and comment on the topic, thereby allowing cultural, grammatical, and lexical work to be woven together. Indeed, it was this more open approach to vocabulary choices that allowed the project to take shape at all. Rather than adding yet another layer of constraints to our choices regarding vocabulary distribution, it freed us to use a very different organizational principle, one that elevated the cultural topic in place of a neat set of semantically related words. As members of the team wrote the contents for the *Interaktionen* throughout the curriculum, we came to see that with very few exceptions, semantically unrelated words from the frequency list could be used to discuss almost any given topic.

Vocabulary Review

In designing the vocabulary reviews that are built into the curriculum, we relied on several guidelines suggested in the L2 vocabulary literature: multiple exposures (Rott, 1999; Schuetze, 2017), deliberate, intentional instruction (Elgort, 2011; Ellis, 1995), and depth of processing, that is, encouraging multiple connections with each word using pronunciation, meaning, and associations with other words (Laufer & Hulstijn; Nation & Newton, 1997; Schmitt, 2008). These considerations formed the background for an array of receptive and productive tasks throughout the curriculum, in keeping with research that shows the importance of both (Webb, 2005, 2007).

1. Receptive tasks (i.e., tasks in which core vocabulary words appear in the task, fostering recognition by users):

    - Match core vocabulary words shown in a box to sentences with missing words.
    - Match core vocabulary with German synonyms or antonyms.
    - Match core vocabulary with extended German definitions.
    - Listen to an audio version of a short text while reading a script with selected core vocabulary words deleted, and fill in the missing words.
    - In a list of four vocabulary words, identify the word that is least related to the other three.
    - While looking at a set of core vocabulary words, listen to a sentence (via audio file) and mark the word(s) from the list that you hear.
    - Read German sentences and translate the underlined core vocabulary words into English (used especially with core vocabulary words that have multiple meanings).
    - Look through a set of core vocabulary words and create a list of all the words that you associate with a given topic.

2. Production tasks (i.e., tasks for which core vocabulary words must be retrieved from memory, or for which core vocabulary words must be used productively)

- Cloze: read a sentence and fill in the blank with a core vocabulary word that fits the context.
- Partial Cloze: read a sentence and fill in the missing letters of a word for which the first and last letters have been provided.
- C-test: read a paragraph in which only the first half of core vocabulary words are given, and write in the remaining letters of the word.
- Read an English definition and provide the core vocabulary word in German.
- Translate English sentences into German, using core vocabulary words.
- Look through two sets of core vocabulary words; choose one word from each set and write a sentence that combines them meaningfully.
- Write a sentence with a given core vocabulary word that shows you know what the word means.
- Complete a crossword puzzle with English definitions serving as the cues.

Vocabulary reviews were inserted into the curriculum with an eye toward the value of "spaced repetition" (Kornell, 2009; Schuetze, 2015). This meant that core vocabulary—especially noncognate—would be encountered by learners not only incidentally in subsequent texts but also deliberately by way of explicit review, and that it would be encountered after increasingly longer intervals of time. Each of the four subsections of a chapter includes a review using one or more of the tasks listed above, targeting the noncognate core vocabulary in a previous chapter. In the first eight chapters (beginning in chapter 3), the following sequence was used in each of the four *Themen* (topics) that served as a vehicle for the cultural content of the chapter:

- Thema 1: noncognate core vocabulary from two chapters before the current chapter
- Thema 2: noncognate core vocabulary from three (or more) chapters before the current chapter
- Thema 3: noncognate core vocabulary from the previous chapter
- Thema 4: all core vocabulary from current chapter, in the form of a crossword puzzle

Over the course of chapters 9–16, the *Thema*-level reviews (T1, T2, ...) move from single-chapter to multiple-chapter coverage to ensure that learners encounter noncognate core vocabulary at least five times over the course of the semester (see Fig. 6.10):

Student Responses

Though it has not yet been possible to conduct a comprehensive, controlled study to judge the relative benefits of this approach, we have used evaluations and

9	T1: Ch 1 T2: Ch 2 T3: Ch 3 T4: Ch 9	13	T1: Ch 1-2-3 T2: Ch 4-5-6 T3: Ch 7-8 T4: Ch 13
10	T1: Ch 4 T2: Ch 5 T3: Ch 6 T4: Ch 10	14	T1: Ch 9-10 T2: Ch 11-12 T3: Ch 13 T4: Ch 14
11	T1: Ch 7-8 T2: Ch 9 T3: Ch 10 T4: Ch 11	15	T1: Ch 12 T2: Ch 13 T3: Ch 14 T4: Ch 15
12	T1: Ch 9 T2: Ch 10 T3: Ch 11 T4: Ch 12	16	T1: 9-10-11 T2: 12-13-14 T3: 15 T4: 16

Figure 6.10. Sequence of noncognate core vocabulary review in *der | die | das*, chapters 9–16, showing spaced repetition

surveys to solicit feedback and ideas for improvement from student users. During and after the pilot course, we asked students to respond anonymously to specific questions regarding ease of use, personal engagement, perceptions of improvement, and comparison with other textbook or vocabulary learning formats. Following the pilot course, we carried out an interview-driven study of students' personal approaches to vocabulary learning. The results of these three feedback sources are presented below.

Students in the pilot course suggested revising this or that topic, clarifying a grammatical point, or in one very specific case moving the word *kriegen* (*informal*: to get, obtain) to an earlier chapter ("my friends in Germany say they use it all the time!"). On a broader scale, however, they articulated a two-fold benefit. Many of them noticed that they could begin reading and comprehending authentic texts—especially journalistic digital media—in a surprisingly short amount of time:

- *As we started reading longer texts, I found that I was able to read these examples of actual German prose—regardless of which genre they came from—with increasing ease and retention.*
- *Even during the fall semester, I found that I was able to read articles from* Der Spiegel, Die Süddeutsche Zeitung, *or other major German newspapers without having to consult the dictionary for every sentence.*
- *I've spoken French for ten years and am basically fluent, but often find myself searching for useful words. This happens less frequently in German.*

Equally prominent in the initial feedback were testimonies to the motivational value of knowing that the vocabulary learned will be encountered frequently, unlike much of the topically driven vocabulary in most textbooks:

- *Knowing that what I was learning was "high-frequency vocabulary" was immensely helpful. When learning languages in the past, I found that too often vocabulary was organized in terms of generic "subjects" (e.g., household chores, ordering food at restaurants) rather than usefulness.*
- *I found myself retaining [the vocabulary] much better than I had in other language courses, where the words were chosen arbitrarily based on a certain theme. Words like "spatula" or "avocado" are quickly forgotten.*
- *Knowing that I was learning high-frequency vocabulary led me to dedicate more time and energy to the learning process.*
- *Following my experience with [der | die | das], learning Portuguese with a traditional textbook frustrated me because I knew I would only rarely come across many words on the vocabulary lists.*
- *I appreciated the fact that words were chosen based on their frequency of use in the language. It was encouraging to know that the words I was learning were ones I would need often in order to communicate rather than ones that rarely come up in conversation or writing.*

For the subsequent study on students' approaches to vocabulary review, students were informed at the beginning of the course about various options for reviewing vocabulary, ranging from old-school paper flashcards (cf. Wissman, Rawson, & Pyc, 2012) to Quizlet (directly connected to the *der|die|das* site[6]), Anki (https://ankiweb.net), StudyBlue (https://www.studyblue.com), and similar online flashcard review engines. Instructors emphasized that regular study and review were essential, but that students should feel free to find a method that appealed to them personally, following Schmitt (1997). Two-thirds of the way through the semester, students were interviewed one-on-one to elicit information about which review programs they preferred and why. The results, as expressed in the course feedback, indicate a wide variety of approaches, largely driven by students' previous language learning experience, for example, in high-school courses:

- *I learned the vocabulary by using Quizlet before class, and then practicing the vocabulary in class exercises.*

---

[6] Quizlet (https://quizlet.com) is a widely used Internet application that allows users to create flashcards and learning games. A computer science student in the pilot course suggested—and personally implemented—a set of Quizlet flashcards and games that can be directly accessed from the website.

- *I personally created a system, albeit a bit old-fashioned, and stuck with it throughout both semesters. With each "Thema" I would create flashcards for all the core vocabulary and color code them based on part of speech (i.e., red for nouns, blue for verbs, etc.).*
- *The strategy that I found most effective was to run through the new words on the built-in Quizlets before each section and then focus on seeing how each word was used in context throughout the following Interactions. This helped me combine rote memorization with some understanding of how the words were supposed to be used.*
- *When preparing for exams, I used StudyBlue to review vocabulary.*
- *I love Anki! It keeps track of which words I know and don't know as well, and keeps showing me the words I need to review.*
- *While many of my classmates learned the vocabulary with physical or online flashcards, I preferred making lists on lined paper with English on the left and German on the right. To study, I would hide the German terms and try to produce them from my head. To engrain the words in my mind it was most helpful to write my own original sentences utilizing different vocabulary.*
- *I learned the vocabulary by making and drilling flashcards. [...] I would then study the cards, going from German to English and then from English to German and making sure that I knew all the information that I had written on the card. I found this way of learning very helpful, and I would highly recommend it to others.*

One point of criticism emerged from students in the pilot course who then continued their language study in Germany: *The high-frequency words are helpful for reading, but I still struggle trying to order food in a restaurant!* This is a valid point, and one that we are currently addressing. While the J–T list is based in part on transcriptions of naturally occurring native-speaker speech, its primary sources are written language, yielding a vocabulary repertoire that is skewed toward journalistic or literary genres. We do not see this as a shortcoming—cultural literacy is, after all, one of the main goals of our department—but as a challenge for providing a balance of useful practical vocabulary in the accompanying daily classroom interactions.

Conclusion

Der|die|das represents an attempt—admittedly one with ample room for improvement—to build a curriculum from the ground up that reflects current research findings in second language acquisition (SLA), specifically the research findings revolving around L2 vocabulary acquisition. It is of course not the first attempt to base a curriculum on an SLA theory—one needs to go back only a few decades to the textbooks emanating from Audiolingualism—but it hopes to avoid the pitfalls of former projects by relying on the relatively broad base of research support, including decades of vocabulary studies and quantitative research into memory and retention, as cited above. That said, it is clear that more quantitative work needs to be done on the use of *der|die|das* itself. Going forward, we have several goals:

- While the basic framework of the curriculum is in place, the cultural components are in constant need of updating and refreshing. We have already engaged focus groups of student users and instructors from the institutions using the program to suggest where texts should be replaced or revised.
- The anecdotal responses of student users are helpful, but they cannot take the place of a rigorously conceived, quantitative survey of all users—with comparative data across cohorts of users to detect trends of attitudes or usage patterns.
- Even more important would be a large-scale study of how a lexically driven curriculum affects overall student learning. Comparative methodology studies are, of course, notoriously difficult to conduct, given the serious reliability and validity issues they entail—not to mention the related logistical and ethical concerns. One possibility would involve testing a cohort of students in an institution after using a different curriculum, and then testing the next year's cohort—which would be similar in background, and taught by the same teachers—to detect any significant differences.

We ultimately want to know whether there are durable learning benefits that derive from a lexically driven approach: Does it actually work, that is, can learners using a lexically driven curriculum read more fluently than other learners? And what benefits might accrue in other areas (e.g., lexical variety in spoken and written discourse, grammatical accuracy, and ability to produce more complex language) in a curriculum that seeks to teach not only breadth of lexis, but also cultural understanding, grammatical knowledge, and functional language use? The larger question in play here is one that affects all of us: How can we make the most effective use of the research findings in our everyday teaching?

For some instructors and program directors, the questions in play may be more localized and specific: How do I develop lexically focused materials for use within an established curricular framework? What resources do I need in order to create and implement them? An initial step toward answering the first question would be to implement (some of) our adaptations to the existing curriculum at the very beginning stages of the *der|die|das* project in order to gauge student response:

- Using the J–T list, identify high-frequency words in the textbook lists.
- Add topic-appropriate words from the J–T list to the textbook lists.
- Emphasize these high-frequency words explicitly in classroom tasks through visual stimuli (e.g., PowerPoint slides), frequent input exposure, priority in assessments, and so forth.
- Create receptive and productive classroom tasks such as matching, crossword puzzles, and audio prompts using the rubrics listed above under "Vocabulary Review"
- Encourage students to make use of web-based flashcard programs such as Anki, Quizlet, or StudyBlue.

The question of resources is closely tied to the level of technical sophistication desired. Creating PowerPoint slides for classroom use, for example, calls merely for a basic working knowledge of PowerPoint. Creating classroom applications for Anki or Quizlet may require an initial technical presentation for instructors, ongoing consultation among instructors to share ideas and classroom reactions, and institutional support for these or similar apps. At the far end of the resource spectrum, creating a functional website with text, audio and video input, and a database for storing student responses will require at the very least a content expert, ideally someone with experience in writing textbook-style pedagogical tasks, a graphic designer, a programmer, and local instructional media personnel for uploading and maintaining the servers or cloud resources that host the site. *Der|die|das* represents our attempt at creating this kind of site, in hopes of answering the question posed above: How can we translate the research on vocabulary acquisition into a workable curriculum? We believe that the site is a useful tool toward that end—but only a tool, and one whose success depends on the interactions of students and instructors in real classrooms.

References

Barcroft, J. (2004). Second language vocabulary acquisition: A lexical input processing approach. *Foreign Language Annals, 37,* 200–208.

Browne, C., Culligan, B., & Phillips, J. (2013). *The new general service list.* Retrieved from http://www.newgeneralservicelist.org

Carroll, B. J., Davies, P., & Richman, B. (1971). *The American Heritage word frequency book.* New York: American Heritage Publishing Co. Inc.

Coady, J. (1997). L2 vocabulary acquisition through extensive reading. In J. Coady & T. Huckin (Eds.), *Second language vocabulary acquisition* (pp. 225–237). Cambridge, UK: Cambridge University Press.

Cobb, T. (2007). Computing the vocabulary demands of L2 reading. *Language Learning & Technology, 11,* 38–63.

Davies, M., & Gardner, D. (2010). *A frequency dictionary of contemporary American English.* London & New York: Routledge.

De Groot, A. M. B., & Keijzer, R. (2000). What is hard to learn is easy to forget: The roles of word concreteness, cognate status, and word frequency in foreign-language vocabulary learning and forgetting. *Language Learning, 50,* 1–56.

Dollenmayer, D., & Hansen, D. (2008). *Neue Horizonte* (7th ed.). Boston: Houghton Mifflin.

Dupuy, B., & Krashen, S. D. (1993). Incidental vocabulary acquisition in French as a foreign language. *Applied Language Learning, 4,* 55–63.

Elgort, I. (2011). Deliberate learning and vocabulary acquisition in a second language. *Language Learning, 61,* 367–413.

Ellis, N. C. (1995). The psychology of foreign language vocabulary acquisition: Implications for CALL. *Computer Assisted Language Learning, 8*(2–3), 103–128.

Ellis, N.C. (2005). At the interface: Dynamic interactions of explicit and implicit language knowledge. *Studies in Second Language Acquisition, 27,* 305–352.

Erten, I. H., & Tekin, M. (2008). Effects on vocabulary acquisition of presenting new words in semantic sets versus semantically unrelated sets. *System, 36,* 407–422.

Folse, K. (2004). *An examination of what intensive ESL students perceive as important in the curriculum.* Unpublished manuscript.

Folse, K. (2008). *Vocabulary myths: Applying second language research to classroom teaching.* Ann Arbor: University of Michigan Press.
Green, D., & Meara, P. (1995). Guest editorial. *Computer Assisted Language Learning, 8*(2–3), 97–101.
Griffin, G. F., & Harley, T. A. (1996). List learning of second language vocabulary. *Applied Psycholinguistics, 17,* 443–460.
Horst, M., Cobb, T., & Meara, P. (1998). Beyond a clockwork orange: Acquiring second language vocabulary through reading. *Reading in a Foreign Language, 11,* 207–223.
Hu, M., & Nation, P. (2000). Unknown vocabulary density and reading comprehension. *Reading in a Foreign Language, 23,* 403–430.
Jones, R. L. (2004). Corpus-based word frequency analysis and the teaching of German vocabulary. *Fremdsprachen Lehren und Lernen, 33,* 165–175.
Jones, R. L. (2006). An analysis of lexical text coverage in contemporary German. In A. Wilson, D. Archer & P. Rayson (Eds.), *Corpus linguistics around the world* (pp. 115–120). Amsterdam: Rodopi.
Jones, R. L., & Tschirner, E. (2006). *Frequency dictionary of German.* London and New York: Routledge.
Kaeding, F. W. (1898). *Häufigkeitswörterbuch der deutschen Sprache.* Steglitz: E.S. Mittler & Sohn.
Kornell, N. (2009). Optimizing learning using flashcards: Spacing is more effective than cramming. *Applied Cognitive Psychology, 23,* 1297–1317.
Krashen, S. D. (1989). We acquire vocabulary and spelling by reading: Additional evidence for the input hypothesis. *Modern Language Journal, 73,* 440–463.
Kucera, H., & Francis, W.N. (1967). *Computational analysis of present-day American English.* Providence, RI: Brown University Press.
Laufer, B. (1992). How much lexis is necessary for reading comprehension? In P. J. L. Arnaud & H. Béjoint (Eds.), *Vocabulary and applied linguistics* (pp. 126–132). London: Macmillan.
Laufer, B., & Hulstijn, J. H. (2001) Incidental vocabulary acquisition in a second language; The construct of task-induced involvement. *Applied Linguistics, 22,* 1–26.
Laufer, B., & Nation, P. (1995). Vocabulary size and use: Lexical richness in L2 written production. *Applied Linguistics, 16*(3), 307–322.
Laufer, B., & Girsai, N. (2008). Form-focused instruction in second language vocabulary learning: A case for contrastive analysis and translation. *Applied Linguistics, 29,* 694–716.
Lipinski, S. (2010). A frequency analysis of vocabulary in three first-year textbooks of German. *Die Unterrichtspraxis, 43*(2), 167–174.
Mayer, R. E. (2009). *Multimedia Learning.* Cambridge, UK: Cambridge University Press.
McQuillan, J. (2016). What can readers read after graded readers? *Reading in a Foreign Language, 28,* 63–78.
Meara, P. (1980). Vocabulary acquisition: A neglected aspect of language learning. *Language Teaching and Linguistics: Abstracts, 13,* 221–246.
Moeller, J., Hoecherl-Alden, G., Adolph, W., & Berger, S. (2009) Deutsch heute (9th ed.). Boston: Houghton Mifflin.
Nation, P. (1993). Vocabulary size, growth and use. In R. Schreuder & B. Weltens (Eds.), *The bilingual lexicon* (pp. 115–134). Amsterdam: John Benjamins.
Nation, P. (2001). *Learning vocabulary in another language.* Cambridge, UK: Cambridge University Press.
Nation, P. (2006). How large a vocabulary is needed for reading and listening? *Canadian Modern Language Review, 63,* 59–81.
Nation, P., & Newton, J. (1997). Teaching vocabulary. In J. Coady & T. Huckin (Eds.), *Second language vocabulary acquisition* (pp. 238–254). Cambridge, UK: Cambridge University press.

Nation, P., & Waring, R. (1997). Vocabulary size, text coverage and word lists. In N. Schmitt & M. McCarthy (Eds.), *Vocabulary: Description, acquisition and pedagogy* (pp. 6–19). Cambridge: Cambridge University Press.

Prince, P. (1996). Second language vocabulary learning: The role of context versus translations as a function of proficiency. *Modern Language Journal, 80*, 478–493.

Quasthoff, U., Fiedler, S., & Hallsteinsdóttir, E. (2011). *Frequency dictionary German/Häufigkeitswörterbuch Deutsch*. Leipzig: Leipziger Universitätsverlag.

Raether, T. (2017, November 29). Braunschweig: Der perfekte Plan B. *Zeit-Online*. Retrieved from http://www.zeit.de/entdecken/reisen/merian/braunschweig-schoenheit-till-raether

Rosengren, I. (1972). *Ein Frequenzwörterbuch der deutschen Zeitungssprache*. Lund: CWK Gleerup.

Rott, S. (1999). The effect of exposure frequency on intermediate language learners' incidental vocabulary acquisition and retention through reading. *Studies in Second Language Acquisition, 21*, 589–620.

Schmitt, N. (1997). Vocabulary learning strategies. In N. Schmitt & M. McCarthy (Eds.), *Vocabulary: Description, acquisition, and pedagogy* (pp. 199–227). Cambridge: Cambridge University Press.

Schmitt, N. (2008). Instructed second language vocabulary learning. *Language Teaching Research, 12*, 329–363.

Schmitt, N., Jiang, X., & Grabe, W. (2011). The percentage of words known in a text and reading comprehension. *The Modern Language Journal, 95*, 26–43.

Schuetze, U. (2017). Efficiency in second language vocabulary learning. *Die Unterrichtspraxis, 50*(1), 22–31.

Schuetze, U. (2015). Spacing techniques in second language vocabulary acquisition: Short-term gains vs. long-term memory. *Language Teaching Research, 19*(1), 28–42.

Tinkham, T. (1993). The effects of semantic clustering on the learning of second language vocabulary. *System, 21*(3), 371–380.

Tinkham, T. (1997). The effects of semantic and thematic clustering on the learning of second language vocabulary. *Second Language Research, 13*, 138–163.

Tschirner, E., Nikolai, B., & Terrell, T. (2009). *Kontakte: A communicative approach* (6th ed.). Boston: McGraw-Hill.

Tschirner, E. & Nikolai, B. (2017). Kontakte: A communicative approach (8th ed.) New York: McGraw-Hill Education.

Tussing, M., & Zimmermann, J. (1977). Vocabulary in first-year German texts. *Die Unterrichtspraxis, 10*, 65–73.

Tussing, M., & Zimmermann, J. (1980). Vocabulary in intermediate German texts. *Die Unterrichtspraxis, 13*, 76–86.

Waring, R. (1997). The negative effects of learning words in semantic sets. *System, 25*(2), 261–274.

Webb, S. A. (2005). Receptive and productive vocabulary learning: The effects of reading and writing on word knowledge. *Studies in Second Language Acquisition, 27*, 33–52.

Webb, S. A. (2007). Learning word pairs and glossed sentences: The effects of a single context on vocabulary knowledge. *Language Teaching Research, 11*, 63–81.

West, M. (1953). *A general service list of English words*. London: Longman.

Wissman, K., Rawson, K., & Pyc, M. (2012). How and when do students use flashcards? *Memory, 20*(6), 568–579.

Chapter 7
Language Corpora for L2 Vocabulary Learning: Data-Driven Learning Across the Curriculum

Nina Vyatkina, University of Kansas

Introduction

Empirical instructed second language acquisition (ISLA) research on second language (L2) vocabulary has shown that data-driven learning (DDL), or teaching and learning languages with the help of corpora (large, structured electronic collections of texts), is beneficial for L2 vocabulary acquisition. Nevertheless, it is still far from becoming a common pedagogical practice, not least because few pedagogical manuals and user-friendly corpus tutorials have been published to date.

This chapter describes how DDL with an open-access German language corpus has been used across the curriculum in a German Studies program at a North American university. I report empirical results and present specific pedagogical suggestions and activities for using a corpus to enhance L2 vocabulary knowledge at all proficiency levels and show how DDL can help learners improve not only the breadth of their L2 vocabulary knowledge (the number of words the basic meaning of which the learner knows) but also the depth of this knowledge (Nation, 1990), including collocations, frequency, and grammatical patterns. Although this chapter uses a German program as a case study, its pedagogical suggestions can be applied to teaching any language for which open-access electronic corpora are available.

In what follows, I provide a brief overview of intersections between corpus linguistics and L2 vocabulary research and then focus in on ISLA and DDL. Next, I describe empirical DDL research results and how to connect it to teaching practice for L2 vocabulary. The rest of the chapter is devoted to a curricular proposal for DDL activities to teach vocabulary across an L2 curriculum, concluding with a brief summary and outlook.

Corpus Linguistics and L2 Vocabulary Research
There are numerous intersections between corpus linguistics and L2 vocabulary teaching and research. This is not surprising as corpus linguistics is predicated upon the postulate of the primacy of lexis (words and coselection of words) over

grammar in terms of meaning creation (Sinclair, 1987, 1991), and thus both disciplines share their major object of study. First, corpus analysis results have been used in L2 vocabulary research for reference purposes. Word frequency lists have been extracted from native corpora of different languages and used as a baseline for measuring L2 learners' vocabulary size (Laufer & Nation, 1995). Second, L2 textbook writers have used corpus-derived information for making decisions on what vocabulary to include and in what curricular progression. Third, more direct applications of corpora in teaching languages in general and L2 vocabulary in particular have been expanding since the 1980s. This teaching method and the associated research field became known as data-driven learning, or DDL (Johns, 1990). According to Boulton and Cobb (2017), DDL is academic inquiry "into the effectiveness of using the tools and techniques of corpus linguistics for second language learning or use" (p. 348).

It is also of note that the concept of lexis has been developing along similar lines in both corpus linguistics and L2 vocabulary research. Corpus linguists have argued against a strict separation of lexis and grammar and, instead, referred in their work to "lexico-grammar" (Sinclair, 1991), that is, tendencies of certain words to occur in certain grammatical patterns. This notion agrees with the concept of "depth" of L2 vocabulary knowledge, first put forth by Nation (1990, 2001). Whereas much of earlier research explored only the "size" of L2 vocabulary knowledge at the level of minimal form–meaning mapping (L1–L2 word translation), Nation has argued that many additional aspects must be included, such as the word's grammatical functions, usage frequency, register, semantic associations, and collocations. On a theoretical level, these approaches clearly align themselves with usage-based language learning theories (e.g., Ellis, 2014), which posit that languages are learned through repeated exposure to usage examples, progressing from individual items (words) to lexico-grammatical patterns to generalizations about abstract categories and principles (grammatical rules).

ISLA and DDL Principles Relevant to L2 Vocabulary Learning

Specific pedagogical principles that are beneficial for L2 vocabulary acquisition in instructed settings have been explored in empirical ISLA studies. Laufer (2017) summarizes these main principles as "The Three 'I's" necessary for successful vocabulary learning: *Input, Instruction*, and *Involvement*. More specifically, the focus of attention has been shown to be critical to what is learned (Barcroft, 2003) and form-focused instruction has been found to be effective (Peters, 2014; Webb & Kagimoto, 2011). Next, studies have shown that repeated exposure (Laufer & Rozovski-Roitblat, 2011), visual input enhancement (Peters, 2012; Sharwood Smith, 1993; Sonbul & Schmitt, 2013), and high involvement load (Kim, 2011; Laufer & Hulstijn, 2001) all lead to more L2 vocabulary learning. As such, these research results lend credence to Schmidt's (1990, 2001) noticing hypothesis, which states that L2 units and features are better learned if they are attended to and noticed at some level of awareness.

Empirical DDL research has been developing mostly in parallel to mainstream ISLA research with few DDL scholars explicitly situating their studies within SLA frameworks (see Flowerdew, 2015, for a discussion). Nevertheless, many of DDL research designs and findings can be explained with a reference to the aforementioned theoretical and pedagogical principles. Typically, learners in DDL get exposed to Laufer's (2017) first "I" condition for successful L2 vocabulary learning, *Input*, through so-called concordances: stacked lines of text with the search item highlighted (e.g., bolded or colored) and centered (Figure 7.1). Concordances provide learners with several to hundreds to millions of examples (depending on how representative of the search item the chosen corpus is). This input is thus rich, repeated, concentrated, and graphically enhanced, which draws the learner's attention to the language patterns (Schmidt, 2001). Corpus examples also have the added benefit of representing naturally occurring language (vs. artificially created textbook examples). As Boulton and Tyne (2015) remark, "corpora bring to the fore a distilled set of authentic uses that the individual would be hard pressed to tease out of the data manually or based on occasional incidental encounters" (p. 303).

Laufer's second "I," *Instruction*, is primarily realized in DDL through the method of guided induction (Herron & Tomasello, 1992), "in which teachers help learners co-construct rules by directing their attention to relevant aspects in the input and asking guiding questions" (Cerezo, Caras, & Leow, 2016, pp. 265–266). Guided induction is operationalized in DDL as another set of "The Three 'I's" (Carter & McCarthy, 1995)—*Illustration* (learners are being exposed to corpus examples), *Interaction* (learners analyze the data and discuss the patterns), and *Induction* (learners induce rules from data analysis)—as well as the fourth "I" of the teacher's *Intervention* (Flowerdew, 2009). Several recent ISLA studies

Ein Extraleben bekommen gute Spieler vom	**Computer**	geschenkt, wenn sie eine besonders hohe Punk
Ich kann nur im	**Computer**	nachsehen, wenn Sie mir die Nummern sagen.
Er setzte sich wieder vor den	**Computer**	, legte eine neue Seite unter den Deckel und st
so nicht wegen des Computers, sondern trotz des	**Computers**	.
Verzweifelt versucht jeder zweite Brite, mit dem	**Computer**	zu sprechen - so eine Microsoft-Studie.
:m Vorbild der Mobilfunkanbieter ihren Kunden die	**Computer**	kostenlos oder zu einem symbolischen Niedrigp
Der Vater kann auch in Herzhöfel am	**Computer**	arbeiten, und die Mutter ist nur vier Tage bescl
Um Viertel nach fünf stand er auf, schaltete den	**Computer**	ein und begann, Seite für Seite von Alfred Dust
/ahren Bedürfnisse des Menschen im Umgang mit	**Computern**	und in der vernetzten Welt.

Figure 7.1. Excerpt from the DWDS corpus search results for *Computer* [1]

---

[1] Hyperlinks to all corpus search results, excerpts from which are represented in the figures, are listed as Figure References at the end of the chapter.

convincingly demonstrate that guided induction is superior to purely deductive or inductive teaching methods while focusing on lexico-grammar (see Cerezo et al., 2016, for an overview). Further, this method has been shown to be associated with learners' deep processing of and high cognitive engagement with the material (Leow, 2015), which accounts for Laufer's *Involvement*, the final "I" condition for successful L2 vocabulary acquisition. To summarize, Laufer's (2017) three conditions necessary for vocabulary learning are realized in DDL as follows:

- Input
  - Rich
  - Repeated
  - Concentrated
  - Enhanced
  - Authentic
- Instruction (guided induction)
  - Illustration
  - Interaction
  - Intervention
  - Induction
- Involvement
  - Cognitive engagement
  - Deep processing

Empirical DDL Research

Most DDL studies have employed variations of the guided induction method in their teaching interventions and explored the effectiveness of these variations in comparison with either one another or with non-DDL teaching methods, most frequently, deductive methods. To date, this research has accumulated a substantial body of evidence that DDL is a viable teaching approach. A detailed review of this literature is beyond the scope of this chapter, and the interested reader is referred to available narrative surveys (e.g., Boulton, 2017; Römer, 2011) and the first comprehensive meta-analyses (Boulton & Cobb, 2017; Lee, Warschauer, & Lee, 2018). Only a few relevant summative findings are discussed here. Boulton and Cobb's (2017) meta-analysis of research published until June 2014 shows that DDL is "a strong methodology for learning language per se, including lexicogrammar" (p. 381). More specifically, the meta-analysis demonstrates a large effect size of learners' improvement in their knowledge of single words and collocations following DDL interventions, and a medium effect size for DDL advantage over traditional materials and teaching methods. Boulton and Cobb also found that both hands-on DDL (learners' direct use of concordancers) and hands-off DDL (learners' work with teacher-printed concordances) are effective, with the hands-on method being somewhat more efficient. Finally, the meta-analysis showed that DDL works not only for advanced but also for intermediate L2 learners. Lee et al. (2018) have confirmed and expanded Boulton and Cobb's (2017) findings in their meta-analysis that specifically targeted DDL vocabulary studies published through 2016. They found "a medium-sized effect on L2 vocabulary learning, with the greatest benefits for promoting in-depth knowledge to learners who have at least intermediate L2 proficiency" (p. 25) and also singled out a number of moderating variables such as corpus types and task types.

While these results are encouraging, the research syntheses also highlight some limitations of the field. The most drastic one relates to the target language: the overwhelming majority of DDL studies target English as a foreign language or an L2. Out of 64 studies that met Boulton and Cobb's (2017) criteria for their meta-analysis, only two addressed languages other than English (one Spanish, one mixed). All articles in the most recent journal special issue on DDL (Vyatkina & Boulton, 2017) also focus on English. While this trend reflects the worldwide spread and importance of English, the scarcity of documented DDL applications to other languages is regrettable because there are many excellent corpora in many languages that are being taught around the globe. This limitation is strongly interconnected with another one, namely, a limited understanding of lexico-grammar in DDL research. Since English is an analytic language without much inflection, DDL studies have primarily focused on the appropriate selection of content and function words but rarely on accuracy in inflectional morphology (Boers & Lindstromberg, 2012). Therefore, it is less clear how DDL fares with other languages. There are some notable exceptions, but overall, DDL studies and pedagogical suggestions for L2s other than English are few and far between (See, for example, Furniss, 2016, for Russian; Kennedy & Miceli, 2010, 2017, for Italian; Kerr, 2009 and Tyne, André, Benzitoun, Boulton, & Greub, 2014, for French; Mendikoetxea, 2014, for Spanish; and Neary-Sundquist, 2015 and Schaeffer-Lacroix, 2016, for German.)

The author of this chapter has contributed to filling this gap by conducting DDL studies using an open-access corpus to teach German to learners at different L2 proficiency levels at a U.S. university. In the first exploratory study, Vyatkina (2013) showed how this corpus was used with advanced learners (mostly graduate students) and outlined the progression of corpus-based activities from more teacher mediation to more learner autonomy. The next two studies focused on German verb–preposition collocations, a difficult lexico-grammatical construction for learners whose first language (L1) is English. Vyatkina (2016a) compared the effectiveness of teaching these collocations with hands-off DDL (printed concordances) and with a deductive method from the course textbook to low-intermediate learners. The study showed that the DDL method was better than traditional instruction for learning new collocations, but both methods were equally effective for improving the knowledge of previously learned collocations. Vyatkina (2016b) compared the effectiveness of hands-on and hands-off concordancing for teaching the same verb–preposition collocations, but this time to high-intermediate learners. The results showed that both methods were equally effective. Some gains were also durable as evidenced on a delayed posttest. This study also found that learners improved regardless of their overall L2 proficiency, although there were some fine-grained differences depending on the test task and proficiency level. Furthermore, the study found that most learners very much liked DDL activities, and that even those who liked them less benefited from them. Finally, Vyatkina (2018) explored the feasibility of using corpus tools beyond concordancing for teaching different aspects of vocabulary knowledge to high-intermediate learners. This study found that learners successfully used a suite of DWDS tools (thesaurus, concordance, word profile, collocations) for researching German verb–noun collocations. As a result, they significantly improved their depth of knowledge of these collocations. It is important to note that these gains were equal to gains achieved from working with printed concordances in regard to word and collocation recall and surpassed paper-based gains in regard to morphological accuracy. Collectively, these studies have shown how an open-access German corpus was successfully used for teaching L2 vocabulary to learners at different L2 proficiency levels.

DDL Research and Practice

One final limitation of DDL research that is directly relevant for this chapter is that a great majority of studies reporting on teaching interventions are conducted by the researchers themselves. Although a few studies did (successfully) involve regular teachers (e.g., Vyatkina, 2016a; Boulton, 2010), it is common for DDL researchers to "lament the fact that corpora have not become widespread in language education" (Boulton & Tyne, 2015, p. 305; see also Frankenberg-Garcia, 2012; Römer, 2011). The main reason for this resistance of language educators to DDL is that using corpora may require substantial corpus linguistic skills on the part of both teachers and learners. Even if teachers were willing to invest their time and effort into learning these skills (in order to share them later with their students), they would be hard-pressed to find appropriate manuals. Although a number of general teacher guides on using corpora and sample DDL exercises have been published (Bennett, 2010; Frankenberg-Garcia, 2012; Kerr, 2009; Thurstun & Candlin, 1997; see also http://sites.psu.edu/calpercorpusportal/corpus-tutorial), tutorials that accompany specific corpora are frequently fairly technical and may be found daunting by teachers (but see Shaw, 2011, for a notable exception). As Boulton and Tyne (2015) note, "it is surprising that there are not more materials to exploit the interactive potential of hands-on corpus use" (p. 308). Such guides could go a long way toward "bringing corpora to the masses" (Boulton, 2011, p. 69) if they capitalize on what is familiar and usual in corpus explorations as opposed to what is unfamiliar and unusual. As Boulton (2011) argues, corpus tools have much in common with other widespread electronic tools (e.g., dictionaries and Google search), and the web itself can be considered a type of corpus. As most language teachers and learners habitually engage in using these tools and materials, tutorials drawing on such parallels could provide step-by-step guidance for using increasingly more sophisticated corpus tools. Finally, teachers and language program directors (LPDs) may shy away from DDL simply because they do not see how they can incorporate them in their already full and busy syllabi and curricula, so modular proposals for incorporating DDL activities into regular syllabi are needed.

This chapter presents such a first attempt as a roadmap for using an open-access corpus and a suite of associated electronic tools for teaching L2 vocabulary across the curriculum.

A Curricular Proposal for Teaching L2 Vocabulary with Corpus-based Resources

The *Digital Dictionary of the German Language*

The electronic resource used in this curricular proposal is more than just a corpus. It is a suite of lexicographic resources titled the *Digital Dictionary of the German Language (Digitales Wörterbuch der Deutschen Sprache)*, henceforth, DWDS (http://dwds.de). It is an open-access resource, supported and regularly updated and expanded by the Berlin-Brandenburg Academy of Sciences in Germany. The DWDS front page reflects these updates by listing links to a word of the day (*Wort des Tages*) and the newest entries (*neueste Artikel*). The empirical basis of DWDS comprises a number of large-scale German corpora that include historical corpora that go as far back as the 17th century, several newspaper corpora, and a number of specialized corpora such as transcribed oral interviews, film subtitles, and blogs. Some of the corpora are annotated for various linguistic categories. Most notably, the core corpus (*Kernkorpus*) of the 20th- and 21st-century German is annotated for parts of speech (POS). It is also equipped with tools that allow the user to search for collocations of a particular word with nouns, adjectives, verbs, and other POS separately. Moreover, the core corpus is balanced by time and text type: each decade is represented by approximately 100,000 words, which are in turn equally divided between four text types: fiction, nonfiction (e.g., guides and manuals), science, and newspaper. While all these corpora can be searched in DWDS, the website also integrates other resources, including electronic dictionaries and visualization tools. The interface is intuitive and user-friendly. The entry page for each word contains its definition, etymology, pronunciation, relevant grammatical information, compounds containing this word, synonyms, collocates (words frequently occurring together with the search word), example sentences, and more. By clicking different links on the front page and setting search filters, the user can find statistical information on the word frequency in different genres, at different time points, in comparison with other words, and more. Due to the richness of DWDS information and presentation formats, it can suit the needs of both scholars (e.g., corpus linguists and lexicographers) and nonspecialist users (e.g., teachers and learners of German). For example, while specialists may be interested in conducting searches that require a sophisticated search syntax (e.g., find all nouns with the ending -*er* separated by two words from the beginning of the sentence but excluding the word *Computer* in all science texts from the 1980s), nonspecialist users can elicit meaningful information from a few typical example sentences containing the search word or commonly used visualization tools, such as the time line or word cloud (illustrated in Figures 7.4 and 7.5, respectively). Over recent years, the DWDS interface has undergone several rounds of substantial revamping to make it more user-friendly. The DWDS website contains links to instructions for using all its resources as well as to publications about the resources and studies conducted with their help. While these references are extremely helpful to specialist users, many of them are too technical for nonspecialist users. Moreover, there currently is no user guide in English, which is a serious obstacle for German learners at lower levels of proficiency. The desire to make this rich vocabulary-learning resource and similar resources more accessible to language teachers and learners provided the main impetus for writing this chapter.

Pedagogical Principles

This proposal is based on the pedagogical principles discussed above that have been shown to benefit L2 vocabulary learning in both ISLA and DDL research. It consists of form-focused teaching modules all of which follow the guided induction method with teacher scaffolding adjusted to each respective curricular level. It is intuitive that tasks should progress from more scaffolded and controlled to less scaffolded and independent ones, also termed "soft" and "hard" DDL, respectively (Gabrielatos, 2005). However, as Boulton and Tyne (2015) note, "there is no single 'right' way to use corpora. It is important for each teacher to choose what is appropriate for him/herself given the learners' needs and available resources" (p. 309). Although activities are presented here according to the L2 proficiency level—from novice to advanced—learner familiarity with corpora should also figure into the equation. For example, if corpora are introduced to advanced L2 learners for the first time, the teacher will want to start with softer DDL versions. In contrast, even low-intermediate L2 learners can complete independent corpus searches after a certain amount of DDL practice. Respectively, all tasks presented here can be varied in regard to the presentation format (teacher-fronted presentation, partner work, individual work), task outcome (open-ended or closed-ended), medium (printed paper materials or online corpus searches), and other characteristics. The selection of vocabulary to be explored will depend on the course goals. Students can complete such worksheets with words preselected by the teacher in accordance with the topics covered in class or from textbook vocabulary lists as well as with self-selected words from class readings or independent readings. While working with textbook vocabulary, the tasks may involve both expanding the depth of knowledge and verifying textbook information with real-life data. The following sections present sample DDL tasks as modules, each titled according to the DWDS tool used and the task to be completed.

DDL Tasks for Novice L2 Learners and/or Novice Corpus Users

Although there may be many ways of introducing corpora, this chapter presents an approach in which learners receive "a gentle introduction [to] corpus use rather than being dropped in at the deep end" (Boulton & Tyne, 2015, p. 308). To introduce DWDS to the students, the teacher can project its main page on a big screen and explain that this is a new generation electronic dictionary that provides many different types of information about words. The key to success is referring to operations and tools that are familiar to students from their everyday technology use, such as Internet and electronic dictionary searches, word clouds, time lines, and so forth. The teacher also needs to explain that DWDS is a monolingual resource; that is, it does not provide L1–L2 translations. For those, learners should use bilingual dictionaries (e.g., http://dict.leo.org/englisch-deutsch/).

Basic search: Form and meaning.

Many foreign language programs start introducing target language vocabulary with cognates: words that have similar meaning and form in both the L1 and L2 (either as borrowings or due to the shared historic origin, as is often the case for German and English, two Germanic languages). Starting on the very first day of a beginning German class, the teacher can enter the cognate word *Internet* in the DWDS search line and then draw the students' attention to the very top line of the resulting page (Figure 7.2) that will list *Internet, das*. The teacher can explain that German has many English borrowings, particularly in the fields related to electronic technology. The teacher may want to point out that the spelling of these borrowings in German is often similar to English, but all nouns in German have to be capitalized and assigned grammatical gender (therefore, one needs to learn German nouns together with their articles—*der, die, das*). The teacher may also click on the speaker icon to listen to the pronunciation of the word. In addition to cognates, good candidates for corpus demonstrations even at beginning stages of German proficiency are so-called pseudoborrowings, or false anglicisms (Furiassi & Gottlieb, 2015), that is, words that have an English form but a different meaning or no meaning in English (e.g., *Handy*—"cell phone," *Twen*—"person between 20 and 30 years of age," *zappen*—"to flip through channels").

Time line: Word frequency over time.

Next, the teacher can point to the word frequency (*Worthäufigkeit*) tool represented as a time line graph in the upper-right corner of the screen (Figure 7.3). Some students may be familiar with this visualization technique from the Google

Internet, das

Grammatik	Substantiv (Neutrum) · Genitiv Singular: **Internet/Internets** · wird nur im Singular verwendet
Aussprache	🔊
Worttrennung	In-ter-net
Herkunft	Englisch
Wortbildung	mit ›Internet‹ als Erstglied: ↗Internet-Adresse ... 86 weitere

[Bedeutung] [Thesaurus] [Typische Verbindungen]

Figure 7.2. Top part of the DWDS vocabulary entry page for *Internet*

selten ▬▬▬▬▬ ▭ ▭ *häufig*

Wortverlaufskurve

| ab 1600 | ab 1945 |

Frequenz / Mio Tokens

7.5

5

2.5

0
1600 1700 1800 1900 2000

Figure 7.3. Word frequency time line graph for *Internet*

Books Ngram Viewer tool (https://books.google.com/ngrams) or any time line graph. It should be easy to interpret this DWDS view that illustrates that German did not have the word *Internet* until the mid-20th century but that its frequency has been growing exponentially. At this point, the teacher may want to mention that all examples and visualizations in DWDS draw from millions of words from texts from historical and contemporary German in different genres. Differences between curated corpora such as DWDS and the web are also worth noting. Frequency data retrieved with this DWDS tool is stable and controlled, and the user can easily access source texts from which this numerical data has been harvested (including examples in context, bibliographic citations for each text, and sometimes the full text if freely available on the Internet). In contrast, frequency data retrieved from the web with the Google Books Ngram Viewer is unstable (it may change any day if new texts are added), largely undifferentiated by text type, and not traceable back to the original texts.

Word cloud: Collocations.

Finally, the teacher can scroll down to the word cloud view that shows typical word combinations (*Typische Verbindungen*), or collocates, of the search word (Figure 7.4). Many students will be familiar with the word cloud view as well, so volunteers can be called on to explain that the words that most frequently appear together with *Internet* are represented in larger letters. While looking at the collocates of *Internet*, the students will recognize further English borrowings such as *Computer* and *Homepage* and other cognates such as *Telefon, Informationen,* and *Adresse*. Students may also notice that the word cloud contains both the forms *Surfen* and *surfen*. The teacher can explain that the first one stands for the noun ("surfing")—because it is capitalized—and the second one for the verb ("to surf"). In other words, this corpus tool differentiates between different POS.

Activities similar to those described above are a good starting point for introducing corpus-based activities to learners at any L2 proficiency level if they are not familiar with corpora or with this particular corpus. For intermediate and advanced learners, corpus-based activities can then be expanded to include more independent work and analysis as well as progressively more sophisticated DWDS tools. Sample activities are described in the following sections.

Adresse   **Computer**   E-Mail   **Fernsehen**

Handel   Handy   **Homepage**

Informationen   **Infos**   Medien   Mobilfunk

Nutzung   **Surfen**   **Telefon**   **Zugang**

abgerufen   abgewickelt   **anbietet**   **bestellen**

buchen   ermöglicht   **heruntergeladen**   informieren

mobile   nutzen   **surfen**   **verbreitet**

vertreiben   **veröffentlicht**   übertragen

Figure 7.4. Collocates of *Internet*

DDL Tasks for Intermediate L2 Learners and/or Intermediate Corpus Users

Concordances: Lexico-grammatical analysis.

Concordancers and concordances are the most frequently used corpus tools and output format in DDL applications. The introduction to concordancing activities should, like with any new tools and activities, begin with a teacher's demonstration on the big screen. To show students specific usage examples of the search word, the teacher can scroll down below the time line and display the list of corpora with associated search word frequencies (Figure 7.5). If, for instance, *chatten* ("to chat") is the search word, students can see at a glance that there are hundreds of examples of this verb in corpora of newspapers, blogs, and film subtitles. By clicking on a hyperlink associated with a corpus, the teacher can display these examples in the form of concordances (Figure 7.6a). The first view displays complete sentences containing the search word, but an extended cotext view or a Key Words In Context (KWIC) view can be selected as well (Figures 6b and 6c). The KWIC view lends itself to form-focused tasks, such as the one described in this section. By seeing different verb forms—which are bolded and centered—*chatten, chattet, chattete, gechattet,* students become aware of how a verb borrowed from English takes on German morphology. Students can be asked to identify specific verb forms (past tense, third-person singular, etc.). The teacher should underscore that at this stage of the analysis, the students should be concerned not with translating each example sentence but rather with identifying general patterns of usage. In contrast, the sentence view or the extended context view lends itself to activities that combine the focus on both meaning and form (described later in this chapter). The activity described here can be conducted in a teacher-fronted format with concordances displayed on a big screen. Alternatively, the teacher may print preselected concordances and assign them to partner groups or as individual homework. The latter format will be especially productive if the aim is to cover several different words as they can be divided between groups or individual students and the results can be later shared with the whole class.

The same procedure can be followed for analyses of lexico-grammatical collocations rather than individual words. A good candidate is verb–preposition collocations (e.g., *warten auf*—"to wait for"), a notorious area of difficulty for English learners of German (see Ecke, 2015, p. 99; Ecke & Hall, 2000, p. 31). In the first iteration of this activity, students work with teacher-printed concordances that best illustrate the usage of the focal collocations. Later (as with any activity presented in this chapter), the assignment can be changed to student online searches for the target verb–preposition collocations in the corpus. Detailed guidelines and sample worksheets for these activities are available in Vyatkina (2015a, 2015b), an open-access online publication.

Korpustreffer

Referenzkorpora

- DWDS-Kernkorpus (1900–1999) (5)
- DWDS-Kernkorpus 21 (2000–2010) (30)
- Deutsches Textarchiv (1473–1927) (8)

Zeitungskorpora

- Berliner Zeitung (1994–2005) (135)
- Tagesspiegel (1996–2005) (197)
- Die ZEIT (1946–2016) (310)

Spezialkorpora

- Referenz- und Zeitungskorpora (aggregiert) (685)
- Blogs (396)
- Polytechnisches Journal (2)
- Filmuntertitel (68)

Figure 7.5. Frequencies of *chatten* in different DWDS subcorpora

Die Zeit, 24.10.2016 (online)
Der Münchner Amokschütze hat im Vorfeld seiner Bluttat im Internet vermutlich mit sich selbst **gechattet**.

Die Zeit, 13.10.2016, Nr. 43
Im Netz wird gesurft, gespielt, **gechattet** – und leider oft auch gehasst.

Die Zeit, 27.09.2016 (online)
Am Ende liegt es im Ermessen der Nutzer, ob sie lieber abhörsicher(er) **chatten** und dafür auf Komfort verzichten.

Die Zeit, 14.08.2016 (online)
Wir wissen nicht, wer miteinander **chattet**", sagte Maaßen.

Figure 7.6a. Concordances with *chatten* (sentence view)

Suite of tools: Get to know a word.

With the help of DWDS, students can significantly deepen their knowledge of both new and previously learned words, since each entry page contains a plethora of lexicographic information. Students can be assigned a word and asked to complete a worksheet in which they list its definition, relevant grammatical information, compounds containing this word, synonyms, collocates, and example sentences with

Die Zeit, 13.10.2016, Nr. 43

Im Netz wird gesurft, gespielt, **gechattet** – und leider oft auch gehasst.
Doch Vorsicht: Wer fiese Kommentare und Fotos postet, kann sich strafbar machen und Besuch von der Polizei bekommen. von Johanna Schoener

Die Zeit, 27.09.2016 (online)
Die künstliche Intelligenz, mit der Facebook und Google seine Dienste in Zukunft für Nutzer verbessern möchten, steht also gewissermaßen der sicheren Kommunikation im Weg.
Am Ende liegt es im Ermessen der Nutzer, ob sie lieber abhörsicher(er) **chatten** und dafür auf Komfort verzichten.
Oder ob Chatbots und der Versand von Gifs für sie unerlässlich sind.

Figure 7.6b. Concordances with *chatten* (extended view)

Wir wissen nicht, wer miteinander	chattet	", sagte Maaßen.
...ht zufolge mit möglichen IS-Kontakten in Saudi-Arabien	gechattet	.
... Person, die etwas tun könnte, sitzt in New Jersey und	chattet	mit ihrer Facebook-Gemeinde!"
	Gechattet	hatte sie demnach mit einem der Verdächtig
...chten beantworte, swipen sie nach links oder rechts und	chatten	mit ihrenmatches . Für Sex, für Romantik, m
Mit Luther per SMS	chatten	oder Buchstaben fühlen - in der Grimmwelt t
...Sie Ihr Snapchat-Videos, folgen Sie Ihr auf Instagram,	chatten	Sie bei WhatsApp mit ihr.

Figure 7.6c. Concordances with *chatten* (KWIC view)

this word. As a final task, the students can write their own example sentences with the word. These worksheets can be compiled in a vocabulary log to be submitted to the teacher iteratively over a semester, or students can be asked to enter this information in a class Wiki for everybody to see. As opposed to all activities described above, this activity can lead to divergent results as learners will search the corpus directly and independently and have a choice of which hyperlinks to click and which examples to select. The key to this activity's success is careful scaffolding. First, the students should be warned that DWDS provides a large amount of information about each word, and covering all of this information would be beyond the limits of this particular assignment. Next, they should be given clear directions and a model—a completed worksheet prepared in advance by the teacher. Ideally, the class would meet in a computer lab (or in a regular room with each student having a laptop, tablet, or smartphone with Internet access) where the teacher could demonstrate the completion of the assignment for the model word on the big screen with students mirroring all steps on their individual computers. In this way, they will learn how to be selective and not become overwhelmed by the richness of information in DWDS. This guided induction approach, in which students receive careful teacher guidance and then work with corpora independently and inductively, has been shown to lead to higher levels of learner engagement with and attention to the L2 material. This results in higher learning gains in comparison with deductive methods in which the teacher provides all information to the students (see Section "ISLA and DDL Principles Relevant to L2 Vocabulary Learning").

DDL Tasks for More Advanced L2 Learners and Corpus Users

More advanced students, after they have become familiar with DWDS by completing some of the activities described above, can be assigned more complex DDL tasks that are open ended and independent as well as involve more sophisticated DWDS tools. In what follows, the target L2 proficiency level will be referred to as "advanced," although this designation is relative depending on the definition of the term. For example, Vyatkina (2016b) has shown that students who have reached the German proficiency at or above the Common European Framework of Reference (Council of Europe, 2001) B1 level (or intermediate high on the ACTFL scale) can successfully complete such tasks if given sufficient initial guidance by the teacher.

Word profile: Lexico-grammatical collocations.
Research results show that although advanced learners have good receptive knowledge of collocations (i.e., they understand their meaning), they have much poorer productive knowledge (Schmitt, 2010). For example, students of German can easily translate the verb–noun collocation *Hausaufgaben machen* as "to do homework" because they are being exposed to the noun *Hausaufgaben* early on and repeatedly. In contrast, in their own German production, calque errors (i.e., using a cognate in contexts that require a noncognate) are frequent because the prototypical translation of "to do" is *tun* and not *machen* (Nesselhauf, 2003; Rott, 2016). Moreover, many learners are not aware that the collocation *Hausaufgaben erledigen* ("to complete homework") is much more frequent than *Hausaufgaben machen* and that the noun is predominantly used in German in its plural form. Form-focused DDL activities can help raise learners' awareness of the verb component in such collocations and improve their productive knowledge (Vyatkina, 2018). As usual, the activity should first be demonstrated by the teacher, then completed by learners under teacher's supervision, and only then assigned as partner work or an independent task.

For this task, the learners will work with the DWDS word profile (*Wortprofil*) tool. By iteratively clicking certain hyperlinks, the user is taken to the word cloud view (Figure 7.7a), then to the view that arranges collocations in ranked lists according to their POS and syntactic role (Figure 7.7b), and then to concordances with usage examples for each collocation (Figure 7.7c). This last step is important because it shows that members of a verb–noun collocation (bolded in this view), though directly connected syntactically, can be separated in a sentence by a considerable number of words due to the German word order rules (Rott, 2016). The instructions direct the learners' attention to the most frequent verbs that go together with the search noun and typical usage patterns, including word order and inflectional morphology. As a result, learners remember more verb collocations of the target nouns and use them more accurately in subsequent production tasks (Vyatkina, 2018).

Erledigen   Erledigung

Klassenarbeiten   Klausuren   Mittagessen

Referate   abfragen   abgearbeitet   abschreiben

aufbekommen   aufhatte   aufkriegen

beaufsichtigen   betreuen   brütet   **erledigen**

erledigte   finanzpolitischen   gemacht

gemachten   haushaltspolitischen   helfen   nachgeholt

nichtgemachte   strukturpolitischen

unerledigten   vernachlässigt

Figure 7.7a. Collocates of *Hausaufgabe* (word cloud)

hat Adjektivattribut	logDice	Freq.
1. unerledigt	9.9	50
2. erledigt	9.2	26
3. nichtgemacht	8.2	7
4. strukturpolitisch	7.6	9
5. gemacht	6.1	25
6. finanzpolitisch	5.9	16
7.	5.3	5

ist Akk./Dativ-Objekt von	logDice	Freq.
1. erledigen	10.4	666
2. machen	6.5	3096
3. vernachlässigen	6.2	22
4. aufhaben	6.1	12
5. aufbekommen	5.7	7
6. abschreiben	5.6	13
7. nachholen	5.6	11

hat Genitivattribut	logDice	Freq.
1. Kind	2.6	14
2. Politik	1.9	7

in Koordination mit	logDice	Freq.
1. Klassenarbeit	11.5	16
2. Referat	9.3	19
3. Note	7.5	8
4. Unterricht	7.2	12

Figure 7b. Collocates of *Hausaufgabe* by POS/syntactic role (word profile)

14: Die Welt, 17.09.2004
   Ganztagsschulen sollten eingeführt, **Hausaufgaben** zusammen mit den Lehrern **erledigt** werden.

15: Bild, 21.08.2004
   Doch für unseren Traum vom Pokal-Endspiel müssen wir solche **Hausaufgaben erledigen**.

16: Der Tagesspiegel, 08.07.2004
   Vor allem aber begutachten sie, wie Leth seine **Hausaufgaben erledigt** hat.

17: Berliner Zeitung, 21.06.2004
   Wichtig dabei ist, dass man vorher seine **Hausaufgaben erledigt** hat.

18: Die Welt, 14.05.2004
   Bevor Mehdorn mit einem Börsengang liebäugelt, sollte er endlich seine **Hausaufgaben erledigen**.

19: Der Tagesspiegel, 09.05.2004
   Und dann hat Ihr Sohn auch noch seine **Hausaufgaben** nicht **erledigt**, obwohl Sie ihn fünf Mal ermahnt haben.

Figure 7c. Concordances for the collocation *Hausaufgaben erledigen*

Word profile: Semantic prosody of near-synonyms.
The word profile tool also supports comparisons of the usage patterns of near-synonyms, or words with very similar meanings (Storjohann, 2009). In particular, students can explore the "semantic prosody" (Louw, 2000) of such words, or their tendency to appear with similar or different collocates. For example, if one explores the word profile of the adjective *gewaltig* ("powerful, enormous"), one can enter its near-synonym *heftig* ("forcible, fierce") in the field *Gemeinsamkeiten mit* ("commonalities with") on top of the page (Figure 7.8a). The resulting view displays lists of common collocates for *gewaltig* and *heftig*. One can see that both adjectives frequently appear together with nouns from the semantic fields "natural disasters; explosions."

If, instead, the operator is changed from "commonalities" to "differences" (*Unterschiede zu*), one can see that while *gewaltig* appears much more frequently with nouns such as *Summe, Ausmaß* (finances), *heftig* goes together with *Kontroverse, Auseinaderstzung, Debatte* (polemics) (Figure 7.8b). All these collocations can be explored in context by clicking on each collocate and perusing the resulting concordance view. Students can be asked to note and discuss their findings with their partners and then share the results with the class. The teacher can select pairs of near-synonyms for this task from relevant curricular topics and texts as well as with the help of DWDS itself, as front pages for each word entry (*Wortinformation*) contain lists of synonyms.

Time line: Word usage history.
To quote DWDS developers, their time line tool supports explorations of "word careers" (*Wortkarrieren*) over more than 400 years (https://www.dwds.de/d/neues). The time trajectory of the word usage frequency allows for tracking a word's emergence, waxing and waning, and even disappearance from the German language. The basic time line view (Figure 7.2) automatically appears in the upper-right corner of the front page for each word entry and presents the word history at a glance

Lemma				optional: Wortvergleich			Lemma Vergleich	
gewaltig				Gemeinsamkeiten			heftig	
Wortart	min. *logDice*		min. Frequenz	Sortierung	Ansicht		Kollokationen	
Adjektiv	0		5	logDice			20	

Überblick	*logDice*	*logDice*	Freq.	Freq.	
1. Explosion	7.5	6.1	717	413	is
2. Sturm	5.1	6.5	151	595	
3. Schlag	4.8	5.3	148	294	
4. Erdbeben	5.1	5.2	113	195	
5. derart	4.6	5.8	83	310	
6. Ausbruch	4.8	5.0	109	190	
7. so	4.4	5.8	1955	5282	
8. Erschütterung	4.6	4.6	69	120	

Figure 7.8a. Common collocates of *gewaltig* and *heftig* (word profile)

Lemma				optional: Wortvergleich			Lemma Vergleich	
gewaltig				Unterschiede zu			heftig	
Wortart	min. *logDice*		min. Frequenz	Sortierung	Ansicht		Kollokationen	
Adjektiv	0		5	logDice			20	

Überblick	*logDice*	*logDice*	Freq.	Freq.	
1. Summe	6.9	-	750	-	is
2. Ausmaß	6.8	-	586	-	
3. irren	6.8	-	353	-	
4. Schneefall	0.9	7.5	5	828	
5. Regenfall	1.8	8.5	10	1790	
6. Kontroverse	1.4	8.1	8	1404	
7. Auseinandersetzung	0.9	8.1	18	3262	
8. Debatte	0.2	7.9	12	3072	

Figure 7.8b. Different collocates of *gewaltig* and *heftig* (word profile), marked by different colors (not visible here)

while also marking whether it is rare or frequent (*selten* or *häufig*). This line graph is easily interpretable for users at any proficiency level. More advanced learners can explore further functionalities of this tool. By clicking on the graph, the user gets to a full-screen view in which one can set various filters. For example, while researching the word *Herausforderung* (challenge), one can select a view containing separate time lines for the relative word frequency (per million words) in different text types (Figure 7.9). One can see that the word first emerged around 1765 in newspaper texts. Its frequency was slowly growing over the next centuries but it really took off after the 1970s. A divergence between text types is also noticeable, with the newspaper frequencies growing rapidly and frequencies in other text types lagging behind. Further, by moving the cursor over the curves, one can see frequencies of the word at each specific point in time. Figure 7.9 shows that in the present decade's newspaper texts, *Herausforderung* has so far been used with an average frequency of 36.59 times per million words, which amounts to 11,978 occurrences in total. If the user clicks the box with this information, a link to corpus examples from the respective decade and in the respective text genre appears. By following this link, the user gets the view of concordances and can explore the use of *Herausforderung* in context. A comparison of the 17th–19th-century examples with more contemporary examples will lead the user to conclude that while, earlier, this word was used in reference to fights and wars (as in "challenge to a duel"), its contemporary usage is almost exclusively restricted to the meaning of "challenge" in the sense of "an issue to be overcome" which had originally been absent in German but was relatively recently borrowed from English (see Kramsch, 1993, pp. 31–32). The teacher can assign such a historical analysis of different words to different students, who will then share the results of their research with the class.

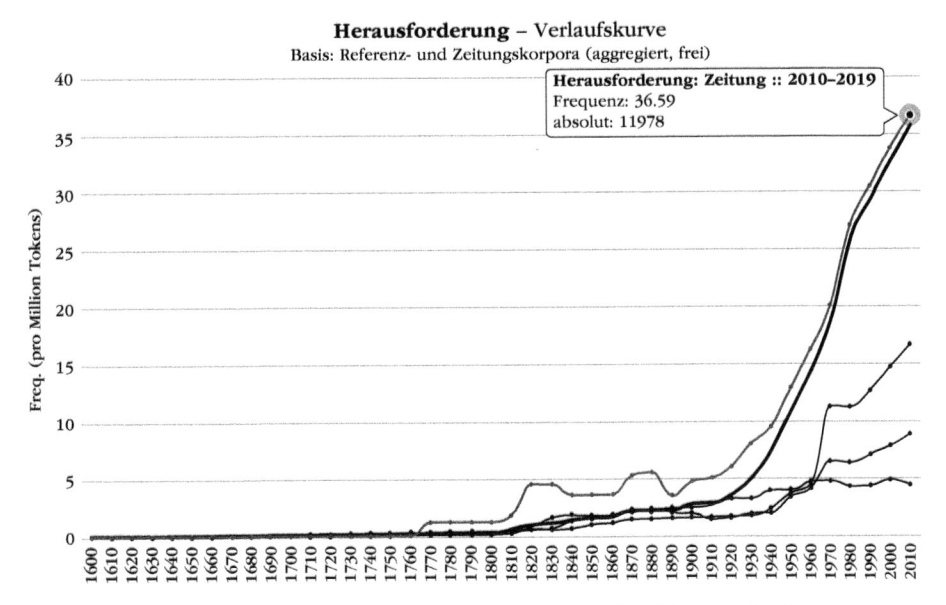

Figure 7.9. Extended view of the time line graph for *Herausforderung*. Curves for different genres are marked by different colors (not visible here)

Beyond a historical-linguistic interest, such activities have practical implications for learners' choice of words in their own L2 use. For example, dictionaries list *obwohl* and *obgleich* as alternatives for translating the English adverb "although." However, the DWDS time line tool shows that whereas the frequencies of the former have been continuously rising since 1800 throughout the 20th century, the picture for the latter is exactly the opposite (see Vyatkina, 2013). This information provides a clear indication that *obwohl* is the preferred alternative today, which may lead the learner to opt in favor of using *obwohl* instead of *obgleich*.

Suite of tools: Long-term student projects.

Finally, advanced students may be assigned group projects or individual projects that can last from several weeks to an academic term. For example, students can keep vocabulary logs in which they record various types of information about newly learned words or expanded information about previously learned words. This activity can be further modified if applied to course texts that are incorporated in the target corpus. In such cases, the teacher can design DDL activities in which learners focus on specific words they encountered while reading, taking a top-down, text-to-corpus approach (Charles, 2007; Johns, Hsingchin, & Lixun, 2008; Vyatkina, 2016b). Such an approach would address Widdowson's (2000) notorious criticism of corpus examples being taken out of a larger context and thus lacking relevance to learner interests. Further, if deemed necessary for the course goals, advanced students may also be taught how to use more advanced search filters (e.g., https://www.dwds.de/d/suche). Another idea for a project is using corpora as a reference resource while completing writing assignments. Students can be asked to work on the appropriateness of their vocabulary use by consulting corpora. They can be instructed to document their searches and attach brief descriptions of these searches and corpus snapshots to their rough or revised writing assignment drafts. Although a detailed outline of such projects is beyond the scope of this chapter, a number of DDL studies attest to their benefits (see Yoon, 2016, for a recent study and overview). Finally, a group project can be designed in which students create multimedia tutorials for teaching languages with corpora and which would culminate in end-of-semester presentations and/or posting the tutorials online (see https://scholarblogs.emory.edu/germangrammar/ for outcomes of a similar project). Such projects would prepare students for life-long learning with corpora and using them as a reference resource beyond the classroom.

Conclusion

Empirical research has by now convincingly demonstrated that DDL with electronic corpora is effective for many areas of ISLA including vocabulary. All necessary conditions for successful L2 vocabulary acquisition are present in DDL; corpora and associated visualization tools provide learners with rich, dense, and authentic input, and the preferred DDL method—guided induction—ensures high levels of learner involvement with and deep processing of this input. However, the paucity of accessible DDL application models for language teachers, especially for languages other than English, has so far hindered a wide spread of DDL in teaching practice. LPDs may be especially hesitant to implement DDL in their programs thinking that it may require a complete revamping of the curriculum.

This chapter intended to counter this misconception and contributed to building a bridge between DDL research and teaching practice. It presented sample modules using an open-access corpus and a suite of associated electronic tools for teaching German vocabulary across the curriculum. Preparation of a more comprehensive teacher guide is currently underway. This proposal presents a case study situated in a specific local context: teaching German as a foreign language to North American university students with a specific electronic resource. All activities described here (or their variations) have been used in a German Studies program in German courses at different proficiency levels and the results were very positive (Vyatkina, 2013, 2016a, 2016b, 2018). However, the principles and activities described here can be adapted to various target languages for which electronic corpora are available.[2] The model presented here conceives of DDL as a "corpus apprenticeship" (Kennedy & Miceli, 2010) that is introduced into a curriculum in a gradual way without radically changing the existing teaching approach. It is hoped that this proposal will help language teachers and program directors become familiar with open-access corpus resources and tools and start using their rich potential in DDL applications to the benefit of their learners.

Figure References (hyperlinks to DWDS search results retrieved May 26, 2018)
Figure 7.1: https://www.dwds.de/r?q=Computer&corpus=korpus21&date-start=2000&date-end=2010&genre=Belletristik&genre=Wissenschaft&genre=Gebrauchsliteratur&genre=Zeitung&format=kwic&sort=random&limit=50
Figure 7.2–7.4: https://www.dwds.de/wb/Internet
Figure 7.5: https://www.dwds.de/wb/chatten
Figure 7.6a: https://www.dwds.de/r?corpus=zeit;q=chatten
Figure 7.6b: https://www.dwds.de/r?q=chatten&corpus=zeit&date-start=1946&date-end=2016&format=max&sort=date_desc&limit=50&p=1
Figure 7.6c: https://www.dwds.de/r?q=chatten&corpus=zeit&date-start=1946&date-end=2016&format=kwic&sort=date_desc&limit=50&p=1
Figure 7.7a: https://www.dwds.de/wb/Hausaufgabe
Figure 7.7b–7.7c: https://www.dwds.de/wp/Hausaufgabe

---

[2] For example, American English (COCA, https://corpus.byu.edu/coca/), Portuguese (http://www.corpusdoportugues.org/), Russian (http://www.ruscorpora.ru/en/), Spanish (http://www.corpusdelespanol.org/).

Figure 7.8a: https://www.dwds.de/wp?q=gewaltig&comp-method=intersection&comp=heftig&pos=0&minstat=0&minfreq=5&by=logDice&limit=20&view=table

Figure 7.8b: https://www.dwds.de/wp?q=gewaltig&compmethod=intersection&comp=heftig&limit=20&minstat=0&minfreq=5&by=logDice&view=table

Figure 7.9: https://www.dwds.de/r/plot?view=1&norm=date%2Bclass&smooth=spline&genres=1&grand=1&slice=10&prune=0&window=3&wbase=0&logavg=0&logscale=0&xrange=1600%3A2016&q1=Herausforderung

References

Barcroft, J. (2003). Effects of questions about word meaning during L2 Spanish lexical learning. *The Modern Language Journal, 87*(4), 546–561.

Bennett, G. R. (2010). *Using corpora in the language learning classroom: Corpus linguistics for teachers.* Ann Arbor, MI: University of Michigan Press.

Boers, F., & Lindstromberg, S. (2012). Experimental and intervention studies on formulaic sequences in a second language. *Annual Review of Applied Linguistics, 32*, 83–110.

Boulton, A. (2010). Data-driven learning: Taking the computer out of the equation. *Language Learning, 60*(3), 534–572.

Boulton, A. (2011). Bringing corpora to the masses: Free and easy tools for interdisciplinary language studies. In N. Kübler (Ed.), *Corpora, language, teaching, and resources: From theory to practice* (pp. 69–96). Bern, Switzerland: Peter Lang.

Boulton, A. (2017). Research timeline: Corpora in language teaching and learning. *Language Teaching, 50*(4), 483–506.

Boulton, A., & Cobb, T. (2017). Corpus use in language learning: A meta-analysis. *Language Learning, 67*(2), 348–393.

Boulton, A., & Tyne, H. (2015). Corpus-based study of language and teacher education. In M. Bigelow & J. Ennser-Kananen (Eds.), *The Routledge handbook of educational linguistics* (pp. 301–312). New York: Routledge.

Carter, R., & McCarthy, M. (1995). Grammar and the spoken language. *Applied Linguistics, 16*(2), 141–158.

Cerezo, L., Caras, A., & Leow, R. P. (2016). The effectiveness of guided induction versus deductive instruction on the development of complex Spanish *gustar* structures. *Studies in Second Language Acquisition, 38*, 265–291.

Charles, M. (2007). Reconciling top-down and bottom-up approaches to graduate writing: Using a corpus to teach rhetorical functions. *Journal of English for Academic Purposes, 6*(4), 289–302.

Council of Europe. (2001) *Common European framework of reference for languages: Learning, teaching, assessment.* Strasbourg: Language Policy Unit. Retrieved from http://www.coe.int/en/web/common-european-framework-reference-languages

Ecke, P. (2015). Was (oft lustige) Fehler und Wortfindungsprobleme über Wortschatzlern- und Verarbeitungsprozesse enthüllen. In M. Löschmann & M. Löschmann (Eds.), *Humor im Fremdsprachenunterricht* (pp. 96–111). Frankfurt am Main: Peter Lang.

Ecke, P., & Hall, C. J. (2000). Lexikalische Fehler in Deutsch als Drittsprache: Translexikalischer Einfluss auf drei Ebenen der mentalen Repräsentation. *Deutsch als Fremdsprache, 37*(1), 30–36.

Ellis, N. C. (2014). Cognitive AND social language usage. *Studies in Second Language Acquisition, 36*(3), 397–402.
Flowerdew, L. (2009). Applying corpus linguistics to pedagogy: A critical evaluation. *International Journal of Corpus Linguistics, 14*(3), 393–417.
Flowerdew, L. (2015). Data-driven learning and language learning theories: Whither the twain shall meet. In A. Leńko-Szymańska & A. Boulton (Eds.), *Multiple affordances of language corpora for data-driven learning* (pp. 15–36). Amsterdam, Netherlands: John Benjamins.
Frankenberg-Garcia, A. (2012). Raising teachers' awareness of corpora. *Language Teaching, 45*(4), 475–489.
Furiassi, C., & Gottlieb, H. (2015). *Pseudo-English: Studies on false anglicisms in Europe*. Berlin, Germany: De Gruyter.
Furniss, E. A. (2016). Teaching the pragmatics of Russian conversation using a corpus-referred website. *Language Learning & Technology, 20*(2), 38–60.
Gabrielatos, C. (2005). Corpora and language teaching: Just a fling, or wedding bells? *TESL-EJ, 8*(4), 1–37.
Herron, C., & Tomasello, M. (1992). Acquiring grammatical structures by guided induction. *The French Review, 65*(5), 708–718.
Johns, T. (1990). From printout to handout: Grammar and vocabulary teaching in the context of data-driven learning. *CALL Austria, 10*, 14–34.
Johns, T., Hsingchin, L., & Lixun, W. (2008). Integrating corpus-based CALL programs in teaching English through children's literature. *Computer Assisted Language Learning, 21*(5), 483–506.
Kennedy, C., & Miceli, T. (2010). Corpus-assisted creative writing: Introducing intermediate Italian students to a corpus as a reference resource. *Language Learning & Technology, 14*(1), 28–44.
Kennedy, C., & Miceli, T. (2017). Cultivating effective corpus use by language learners. *Computer Assisted Language Learning, 30*(1–2), 91–114.
Kerr, B. J. (2009). Applications of corpus-based linguistics to second language instruction: Lexical grammar and data-driven learning. In S. L. Katz & J. Watzinger-Tharp (Eds.), *Conceptions of L2 grammar: Theoretical approaches and their application in the L2 classroom* (pp. 128–150). Boston, MA: Heinle Cengage Learning.
Kim, Y. (2011). The role of task-induced involvement and learner proficiency in L2 vocabulary acquisition. *Language Learning, 61*(1), 100–140.
Kramsch, C. (1993). *Context and culture in language teaching*. Oxford: Oxford University Press.
Laufer, B. (2017). The Three "I"s of second language vocabulary learning: Input, instruction, involvement. In E. Hinkel (Ed.), *Handbook of research in second language teaching and learning*, (Vol. 3, pp. 343–354). London: Routledge.
Laufer, B., & Hulstijn, J. H. (2001). Incidental vocabulary acquisition in a second language: The construct of task-induced involvement. *Applied Linguistics, 22*, 1–26.
Laufer, B., & Nation, P. (1995). Vocabulary size and use: Lexical richness in L2 written production. *Applied Linguistics, 16*, 307–322.
Laufer, B., & Rozovski-Roitblat, B. (2011). Incidental vocabulary acquisition: The effects of task type, word occurrence and their combination. *Language Teaching Research, 15*, 391–411.
Lee, H., Warschauer, M., & Lee, J. H. (2018). The effects of corpus use on second language vocabulary learning: A multilevel meta-analysis. *Applied Linguistics*, 1–34. doi:10.1093/applin/amy012
Leow, R. P. (2015). *Explicit learning in the L2 classroom: A student-centered approach*. New York: Routledge.

Louw, B. (2000). Contextual prosodic theory: Bringing semantic prosodies to life. In C. Heffer, H. Sauntson, & G. Fox (Eds.), *Words in context: A tribute to John Sinclair on his retirement* (pp. 48–94). Birmingham, UK: University of Birmingham.

Mendikoetxea, A. (2014). Corpus-based research in second language Spanish. In K. L. Geeslin (Ed.), *The handbook of Spanish second language acquisition* (pp. 11–29). Malden, MA: Wiley-Blackwell.

Nation, P. (1990). *Teaching and learning vocabulary*. Rowley, MA: Newbury House.

Nation, P. (2001). *Learning vocabulary in another language*. Cambridge, UK: Cambridge University Press.

Neary-Sundquist, C. (2015). A corpus-based pedagogy for German vocabulary. In A. J. Moeller (Ed.), *Learn languages, explore cultures, transform lives* (pp. 201–215). Report of the Central States Conference on the Teaching of Foreign Languages, University of Nebraska–Lincoln. Retrieved from http://www.csctfl.org/documents/2015Report/CSCTFL%20Report_2015.pdf

Nesselhauf, N. (2003). The use of collocations by advanced learners of English and some implications for teaching. *Applied Linguistics, 24*, 223–242.

Peters, E. (2012). Learning German formulaic sequences: The effect of two attention-drawing techniques. *Language Learning Journal, 40*, 65–79.

Peters, E. (2014). The effects of repetition and time of post-test administration on EFL learners' form recall of single words and collocations. *Language Teaching Research, 18*, 75–94.

Römer, U. (2011). Corpus research applications in second language teaching. *Annual Review of Applied Linguistics, 31*, 205–225.

Rott, S. (2016, March). *Explicit learning of multi-word chunks: Insights into the development of phraseological competence in L2 German*. Paper presented at the Pennsylvania State University, State College, PA.

Schaeffer-Lacroix, E. (2016). Talking about German verb particles identified in concordance lines–from spontaneous to expert-like metatalk. *Language Awareness, 25*(1–2), 127–143.

Schmidt, R. (1990). The role of consciousness in second language learning. *Applied Linguistics, 11*, 129–158.

Schmidt, R. (2001). Attention. In P. Robinson (Ed.), *Cognition and second language instruction* (pp. 3–32). Cambridge, UK: Cambridge University Press.

Schmitt, N. (2010). *Researching vocabulary: A vocabulary research manual*. Basingstoke, UK: *Palgrave* Macmillan.

Sharwood Smith, M. (1993). Input enhancement in instructed SLA. *Studies in Second Language Acquisition, 15*(2), 165–179.

Shaw, E. M. (2011). Teaching vocabulary through data-driven learning. Provo, UT: Brigham Young University. Retrieved from http://corpus.byu.edu/coca/files/Teach- ing_Vocabulary_Through_DDL.pdf

Sinclair, J. M. (1987). The nature of the evidence. In J. M. Sinclair (Ed.), *Looking up: An Account of the COBUILD Project in Lexical Computing* (pp. 150–159). London: Harper Collins.

Sinclair, J. M. (1991). *Corpus, concordance, collocation*. Oxford: Oxford University Press.

Sonbul, S., & Schmitt, N. (2013). Explicit and implicit lexical knowledge: Acquisition of collocations under different input conditions. *Language Learning, 63*(1), 121–159.

Storjohann, P. (2009). Plesionymy: A case of synonymy or contrast? *Journal of Pragmatics, 41*, 2140–2158.

Thurstun, J., & Candlin, C. N. (1997). *Exploring academic English: A workbook for student essay writing*. Sydney, Australia: National Centre for English Language Teaching and Research.

Tyne, H., André, V., Benzitoun, C., Boulton, A., & Greub, Y. (2014). *French through corpora: Ecological and data-driven perspectives in French language studies.* Newcastle Upon Tyne, UK: Cambridge Scholars Press Ltd.
Vyatkina, N. (2013). Discovery learning and teaching with electronic corpora in an advanced German grammar course. *Die Unterrichtspraxis/Teaching German, 46*(1), 44–61.
Vyatkina, N. (2015a). *Corpus-driven instruction.* Center for Applied Second Language Studies (CASLS), University of Oregon. Retrieved May 26, 2018, from http://caslsintercom.uoregon.edu/content/18926
Vyatkina, N. (2015b). *Corpus activity: German verb-preposition collocations.* Center for Applied Second Language Studies (CASLS), University of Oregon. Retrieved May 26, 2018, from http://caslsintercom.uoregon.edu/content/18927
Vyatkina, N. (2016a). Data-driven learning for beginners: The case of German verb-preposition collocations. *ReCALL, 28*(2), 207–226.
Vyatkina, N. (2016b). Data-driven learning of collocations: Learner performance, proficiency, and perceptions. *Language Learning & Technology, 20*(3), 159–179.
Vyatkina, N. (2018, March). *Data-driven learning for instructed second language acquisition: Deepening the L2 vocabulary knowledge.* Paper presented at the American Association of Applied Linguistics conference, Chicago, IL.
Vyatkina, N., & Boulton, A. (Eds.). (2017). Corpora in language learning and teaching [Special issue]. *Language Learning & Technology, 21*(3).
Webb, S., & Kagimoto, E. (2011). Learning collocations: Do the number of collocates, position of the node word, and synonymy affect learning? *Applied Linguistics, 32,* 259–276.
Widdowson, H. G. (2000). On the limitations of linguistics applied. *Applied Linguistics, 21*(1), 3–25.
Yoon, C. (2016). Concordancers and dictionaries as problem-solving tools for ESL academic writing. *Language Learning & Technology, 20*(1), 209–229.

Chapter 8
Setting the Lexical EAP Bar for ESL Students: Lexical Complexity of L2 Academic Presentations

Alla Zareva, Old Dominion University

Introduction

This chapter concerns the lexical complexity of academic presentations of college students (undergraduate and newly admitted graduate students) who are advanced English-as-a-second- or subsequent-language (ESL) users. Of all proficiency levels in the context of English for academic purposes (EAP), the advanced ESL lexicon has received the least attention in the research literature and instructional materials, a situation that is likely based on the assumption that at that level of language proficiency, learners' lexicons are developed well enough to be functional and do not need special attention. Such an assumption, however, is somewhat misleading because it underestimates the lexical problems that higher proficiency second language (L2) learners often have when they must transition rapidly from university-based ESL programs to degree-granting programs. Unfortunately, language instructors and material designers do not seem to approach lexical complexity as a multidimensional phenomenon and neither teaching materials nor instructional practices focus on the multiple aspects of lexical complexity of language learners' production in order to improve it and raise learners' awareness of the importance of lexical complexity in academic contexts.

The discussion of lexical complexity in this chapter will be based on the English language and will offer specific parameters as guidelines that both ESL instructors and students should consider in oral communication courses that include a focus on academic presentations. However, the framework of lexical complexity that will be introduced here is not language specific and can thus be adopted conceptually by other higher education language programs (LPs), insofar as the framework in question offers an opportunity to establish lexical complexity baselines for various proficiency levels in measurable terms. In addition, although most research on lexical complexity (the notion is discussed in greater detail in the following section) is based on comparisons between texts produced by language learners and texts produced by professional writers or speakers (e.g., articles, textbooks, lectures, and conference presentations), this study is based on data from successful student academic presentations (delivered by both English native speaking and ESL presenters), which is a more realistic way of establishing baselines for various linguistic features. Thus, LP directors and other faculty members engaged in curriculum design and program evaluation may find the methodology of this study useful, especially if their programs offer higher division language courses or prepare language majors for graduate-level coursework. At that level of instruction, university-based ESL programs and foreign LPs seem to share a lot of similarities in their student needs and curricular goals.

What places the student presentation among the important academic genres students need to master is primarily its great potential for disciplinary learning and its special place in the network of genres that college students have to participate in during their studies (Zareva, 2009a). From a learning point of view, preparing an academic presentation is a process that requires the mastery of many academic skills that are shared between different academic genres both in speech and in writing, which is probably one of the reasons why the presentation is frequently used as a graded assignment in academic courses. Thus, knowing more about the various aspects of student presentations (lexical, grammatical, rhetorical, compositional, etc.) will give us valuable insights into how these aspects interact with each other and will allow us to more clearly articulate the learning targets needed for advanced proficiency and skill with this genre.

What makes lexical complexity of academic presentations an interesting aspect of investigation is its contribution to the informational packaging of the presentation content, its discipline-specific appropriateness, and its suitability for the mode of delivery. In other words, given that the academic presentation is largely a monologic speech act that is dense in informational content primarily derived from written academic sources, we should expect that, lexically, it will share features that are typical of both written and oral academic discourse. Surprisingly, however, we still know little about the extent to which these two competing driving forces (i.e., informational packaging and oral mode of delivery) impact the lexical complexity of academic presentations. Such knowledge will give us better insights into the lexical choices student presenters make to display their depth of topic-related knowledge in relation to their sense of mode-of-delivery appropriateness and give us evidence-based feedback, recommendations, and advice for improvement when necessary.

In the rest of the chapter, I will first elaborate on the notion of lexical complexity adopted in the study in order to highlight its multifaceted nature from theoretical, observational, and operational points of view. The review of the current literature will focus on what lexical complexity entails, how the notion is similar to and different from the notion of lexical richness, how lexical complexity is manifested in naturally occurring academic oral and written discourse, and what measures can capture its various dimensions most reliably. Next, I will present the comparative results from a study of a number of lexical complexity features in two corpora of presentations from high-quality native speakers of English (first language or L1) and ESL speakers. The discussion will highlight what is lexically "typical" of successful student presentations; the implications for teaching, material, and course design; and how instructors and students can monitor these features in academic communication courses. Knowing what lexical complexity entails and exploring how its dimensions are realized in successful presentations give us a better sense of "where the lexical bar should be set" in order to make better decisions about how to get language learners to that level.

Lexical Complexity: Operationalization and Measurement

Discussions about lexical richness commonly highlight the value of knowing more about how L2 learners use vocabulary beyond the 2,000 (2K) most frequent words in the English language (Laufer & Nation, 1995; Lu, 2012; Morris & Cobb, 2004; Nation, 2001; Read, 2000; Zareva, 2012). Likewise, L2 instructors and researchers unanimously recognize lexical richness as an important construct that is directly linked to students' ability to function effectively in both speech and writing. Sophisticated lexical usage becomes particularly important in academic contexts where demands for precision and disciplinary relevance are greater and more heightened than in general language usage. Undoubtedly, the 2K most frequent English words provide the greatest coverage of vocabulary used in academic and nonacademic speech and writing (e.g., Laufer & Nation, 1995; Morris & Cobb, 2004; Nation, 2001; Zareva, 2012). However, it is the lexical layers beyond the 2K words (e.g., lower frequency, academic, specialized, and technical vocabulary) that allow proficient L2 users to put their academic and disciplinary knowledge on display in a relevant way (Nation, 2001). This is perhaps one of the main reasons why the lexical richness of students' productively used vocabulary has become an area of considerable research interest in recent years yet not without some terminological and conceptual ambiguities.

To avoid the terminological and conceptual ambiguity associated with the term "lexical richness," the notion of lexical complexity as operationalized by Bulté and Housen (2012) will be used in this study, which bears a great deal of similarity to Read's (2000) understanding of lexical richness. Bulté and Housen (2012) viewed lexical complexity on a broader scale within a larger descriptive and analytic framework of language complexity. The authors strongly emphasized that any analysis of L2 complexity should specify how we can distinguish between simple and complex language features, what is meant by the "complexity" of a linguistic feature, and how "complexity" can be reliably operationalized, measured, and evaluated. At the heart of the notion is the idea that there is a wide range of basic and sophisticated words available to L2 learners that contribute differently to the lexical complexity of their performance. In this sense, it is important to know what the contribution of these words is and how we can measure and evaluate it in order to practically determine, at various proficiency levels, the aspects of learners' lexical knowledge that deserve more instruction and other aspects of that knowledge that are already stable and functional relative to students' academic goals and needs.

Bulté and Housen's (2012) framework includes three of the subcomponents of Read's (2000) model: *lexical density, lexical sophistication,* and *lexical diversity*. The fourth subcomponent they proposed is *compositionality of words* (morpheme and syllable structure), which will likely be useful for evaluating texts produced by young L2 learners or lower proficiency learners but not so much for evaluating the performance of higher proficiency learners. Based on a review of the literature, the authors proposed various measures that can reliably capture each of the aforementioned subcomponents of lexical complexity, some of which are more stable for different text samples than others. In the following paragraphs, I will briefly discuss each of the subcomponents in the lexical complexity framework.

In both Bulté and Housen's (2012) and Read's (2000) models, *lexical density* refers to the ratio of content words or lexical words (e.g., nouns, verbs, adjectives, and adverbs) to the total number of words in a text—a notion that was first introduced by Ure (1971). Thus, lexical density is linked to the idea that a message containing more complex information requires the use of more content vocabulary as compared to grammatical or function words (e.g., articles, prepositions, particles, auxiliary verbs, modal verbs, coordinators, subordinators, and pronouns). In general, spoken texts within the conversational register have a lower lexical density (between 24% and 35% of content words) than written texts (36% to 57%) (Ure, 1971). This is perhaps because spontaneous speech can be influenced by factors such as time pressure, online production, planning, and interactivity. The lexical density of written academic texts (both student- and expert-written) has received a great deal of attention in the research literature; however, the lexical density of oral academic texts has been less well examined.

Lexical sophistication (also called *lexical rarity*) refers to the proportion of lower frequency vocabulary to the total number of words. Thus, it would include technical vocabulary, jargon, subject-specific vocabulary, and other uncommon lower frequency words that may be related to a specific genre, discipline, or topic. Typically, the 2K most frequent words in English are considered to be "basic" vocabulary (e.g., Laufer & Nation, 1995; Lu, 2012; Nation, 2001); however, it should be noted here that these words provide the greatest coverage in both spoken and written texts. For instance, Nation (2001) estimated that the 2K words account for about 90% of the vocabulary in conversation, 87% in fiction, 80% in newspapers, and 78% in written academic texts, which shows their fundamental importance across the registers. Nonetheless, research to date has consistently confirmed that the increased use of academic vocabulary and specialized or technical vocabulary is what sets apart the academic register from the less formal ones.

An important layer of L2 students' lexical sophistication in academic contexts is their knowledge of academic vocabulary. To guide L2 instructors and learners in their selection of academic words for academic writing purposes, Coxhead (2000) compiled the Academic Word List (AWL), which consists of 570 academic word families widely used across different disciplines. In other words, the AWL does not include vocabulary that is technical or field specific. Rather, these are words beyond the 2K vocabulary that comprise approximately 10% of any academic text (written by experts), although they occur less frequently in newspaper articles (about 4.5%) and fiction texts (approximately 1.4%) (Coxhead, 2011). In this regard, Coxhead (2011) has rightly pointed out that the AWL should require special instruction because the reading and analysis of fiction, for example, will not provide sufficient access to this vocabulary for students who need to become effective academic writers.

Although the study of students' use of academic vocabulary in writing has received a good amount of attention in the research literature, the study of students' use of these words in the oral academic genres, including student presentations, is seriously lagging behind. The few of such studies that exist suggest that L2 learners employ much less academic vocabulary in their presentations (2.53% in tokens—i.e., the percentage includes repetitively used vocabulary) compared to L2 expert conference presenters (between 7.25% and 7.87%) (Kao & Wang, 2014) or L1 and L2 advanced degree students' research presentations (approximately 5.7%) (Zareva, 2012). The lack of such research in general, and especially the lack of such research across the various proficiency levels, prevents us from establishing and setting reasonable academic vocabulary use baselines in a way that would serve to align the goals of language teaching with students' needs and outcomes.

Lexical diversity (also called *lexical variation*) is another subcomponent of lexical complexity that is associated with the use of different words in a text versus a limited number of words used repetitively. In other words, it refers to the range and variability of expression as displayed in language performance and, in that sense, lexical diversity reflects the variety of active vocabulary that speakers or writers choose to use as opposed to the vocabulary they have available but do not use (Malvern, Richards, Chipere, & Durán, 2004; McCarthy & Jarvis, 2007). As an aspect of lexical complexity, this dimension has been found to be associated with writing quality, lexical proficiency, general characteristics of speakers' or writers' language competence, and accommodation adjustments that show audience awareness.

Although the importance of lexical diversity as part of L1 and L2 lexical knowledge has been unanimously recognized by both teachers and researchers, there have been many concerns about how to measure it. The type-token ratio (TTR)—that is, the ratio of the number of different words (word types) to the total number of words (tokens) in a text—is a simple measure that has been widely used in both L1 and L2 lexical studies for a long time. However, the measure (and its various transformations) has been rightly criticized in recent years for its sensitivity to text length: The ratio tends to substantially decrease as the size of the text increases, because the longer the text, the less varied vocabulary speakers use (e.g., Lu, 2012; Malvern et al., 2004; McCarthy & Jarvis, 2007; Read, 2000; Treffers-Daller, Parslow, & Williams, 2016). For the purposes of this study, two measures will be used to evaluate the lexical diversity of students' presentations: the number of different words used and the measure of textual lexical diversity (MTLD) (for a detailed review, see McCarthy & Jarvis, 2010). In brief, MTLD is a lexical diversity index of a text, which is evaluated sequentially. The index is calculated as the mean length of sequential strings of words in a text that maintain a 0.720 TTR value—that is, each word of the text is evaluated sequentially for its TTR. This value was selected based on evidence from the testing of various narratives and expository texts, which revealed that their TTR trajectories tended to stabilize at around 0.720 (+/− 0.03) (McCarthy & Jarvis, 2010). One of the greatest advantages of the MTLD compared to other indexes of lexical diversity is that it makes use of the notion of thematic saturation— that is, it evaluates how many words it takes for a text to reach the point of stabilization after which no new vocabulary is used. Thus, the fewer words it takes to get to the point of saturation, the less diverse the text is. In sum, the selection of these two lexical diversity measures was made based on empirical evidence that they are stable with regard to longer texts (of 1,000–2,000 words), and they allow the integrity of naturally occurring texts to be preserved (i.e., no text should be discarded), since instances of natural discourse are rarely of equal length (McCarthy & Jarvis, 2010; Treffers-Daller, et al., 2016).

This study was conducted with three primary goals in mind: first, to determine whether successful L1 and L2 users' presentations (thus qualified based on the grade they received) differ in their lexical complexity; second, to establish guiding baselines of several measures associated with the three-dimensional framework of lexical complexity; and last, to ascertain the relationship between the subcomponents of lexical complexity, which will have implications for the way it is operationalized, studied, and taught. The study therefore aimed to address the following research questions:

1. How do L1 and L2 users compare on the lexical complexity of their academic presentations?
2. What is lexically "typical" of L2 users' successful presentations in terms of lexical density, lexical sophistication, and lexical diversity?
3. What is the relationship between the three subcomponents of lexical complexity (lexical density, lexical sophistication, and lexical diversity) for the L2 group of presenters?

Method

Participants

The study was based on two corpora of individually given L1 and L2 academic presentations ($n = 70$). The data were collected at several U.S. universities during regular classes in which the presentations were scheduled. The participants also completed a questionnaire with some demographic items. The L1 group ($n = 35$) consisted of senior undergraduate and newly admitted graduate students (females = 25; males = 10; $M_{age} = 25$ years old) enrolled in various programs in education, applied linguistics, international studies, and the humanities. The participants were all taking introductory-level courses in language-related areas that were relatively new to them and reported that they had to give approximately four academic presentations per term. They rated their presentation skills at 4.1 on a 6-point Likert scale and reported that they considered it very important to be able to give effective presentations both academically and professionally (5.6 on a 6-point Likert scale).

The L2 presenters ($n = 35$) were of similar composition (females = 27; males = 8; $M_{age} = 28$ years old) from the same disciplinary areas. They were speakers of 15 different languages: Arabic, Chinese, French, Goun, German, Indonesian, Japanese, Korean, Portuguese, Slovenian, Subia, Spanish, Taiwanese, Vietnamese, and Ukrainian. They had all studied English through formal instruction ($M = 9.1$ years) in their native countries before coming to the United States. In order to be admitted to degree-granting programs, the L2 students were required to satisfy the language proficiency requirement of their respective programs by having taken an English proficiency test (e.g., TOEFL) or in some other acceptable ways. The L2 students' paper-based TOEFL scores were in the range of 550 to 647 ($M = 585$) and their Internet-based TOEFL ranged from 83 to 107 ($M = 96$), corresponding to a 557–610 score on a paper-based TOEFL format. Altogether, the proficiency test scores showed that the L2 participants can be considered proficient users of English. They also reported that they had been required to give on average four presentations per term, but they rated their presentation skills lower than the L1 students, at 3.8 on a 6-point Likert scale. Like the L1 participants, they also considered it important to have good presentation skills (4.9 on a 6-point Likert scale).

Data

All presentations were given to satisfy a final project course requirement, so they were delivered toward the end of the semester to showcase students' individual research projects. The presentations were graded as successful and high quality by the respective instructors. To keep the L1 and L2 corpus comparable, several features of the presentations were kept similar to minimize their potential influence on the lexical complexity of the data. For instance, all presentations were based on library research that the students had carried out on topics of interest to them; the topics were related to coursework typically associated with language, education, applied linguistics, and teaching; the presentations included in the analysis were limited to 15–20 minutes of presentation time ($M_{presentation\ time}$ = 15.6 minutes); all presentations were given extemporaneously and the presenters used various visuals and support materials (e.g., PowerPoints, handouts, and flashcards). All in all, these are features that are typical of student presentations in most disciplinary areas where language is used not so much for the sake of language learning but rather for subject-area learning purposes. The presentations were audio-recorded and transcribed orthographically.

Data analysis criteria.

Naturally occurring oral data are not as "clean" and "tidy" as academic writing data. However, the integrity of the presentations was completely preserved so that the analysis could capture features that may be typical of oral academic speech but unlikely to occur in written academic prose (e.g., fillers, hesitations, inserts, and lexicalized expressions). Only the truncated (partially pronounced) words were removed from the data, either because they were part of false starts that were repaired or because the corrected and intended word was provided immediately afterward.

Each of the subcomponents of lexical complexity was captured by various measures typically associated with it:

I. Lexical density was evaluated by
   1. the ratio of lexical/content words to the total number of words in a presentation.

II. Lexical sophistication was evaluated by
   1. the percentage of different words (types) from the AWL (e.g., *agenda, basics, generalize, hostility,* and *standardized*);
   2. the percentage of lower frequency, technical, and specialized vocabulary (in word types) beyond the 2K and AWL, which included discipline-specific vocabulary (e.g., *acculturate, adverb, calligraphy, colloquial, dyslexia, lexicon,* and *syntactically*); names of countries, institutions, languages, scholars (e.g., *Ukraine, NAU, Hindi,* and *Goffman*); acronyms (e.g., *L2, NNS, TOEFL,* and *EFL*); foreign or other words used in examples (e.g., *hablar, velik,* and *ich*).

III. Lexical diversity was evaluated by
   1. the number of different words (types) used by the presenters;
   2. MTLD score (i.e., the range and diversity of vocabulary in a text).

To determine the lexical complexity of the presentations, the data were analyzed in several ways. First, the presentations were run through Cobb's (2002) *VocabProfile* (classic version). The classic version determines the 1K and 2K words in relation to West's (1953) General Service List (GSL) and the AWL based on Coxhead (2000), which contains vocabulary beyond the GSL. Words beyond these three categories are placed into the off-list category, which may contain proper nouns, rare words, specialized or technical words, acronyms, abbreviations, inserts, and so on.

Based on the way different lexical categories were defined for the purposes of this study, some of the measurements were taken as calculated by the *Vocabprofiler* (e.g., total number of words, number of different words, and percentage of word types from the AWL). Others, such as lexical density and percentage of different lower frequency, technical, and specialized vocabulary, had to be recalculated in order to account for the effect of the disfluencies on the measurements—for example, mispronunciations (e.g., *Alabic* [for *Arabic*]); hesitations, fillers, and inserts (e.g., *um, like ah, ts, okay, yeah,* and *wow*); and lexicalized phonological reductions (e.g., *cuz, wanna,* and *kinda*). Details about obtaining the MTLD values can be found in McCarthy and Jarvis (2010). The presentation data for the MTLD analysis was kept fully intact and included the truncated word segments so that the obtained values were representative of the presentations as a whole language event.

Results

To address the first two research questions related to the comparison between the lexical complexity of the L1 and L2 users' academic presentations and the typical complexity characteristics that these presentations revealed, a series of analyses of variance were conducted using the group as an independent variable and the lexical complexity measures as dependent variables. Also, since most of the lexical complexity measures are influenced by text length, it was important to determine whether the L1 and L2 presentations were of similar length by comparing them on the total number of words (tokens). Means and standard deviations are presented in Table 8.1.

There were no significant differences ($p > .05$) between the two groups in the word count of their presentations, which showed that, on average, the presenters attempted to discuss the complex content of their researched topics within a similar word count. Since the presentation narratives were of similar time length (M_{L1} = 15 minutes and M_{L2} = 16 minutes), this means, by extension, that the L1 and L2 presenters maintained a similar rate of speaking—an aspect of prepared oral discourse that is important in academic settings, where many oral assignments have a time limit due to the fast-paced nature of advanced studies.

The comparison between the L1 and L2 presenters along the three lexical complexity subcomponents also showed similarities between the two groups—that is, there were no significant differences ($p > .05$) between them on any of the lexical complexity measures. Thus, the overall results revealed that high-quality

Setting the Lexical EAP Bar for ESL Students 155

Table 8.1. Means and Standard Deviations of the Lexical Complexity Measures Used in the Study across the L1 and L2 Presentations

Subcomponents of lexical complexity	Lexical complexity measures	L1 presentations ($n = 35$) Mean	SD	L2 presentations ($n = 35$) Mean	SD
	Number of words (tokens)	1,959	508	1,994	353
Lexical density	Content/function words (in tokens)	.43	.02	.44	.04
Lexical sophistication	Percentage of AWL word types	12.06	2.89	11.26	3.10
	Percentage of lower frequency, technical, and specialized word types	13.12	2.94	14.98	6.25
Lexical	Number of different words	496	97	484	89
diversity	MTLD	36.87	3.86	36.91	9.96

L1 and L2 presentations shared very similar profiles across all three subcomponents of lexical complexity. The analyses also revealed that the pattern of what can be considered lexically "typical" of successful L2 presentations in terms of lexical density, lexical sophistication, and lexical diversity was similar to that of the presentations of the L1 group (see Table 8.1).

To address the third research question and find out what the relationship was between the three subcomponents of lexical complexity (i.e., lexical density, lexical sophistication, and lexical diversity) and the measures associated with each subcomponent for the L2 presenters, bivariate Pearson correlations were computed for this group. On the one hand, the absence of significant correlations between the measures would show that each of them captures a unique aspect of the presentation. Such a result would also reveal that the three subcomponents of lexical complexity are independent dimensions and will require that special attention, focus, and effort be devoted to each of them individually. On the other hand, the presence of significant correlations between the measures would show that some aspects are related in some ways and, perhaps, gains in one of them will result in gains in the other(s).

Using the Bonferroni approach to control for Type I error across the five variables, a p-value of less than .01 (.05/5 = .01) was required for significance. The results revealed only one weak, significant correlation between the number of different words and the percentage of low frequency, technical, and specialized vocabulary ($r = .440, p < .01$). This correlation suggested that the presenters' use of different vocabulary could explain about 19% (r^2) of the variance in the proportion of their use of lower frequency and specialized vocabulary. Overall, the results implied that the three-dimensional framework of lexical complexity does indeed capture unique aspects of complexity. The implications of the findings will be discussed in the following section.

Discussion

The value of effective and successful presentations in higher education has been fully recognized by instructors and students alike in recent years, because this genre quite often bridges students' academic life with the professional experience they prepare for. At the same time, giving an academic presentation is a linguistically, academically, and intellectually demanding task for students, especially if they have not had previous training and experience with this genre. Thus, some LPs have started to include in their curricula and assessments the development of presentational competence in a foreign language in an attempt to align the intellectual content of general education and foreign language study (see Klee, Melin, & Soneson, 2016). Similarly, ESL programs preparing L2 learners to transition smoothly to degree-granting tertiary education programs have a unique opportunity to provide presentation-giving experience and training to these students, who will be expected to show a reasonable degree of familiarity with this genre once they begin their studies.

One of the most interesting findings from the comparison between the L1 and L2 participants was that they shared overwhelming similarities along the lexical complexity framework used in the study. The similarities suggested that successful presentations do not differ in any notable ways with regard to the choices regarding lexical density, sophistication, and diversity that presenters make regardless of their native language and the context of their previous educational experience. In this sense, the analysis allows us to establish not only the common lexical complexity ground shared by the L1 and L2 presentations but also some lexical baselines that both L2 learners and instructors can monitor in academic communication courses. However, it should be noted here that it took the L2 students an average of about nine years of language study to reach that point of shared lexical complexity of their presentations, which suggests that a solid language background is perhaps a prerequisite for developing successful presentation skills. In the rest of the sections, I will discuss each of the lexical complexity subcomponents separately with regard to the L2 presentations.

Lexical Density of Proficient L2 Academic Presentations

Lexical density is a dimension of lexical complexity that shows the proportion of content vocabulary that speakers or writers use in texts. On average, the proportion of content words in the L2 presentations was 44%, which was close to the proportion of content words found in other studies involving the oral discourse of proficient EAP users (e.g., Kao & Wang, 2014; Lu, 2012; Ure, 1971; Zareva, 2012).

It was also interesting to see that the lexical density of the presentations put this genre closer to the lexical density found in written texts—especially in narrative and expository writing—than to that of spoken texts (e.g., Morris & Cobb, 2004; Ure, 1971). In this regard, Ure (1971) has rightly pointed out that the distinction between oral and written texts can largely be attributed to "the physical conditions of the delivery of the text, in sound, in space and in time" as well as to the time available for preparing a text (p. 447). Thus, the similarity in lexical density of the presentations with written texts can be attributed to several factors. For instance, unlike spontaneous speech, which shows much lower usage of content words (lower than 36% [Ure, 1971]) than writing does, the academic presentation (a) is a prepared discourse; (b) has a content largely based on written academic texts that have been read, analyzed, and summarized in the target language; (c) is revised multiple times during the preparation stage; (d) is usually rehearsed beforehand; and (e) is a monologic speech act—that is, there is no verbal response to other speakers, which seems to be an even more powerful factor than the spoken/written distinction in determining lexical density (Ure, 1971). Overall, the lexical density of the presentations in this study revealed that proficient language users are aware that academic presentations in specialized areas should be as dense in content vocabulary as academic writing in order to convey complex discipline-specific content. However, this awareness should be explicitly developed in language courses because research on the lexical density of lower proficiency learners' oral academic production has shown the density to be lower than the values reported here (e.g., Lu, 2012).

Lexical Sophistication of Proficient L2 Academic Presentations

Lexical sophistication of the presentations was captured by the percentage of different AWL words as well as the percentage of higher frequency, technical, and specialized content vocabulary employed by the presenters. On average, the L2 presenters' use of different AWL vocabulary (types) constituted 11.26% of all different words in their presentations in addition to another 14.98% of lower frequency, technical, and specialized vocabulary. These percentages do not include repetitions and show that, altogether, the sophisticated vocabulary in the presentations accounted for about 26% of different words, which is a substantial vocabulary chunk that presenters need to master and use appropriately to display their subject-area knowledge and convey the complexities of their topic content. In analyzing written academic texts, Nation (2001) reported 8.5% of AWL vocabulary—a percentage that was much higher compared to speaking (1.9%), fiction (1.7%), and newspaper language (3.9%). In addition, he found that the percentage of other vocabulary (including lower frequency, technical, and discipline-specific vocabulary) also increased from 7.8% in speaking to 13.3% in academic writing, so the sum total of sophisticated vocabulary that Nation (2001) reported would be close to the percentage reported here for academic L2 presentations.

It is difficult to fully interpret the lexical sophistication results from this study in comparison to other studies because most of the lexical profiling has been done on written texts and only a few studies have focused on oral academic discourse. To my knowledge, there are only two other studies on academic presentations (Kao & Wang, 2014 and Zareva, 2012) that reported the percentages of AWL vocabulary for expert presenters in tokens (i.e., including the repetitions). Those percentages ranged between 5.6% (Zareva, 2012) and 7.25% (Kao & Wang, 2014). The important point to be made here, though, is that the heightened percentage of sophisticated vocabulary use in academic discourse (both spoken and written) sets it apart from the other registers. Further, mode of delivery (speaking vs. writing), which is generally a very strong influence on many linguistic features of texts (Biber, 2006; Swales, 2004), did not seem to impact the choice of sophisticated vocabulary in the academic register as much as it influenced the choice of other linguistic and rhetorical features.

Since the presentations were within the same disciplinary areas, it was of interest to find out more about the spread of the sophisticated vocabulary across the higher frequency bands. A further analysis revealed that the majority of the lower frequency content words—that is, words beyond the 2K vocabulary and the AWL words—came from the 3K word families (e.g., *agenda, architecture, concrete, disability, exceptionally, household, imported, novels, province, resemble, romantic,* and *urban*), followed by the 4K word families (e.g., *anonymous, consolidated, flaw, senator,* and *spouse*). The discipline- and topic-specific vocabulary was associated primarily with word families below the 3K and 4K frequency bands (e.g., *assimilation, elicitation, imperatives, intelligibility, pedagogical, phonetic, morphology, nasal, socioeconomic, slang,* and *vernacular*) and its repetitive use increased because there are few synonymous substitutes for this kind of vocabulary. This information suggests that for academic presentation purposes, higher proficiency L2 learners should be prompted to master vocabulary layers in the 3K and 4K frequency bands in addition to the specialized lexicon that is part of their disciplinary knowledge to be able to convey their arguments in a discipline-specific and appropriate way. Perhaps the first step in this direction would be to make students explicitly aware of the notion of word frequency and of what vocabulary falls under different frequency bands. One possible way to do so is to introduce them to software that demonstrates word frequency categories in texts (e.g., *VocabProfile* free software) or recommend dictionaries that mark the word frequency of their entries. Either approach will allow L2 learners to independently monitor their lexical choices relative to reliably predetermined frequency baselines.

Lexical Diversity of Proficient L2 Academic Presentations

The lexical diversity of the presentations was captured by two measures: number of different words and MTLD. In presentations that were, on average, about 15 minutes long (which is typically the time limit for presentation assignments in higher proficiency classes), the L2 presenters used on average approximately 2K words, which included repetitions, hesitations, fillers, and so on. When the repetitions were removed, the number of different words was much lower, 484, of which 72.57% were high-frequency content and function words from the 1K and 2K vocabulary bands, 26.24% were sophisticated vocabulary, and 1.19% were lexical disfluencies (e.g., hesitations, mispronunciations, and inserts). The high percentage of vocabulary from the 1K and 2K frequency bands confirms what other lexical studies have previously established: that the first 2K most frequent words (or the "basic words") in the English language provide the greatest word coverage in texts (Laufer & Nation, 1995; Morris & Cobb, 2004; Nation, 2001; Treffers-Daller et al., 2016; Zareva, 2012). Thus, mastering the 1K and 2K lexical bands will have the greatest payoff for L2 learners across the registers. However, these learners will also need to master the academic, specialized, and technical vocabulary layers to be able to put their academic knowledge on display (Morris & Cobb, 2004; Nation, 2001) in contexts where demands for precision and disciplinary relevance are heightened (Zareva, 2012).

The second measure of diversity used in the study—MTLD—determines the lexical diversity value of texts in terms of the average number of words needed for a text to reach a point of saturation where additional repeated words or the introduction of new word types would not significantly influence the TTR (McCarthy & Jarvis, 2010). In other words, this measure accounts for the fact that a text reaches a point of saturation where no additional new vocabulary may be needed or where the rate of adding new words significantly decreases. In general, the fewer words it takes to reach the point of text stabilization, the less lexically diverse a text is in terms of sequential use of lexis. The results from this study revealed that it took L2 presenters, on average, 37 words to reach the point of text stabilization, which is in agreement with Zareva's (2012) findings (range 33–37) for her L1 and L2 participants. This MTLD score, however, was much lower than the MTLD score found in proficient L2 writing where, for instance, Treffers-Daller et al. (2016) found an MTLD score of 88.47 for C1 and an MTLD score of 93.84 for C2-level ESL writers. The notable difference between the MTLD scores in proficient L2 users' speech and writing suggests that the presenters were most likely not striving for lexical diversity in their delivery. Rather, under the cognitive pressures of their online production, their frequent recycling of the same vocabulary seemed to sufficiently serve the purpose of getting their content point across.

Relationship between the Subcomponents of Lexical Complexity

The last research question addressed in the study was whether or not each subcomponent of lexical complexity accounted for an independent aspect of students' presentations. Generally, the answer to this question has implications for at least three interrelated perspectives associated with lexical complexity: theoretical, pedagogical, and research. In other words, if, on the one hand, some of the subcomponents showed strong significant correlation(s), that result would have theoretical implications regarding how lexical complexity is operationalized in terms of number of dimensions. Pedagogically, any interrelated dimensions would suggest that improving one subcomponent will contribute to the improvement of the other(s). From a research point of view, a strong, significant correlation between two variables would imply that measuring only one of them would give us indication about the other; hence, excluding one of the correlated variables from the set of measures would be justified. On the other hand, if the subcomponents of lexical complexity were not significantly correlated or only weakly correlated, this would suggest that theoretically, pedagogically, and research wise each dimension should be approached individually because only in their totality can we have a holistic picture of lexical complexity in a given oral or written text.

Interestingly, there was only one weak correlation for the L2 group between the percentage of their lower frequency, technical, and specialized vocabulary (one of the measures of lexical sophistication) and the number of different words they used in their presentations (one of the measures of lexical diversity). This suggested that the presenters' use of different vocabulary could explain about 19% (r^2) of the variance in the proportion of their use of lower frequency and specialized vocabulary. The weak correlation between the two variables, however, would not warrant excluding any one of the measures from the set of lexical complexity measures. In addition, the fact that no relationship between the second measure of sophistication (percentage of AWL vocabulary) and diversity (MTLD) was found implies that the three-dimensional framework of lexical complexity does indeed capture unique aspects of complexity in student presentations. Overall, the result confirmed findings from other studies (Lu, 2012; Zareva, 2012) and suggested that L2 students should be prompted to consciously work on and develop each dimension of lexical complexity separately (i.e., lexical density, lexical sophistication, and lexical diversity) because improving only one of them, for instance, will not contribute to the improvement of the others. However, if each of the dimensions is well developed, in their totality they create a powerful effect of discipline-specific lexical sophistication in any oral or written text.

Concluding Remarks and Implications

The study presented in this chapter was based on a three-dimensional framework of lexical complexity that can be applied to different languages, genres, and types of texts (oral or written) that L2 learners are expected to be able to produce at different levels of proficiency. The framework also offers an opportunity for LP directors and instructors to establish specific baselines associated with lexical complexity in relation to the specificities of their curricula, the language competencies they aim at developing, their students' proficiency levels and needs, and expected outcomes. One possible way to approach this task is by conducting a critical review of the published literature for a specific target language on the issue and then using the findings to inform instructional and pedagogical decisions. Another possibility would be to collect samples of what counts as "successful" presentations in a given language, proficiency level, or area of specialization and determine the lexical features that are typical of the samples. In this regard, LP directors and faculty engaged in curricular changes and program evaluation may find the methodology used in this study useful because it offers a framework for lexical complexity analysis and a set of specific measures that can be flexibly applied to a variety of languages.

We also strongly encourage the inclusion of presentational competence as one of the main competencies in foreign language studies, insofar as the skills involved in preparing a presentation not only promote depth of learning but are also easily transferable to other areas of study. For instance, some of the skills involved in the process of presentation design include research topic selection, which usually requires some disciplinary knowledge, focused reading, and analysis of complex literature in the target language (e.g., articles, books, chapters, and monographs), as well as identification of main arguments, synthesis of research related to different arguments, establishing a logical connection between the main points, taking a stance, designing visuals, and so on. All these skills are at the core of other language competencies (e.g., interpretive competence and interpersonal competence), and they also "travel" easily across different subject areas.

By and large, the results from the current study suggested that each of the subcomponents of lexical complexity adds unique information to the overall lexical complexity profiles of student presentations. Theoretically, the finding confirmed that lexical complexity is a multidimensional notion and that the dimensions are relatively independent of each other— that is, each aspect of lexical density, sophistication, and diversity should be addressed in language instruction individually. From a research point of view, if the goal is to obtain an optimal set of variables that uniquely describe the different dimensions of lexical complexity, the results from the current study suggest that the set of five lexical measures used in the analysis will sufficiently capture various aspects of the phenomenon.

From a pedagogical point of view, one of the primary goals of the study was to determine the lexical complexity profile of successful ESL users' academic presentations in an attempt to provide guiding baselines for this genre for advanced EAP coursework. In sum, in order to convey the complex content of their topics in a discipline-appropriate manner, the L2 presenters employed a relatively high density of content vocabulary (.44) as well as about 11% of academic vocabulary and another 15% of lower frequency, technical, and specialized vocabulary. They used 484 different words that they recycled frequently and their MTLD score was relatively low (approximately 37). Overall, the effects of the oral mode of delivery were the strongest on the lexical diversity of the presentations, while the other two aspects of lexical complexity— that is, lexical density and sophistication— were closer to values obtained for written academic prose than for speech.

Finally, we would recommend the use of Cobb's (2002) *VocabProfile* free software or other similar software in language classes, not only to raise L2 students' awareness of lexical complexity in academic speech and writing but also to engage them in monitoring different aspects of their lexical uses in texts across a variety of academic genres. *VocabProfile*, which also works with texts in French, is a user-friendly program that instructors can use to demonstrate and discuss with students desirable lexical features of a variety of texts. Students can also use it independently to analyze their own texts and monitor the lexical composition of their own language production. Such an approach can further help instructors and material designers to target specific lexical complexity aspects in content building across the genres and to set realistic vocabulary learning goals that reflect real-life language usage—after all, the way we "set the lexical bar" will strongly impact the process and the outcomes of "getting there."

References

Biber, D. (2006). *University language: A corpus-based study of spoken and written registers*. Amsterdam, Netherlands: John Benjamins.

Bulté, B., & Housen, A. (2012). Defining and operationalising L2 complexity. In A. Housen, F. Kuiken, & I. Vedder (Eds.), *Dimensions of L2 performance and proficiency: Complexity, accuracy and fluency in SLA* (pp. 21–46). Amsterdam, Netherlands: John Benjamins.

Cobb, T. (2002). Web VocabProfile (v. 4 Classic). Retrieved from http://www.lextutor.ca/vp/eng/

Coxhead, A. (2000). A new academic word list. *TESOL Quarterly, 34*, 213–238.

Coxhead, A. (2011). The Academic Word List 10 years on: Research and teaching implications. *TESOL Quarterly, 45*, 355–362.

Kao, S., & Wang, W. (2014). Lexical and organizational features in novice and experienced ELF presentations. *Journal of English as a Lingua Franca, 3*, 49–79.

Klee, C., Melin, C., & Soneson, D. (2016). From frameworks to oversight: Components to improving foreign language efficacy. In J. Norris & N. Mills (Eds.), *Innovation and accountability in language program evaluation* (pp. 131–153). Boston, MA: Cengage Learning.

Laufer, B., & Nation, P. (1995). Vocabulary size and use: Lexical richness in L2 written production. *Applied Linguistics, 16*, 307–322.

Lu, X. (2012). The relationship of lexical richness to the quality of ESL learners' oral narratives. *The Modern Language Journal, 96*, 190–208.

Malvern, D., Richards, B., Chipere, N., & Durán, P. (2004). *Lexical diversity and language development: Quantification and assessment*. Basingstoke, UK: Palgrave Macmillan.

McCarthy, P. M., & Jarvis, S. (2007). *vocd*: A theoretical and empirical evaluation. *Language Testing, 24*, 459–488.

McCarthy, P. M., & Jarvis, S. (2010). MTLD, vocd-D, and HD-D: A validation study of sophisticated approaches to lexical diversity assessment. *Behavior Research Methods, 42*, 381–392.

Morris, L., & Cobb, T. (2004). Vocabulary profiles as predictors of the academic performance of teaching English as a second language trainees. *System, 32*, 75–87.

Nation, P. (2001). *Learning vocabulary in another language.* Cambridge, UK: Cambridge University Press.
Read, J. (2000). *Assessing vocabulary.* Cambridge, UK: Cambridge University Press.
Swales, J. M. (2004). *Research genres: Explorations and applications.* Cambridge, UK: Cambridge University Press.
Treffers-Daller, J., Parslow, P., & Williams, S. (2016). Back to basics: How measures of lexical diversity can help discriminate between CEFR levels. *Applied Linguistics, 39,* 302–327.
Ure, J. (1971). Lexical density and register variation. In G. E. Perren & J. I. M. Trim (Eds.), *Application of linguistics: Selected papers of the second International Congress of Applied Linguistics, Cambridge, 1969* (pp. 443–452). Cambridge, UK: Cambridge University Press.
West, M. (1953). *A general service list of English words.* London, UK: Longman, Green.
Zareva, A. (2009a). Informational packaging, level of formality, and the use of circumstance adverbials in NES and L2 student academic presentations. *Journal of English for Academic Purposes, 8,* 55–68.
Zareva, A. (2012). Lexical composition of effective L1 and L2 student academic presentations. *Journal of Applied Linguistics, 6,* 91–110.

Chapter 9
The Input-Based Incremental Approach to Vocabulary in Meaning-Oriented Instruction for Language Program Directors and Teachers

Joe Barcroft, Washington University in St. Louis

Introduction

New research findings and theoretical advances provide us with opportunities to change the way we view different phenomena in the world and alter different types of practice, such as instructional practices, in order to make them more effective. Whereas changes in practice sometimes involve near or complete replacement of previous ones, other times they only call for modifications in order to integrate the practical implications of the new research findings and theoretical developments in question. With this larger picture in mind, this chapter explains how different types of meaning-oriented language instruction can be improved when they are modified to incorporate input-based incremental (IBI) vocabulary instruction (Barcroft, 2012), an evidence-based approach to vocabulary instruction based on research findings and theoretical advances from the past three decades. The chapter is also aimed specifically toward language program directors and teachers with the goal of breaking down how the IBI approach can be assimilated in courses at different levels across an entire language program, including courses focused on specific areas of content such as linguistics or literary and cultural studies.

The chapter is divided into seven main sections. The first section focuses on how meaning-oriented language instruction, including communicative language teaching (CLT) and task-based instruction (TBI), is by nature equipped to provide learners with what they need for successful second language (L2) acquisition (SLA). The second section highlights issues related to what is needed to learn target words and lexical phrases fully, noting how the IBI approach is poised to help each target word satisfy its lexical *wish list* (as explained in this section) on this front. The third section presents the IBI approach itself, including its 10 principles of effective vocabulary instruction and a seven-item checklist for creating IBI lessons. The fourth section reviews examples of some of the key research findings that provide support for the IBI approach, such as the negative effects of different types of semantic elaboration and forced output without access to meaning during the early stages of word learning and the positive effects of employing increasing acoustic variability in the presentation of target words. The fifth section underscores how the IBI approach is consistent with different varieties of meaning-oriented instruction (MOI), such as TBI, and how it can be seamlessly integrated within them, even when an IBI lesson may involve some explicit discrete-item learning of target vocabulary. The sixth section provides two examples of IBI lessons, illustrating how IBI is consistent with MOI and how it can be incorporated at different proficiency levels. Finally, the seventh section offers a series of recommendations for language program directors and teachers as they work to incorporate the IBI approach.

Why Meaning-Oriented Instruction?

Because language acquisition is the product of the development of form–meaning connections over time, without the presence of meaning, linguistic forms have nothing to which they can attach themselves. Imagine, for example, that in a first-semester L2 Basque class an instructor presents the novel Basque word *zuhaitz* by pronouncing or writing it on a chalkboard without providing sufficient context (visuals, verbal cues, etc.) to infer its meaning or exemplify its usage. What are the students to do if the meaning of a word is not only underspecified but also highly ambiguous? If the word's form is not similar to a corresponding first language (L1) word form, the students have little to no chance of inferring its meaning and making an appropriate form–meaning connection, which in this case should be between the word form *zuhaitz* and the word meaning expressed by the English word *tree*. Therefore, meaning needs to be present in the *input*—that is, in samples of the target language to which language learners are exposed—so that form–meaning connections can begin and continue to develop over time.

In addition, the meaning-oriented input provided to learners needs to be sufficiently comprehensible because otherwise the linguistic forms in question still have little or no meaning to which to attach themselves. For this reason, the provision of input that is meaning-bearing and sufficiently comprehensible is critical for language development. In the above example, if the instructor were to define the word by saying (in Basque) "A *zuhaitz* is . . . ," the definition itself would also need to be sufficiently comprehensible for the students to understand the meaning of the word. As Krashen (1985) asserted, what drives language acquisition is comprehensible input and, most desirably, input at the level of $i + 1$, or input at a level that is slightly above a learner's current level, because input at such a level provides language learners with something new, a potentially new linguistic element—a word, a new syntactic structure, and so on—that can be acquired. Because meaning-oriented language instruction provides learners with input that is meaning-bearing and (hopefully) sufficiently comprehensible, instruction of this nature is well suited to provide learners with what they need to advance, however gradually, in their acquisition of a target language.

In addition to the need for meaning orientation and sufficiently comprehensible input, learners also need sufficient context for inferring word meaning. Imagine that the instructor in our example were to say (in Basque) "I saw a really pretty *zuhaitz* this morning." Assuming that the learners knew all of the other word families in the sentence (including the verb *see* in Basque), what is the chance that they will correctly infer the meaning of *zuhaitz*? Although not as low as with the no-input case above (around 0%), the chance of inferring word meaning correctly from this sentence may still be very low. Notably, research indicates that in the absence of sufficient context needed to infer novel word meaning, learners still attempt to assign meaning to words. They often do so based on the similarity of the novel word form to other words in the learner's L1 or L2 in the case of (a) cognates (words similar in both form and meaning across different languages, such as *historia, storia,* and *histoire* in Spanish, Italian, and French for the English word *history*; see Hall, Newbrand, Ecke, Sperr, & Marchand, 2009, for research in this area) and (b) false cognates (words that may appear to be cognates but are not, such as *carpeta* in Spanish, which means *folder* and not *carpet* in English; see Hall, 2002, for research in this area). When the form of a word bears no similarity to an L1 word form, learners employ other types of "parasitic" processes (in this case non-form-oriented strategies) to infer word meaning (see Hall & Ecke, 2003; Jiang, 2000; and Ecke, 2015, for a review of research on these techniques, which involve searches for translation equivalence), but when meaning is not conveyed, when input is not sufficiently comprehensible, and when context is deficient, these attempts to infer word meaning will always be met with a lack of success or only partial success (e.g., disparities of meaning or syntactic roles between L1 and L2 counterparts). As should become clear in this chapter, the IBI approach helps learners overcome the potentially incorrect assumptions they may make due to lack of meaning orientation, lack of sufficient comprehensibility, lack of sufficient context, or any combination of these.

What are some of the major types of MOI utilized today? As language program directors and teachers will recognize, they include (a) CLT, (b) TBI, and (c) content-based instruction (CBI). In what follows, we consider basic tenets of each of these three varieties of MOI in turn.

Communicative Language Teaching

CLT is characterized by the following tenets (as summarized by the author):

1. Emphasis on developing communicative competence (see Hymes, 1966, regarding the origin of the term) or multiple types of competence, such as linguistic (phonetic/phonological, lexical, morphological, syntactic, pragmatic), sociolinguistic, discourse, and strategic competence (Savignon, 1972, defined communicative competence as "the ability to function in a truly communicative setting—that is, in a dynamic exchange in which linguistic competence [the ability to use grammar,

vocabulary, etc.] must adapt itself to the total informational input, both linguistic and paralinguistic" [p. 8]).
2. Emphasis on the provision of meaning-bearing comprehensible input and language development as the outcome of processing meaning-bearing comprehensible input over long time.
3. Emphasis on learner centeredness, a situation in which the role of the instructor is that of an architect and a model and in which learners become active participants with greater responsibility for their own learning.
4. Emphasis on "real-life" interactions, meaningful tasks, and content.
5. Emphasis on a low anxiety environment (lowering the learner's "affective filter") so that language acquisition is not impeded by anxiety.

Task-Based Instruction

Consistent with the general tenets of CLT, TBI emphasizes engaging learners in meaningful tasks with a focus on task completion instead of linguistic accuracy per se. Proponents of TBI include, for example, Long (2015) and Willis and Willis (2007). Other publications on TBI can be found on the publications web page of the International Association for Task-Based Language Teaching at http://www.tblt.org/publications/. Given its focus on meaning and real-life meaningful interactions, TBI may also be considered one variety of CLT. TBI has inspired the development of meaning-oriented course syllabi based on a series of different types of tasks that learners can learn to complete. The tasks in question commonly include some type of "gap" whose resolution learners need to work on together using appropriate linguistic tools. Some tasks involve consolidating two sources of information, such as when one student has access to some pieces of information and another student has access to other pieces of information. Other tasks may involve group decision, such as when a small group of students must make a reasoned decision (e.g., which individuals stay and go, which items are bought and are not bought, and which places are visited or not) by working together and, of course, by using the target language to communicate about considerations related to the task at hand. Lee and VanPatten (2003) provide a range of examples of different types of tasks that learners can perform and advocate incorporating tasks of this nature within CLT.

When it comes to learning novel vocabulary, as with any approach, TBI cannot obviate the reality that vocabulary learning is *input-first*. If a set of novel vocabulary is needed to perform a given task, such as an information-gap or group-decision task, learners will need to be exposed to it in a pretask phase or access it during the actual task phase. In the latter case, learners might use a bilingual dictionary or some other means of gaining access to the vocabulary that they need to complete the task. Because the IBI approach to vocabulary addresses this issue directly, incorporating this approach within TBI can help learners acquire critical vocabulary effectively and allow them to engage in tasks in a more effective manner by ensuring that they are sufficiently prepared on the lexical front.

Content-Based Instruction

Another major strand of MOI is CBI (see Brinton, Snow, & Wesche, 1989; Brinton, 2003; Lyster, 2011), which harnesses the learning of content to promote significant language development. The target content that one can learn while developing linguistic skills is virtually limitless. Possible content topics include linguistics, literary and cultural studies, history, anthropology, political science, engineering, mathematics, and so forth. CBI is also tied to courses in learning languages (L2s) for specific purposes, such as for business, social science, and so on. CBI is also consistent with CLT and TBI approaches because content is commonly learned in any one of these three meaning-oriented approaches and learning novel content can greatly motivate and engage students.

Treatment of vocabulary in CBI depends on needs dictated by the content in question: Is there a new concept that needs to be learned? If so, is any of the vocabulary that is required for learning that new concept also novel to the learners? How do the learners ascertain the meaning of new terms while learning the content in question? Questions such as these are vital to successful CBI and, as explained in subsequent sections, are addressed by the IBI approach. Given how IBI vocabulary instruction respects the input-first nature of vocabulary learning, harnesses the value of repetition during the provision of meaningful and sufficiently comprehensible input, and provides guidelines for making the best use of input and tasks, incorporating the IBI approach within a larger program of CBI can improve vocabulary learning on a regular basis and increase the overall effectiveness of CBI.

"Knowing" Vocabulary: The Lexical *Wish List* of Every Word

Before presenting the 10 principles of the IBI approach, let us first consider some of the key issues involved in learning and eventually "knowing" a word or multiword lexical phrase. Learning a new word or lexical phrase involves (a) word form, (b) word meaning, and (c) mapping between word form and meaning. Beyond these basics, however, every word has what might be called its *wish list*, or all of the meaning- and usage-related properties that a word can have, including its collocations, both primary and secondary. The lexical wish list for the word *glass* in English includes, for example, collocations such as *glass ceiling*, *glass window*, *glass eye*, and *glass-bottom boat*, as well as idiomatic expressions such as *People who live in glass houses shouldn't throw stones*. It also includes all possible denotative and connotative meanings of the word *glass* and all syntactic projections that a word such as *glass* might have. For example, the lexical wish list of the Spanish word *poner* (to put) includes the fact that this verb requires an object: *poner algo en algún lugar* (to put something somewhere) is acceptable, but *poner algo* (to put something) by itself without an object is not. A notable exception to this rule is the case of *poner huevos* (to lay eggs), for which location is only optional (but in which case the meaning of *poner* changes). All of this information, among a variety of other types of information, make up the lexical wish list of the Spanish word *poner*.

Why is the lexical wish list for each word so important? For one reason, it clarifies that discrete-item intentional vocabulary learning alone will never provide learners with all of the information they need to satisfy the lexical wish lists of all the target words they might like to acquire. Discrete-item intentional learning may be useful, such as for acquiring knowledge of the form and the most frequent meanings of a given set of target words, but in no way can this type of learning replace the information provided by discourse-level input that contains multiple meanings of words, shades of meaning, connotative meanings, and various collocational properties of a given target word. To be fluent in any language, a learner needs to develop implicit knowledge of the collocational and semantic (including conceptual) properties of any given word or combination of words. As should become clear in the following section, IBI vocabulary instruction takes these issues into account and works toward satisfying the wish lists of words or lexical phrases, even though this goal is incremental in nature and may involve long periods of time.

Tenets of the IBI Approach

Input-based incremental (IBI) vocabulary instruction is a meaning-oriented approach that emphasizes the pivotal role of input—in particular, meaning-bearing and sufficiently comprehensible input—as well as the incremental nature of learning multiple aspects of vocabulary knowledge over time. The IBI approach is ambitious in that it targets all L2-specific meanings and uses of words, but it also takes into account the *learning burden* that novel vocabulary implies (Nation, 2001) when selecting the tasks learners should engage in during the early stages of word learning and then gradually over time. The approach also offers suggestions for providing learners with the best type of input possible, including *enhanced input*, for promoting vocabulary learning. Most importantly, the IBI approach is theoretically grounded and based largely on a variety of studies of *lexical input processing* (lex-IP; see Barcroft, 2015), which refers to how learners allocate their limited processing resources when they encounter novel vocabulary (novel words or lexical phrases) in the input, regardless of whether the context of learning is intentional or incidental. This theoretical and evidence-based foundation of the approach is critical to its effectiveness in practice.

The 10 principles of IBI vocabulary instruction appear in Table 9.1. Principle 1 is a logical general principle, but it is one that can be overlooked or forgotten during language program planning. For example, one question faced by language program directors (and textbook authors and publishers) is whether word frequency should be taken into consideration when identifying target vocabulary for a given course or a series of courses within a larger instructional sequence. Should the most frequent 2,000 words of the target language be a particular goal, or should course themes and tasks dictate target vocabulary, given that the most frequent words of any language tend to occur whether or not they are targeted? Other principles are clearly based on research findings, such as Principle 2, which is consistent with the frequency effect in human memory, and Principles 5, 6, and 7, which are based on research on lexical input processing lex-IP, as discussed in the following section.

Table 9.2 presents a seven-point checklist for designing IBI lessons. Note that the checklist items not only emphasize key tenets of the IBI approach but also encourage inclusion of appropriate historical and cultural information when possible. This checklist should be helpful when designing IBI lessons from scratch as well as when designing IBI lessons to complement target vocabulary in existing textbooks.

Table 9.1. Ten Principles of IBI Vocabulary Instruction

1. Develop and implement a vocabulary acquisition plan.
2. Present new words frequently and repeatedly in the input.
3. Promote both intentional and incidental vocabulary learning.
4. Use meaning-bearing comprehensible input when presenting new words.
5. Present new words in an enhanced manner.
6. Limit forced output without access to meaning during the initial stages.
7. Limit forced semantic elaboration during the initial stages.
8. Promote learning L2-specific word meanings and usage over time.
9. Progress from less demanding to more demanding activities over time.
10. Apply research findings with direct implications for vocabulary instruction.

Table 9.2. Checklist for Designing IBI Lessons

___ 1. I defined target vocabulary and materials needed for the activities.
___ 2. I designed the activities to be meaningful, educational, and interactive.
___ 3. I included cultural and historical information when appropriate.
___ 4. I presented target vocabulary repeatedly in the input-first.
___ 5. I increased the difficulty of tasks involving target vocabulary gradually over time.
___ 6. I incorporated a number of the 10 principles of the IBI approach.
___ 7. I included directly applicable research findings.

Some Pivotal Research Findings

The reader is referred to two books by Barcroft (2012, 2015) for more detailed information about the research foundations of the IBI approach. In this section, however, we consider some of the key research findings that support different IBI principles. To begin demonstrations of the benefits of repetition are ubiquitous in research on human memory, but studies by Hulstijn and colleagues (Hulstijn, 1992; Hulstijn, Hollander, & Greidanus, 1996) have provided empirical evidence of these benefits for L2 vocabulary learning in particular and, in this case, for *incidental vocabulary learning*, which is when new vocabulary is acquired without consciously intentending to do so. Consistent with these findings, Rott (2007) also provided telling findings regarding the benefits of increased repetition by demonstrating that the inclusion of four repetitions of target words in a text resulted in significantly more word gain than inclusion of only one repetition.

Principles 6 and 7, although perhaps counterintuitive at first glance, are supported by a series of studies of different types of tasks involving *semantic elaboration* (elaborating on the meaning of a word more than would otherwise be the case) and *output without access to meaning* (see Lee & VanPatten, 2003) at the level of individual words. As for Principle 7, Barcroft (2004) assessed the effects on L2 vocabulary learning of having learners write target words in original sentences (seeing each target word and its picture on a screen and then writing the word in an original sentence in the L2—the control condition was to study the words in the same way but without writing anything). In stark contrast to what might be expected with a general extension of the levels-of-processing framework for research on human memory (Craik & Lockhart, 1972; see Morris, Bransford, & Franks, 1977, for a possible alternative interpretation of early and more recent research findings) to the realm of L2 vocabulary, not only did sentence writing fail to facilitate L2 vocabulary learning, it also decreased it by approximately 100%. In another study, Wong and Pyun (2012) found that the negative effects of the same type of sentence-writing task were even more pronounced when the L2 in question was less formally similar to the learners' L1 (the study contrasted English-speaking learners of L2 Korean [less similar] with English-speaking learners of L2 French [more familiar]). Barcroft (2002) also found negative effects of a semantically oriented pleasantness-ratings task on both free and cued recall of target L2 vocabulary. All these findings are consistent with the predictions of the type of processing-resource allocation (TOPRA) model, one of which cautions that increased semantic processing can decrease processing resources available for form processing and thereby diminish word-form learning.

Another finding that supports IBI Principle 6 is that requiring learners to copy target words (by writing them down) does not facilitate L2 vocabulary learning and, in fact, can decrease learning of this nature (Barcroft, 2006). On the other hand, if learners are provided with opportunities to process target words as input first and then asked to attempt to retrieve the target word forms on their own, their L2 vocabulary learning can be improved, as demonstrated by studies conducted since the 1970s (Barcroft, 2007; McNamara & Healy, 1995; Royer, 1973). These findings on the value of providing learners with opportunities to retrieve target words on their own are consistent with both Principles 6 and 10 because retrieval is not the same as producing output without access to meaning.

Other IBI principles are supported by early (1960s and 1970s) reasoning and theoretical work as related to SLA. Specifically, the proposal of Principle 4 to use meaning-bearing comprehensible input when presenting target words is consistent with Krashen's (1985) input hypothesis and with our understanding of how language acquisition progresses by means of the development of form–meaning connections over time at all levels of linguistic grain.

Lastly, when it comes to L2 vocabulary learning in the spoken mode, studies by Barcroft and Sommers (2005) and Sommers and Barcroft (2007) have demonstrated the benefits of using acoustic variability—specifically, input produced by multiple talkers, input produced by one talker in multiple speaking styles, and input presented at multiple rates—on L2 vocabulary learning. The pedagogical implications of this research are clear: increased acoustic variability can be readily incorporated in online instructional materials as well as in the classroom by individual instructors who understand the value of providing input with variations in, for example, speaking style and speaking rate. The benefits demonstrated in these studies suggest that enhanced spoken input of this nature (note IBI Principle 5) should be of interest to every language program director and L2 teacher. Also intriguing in this area is a study by de Groot (2006), who found that presenting target words while playing classical music in the background led to greater L2 vocabulary learning as compared to when no music was played. Findings such as these can be readily incorporated in L2 instructional programs, not only in one course taught by one instructor but also in all courses at various levels of proficiency and as part of the instructional materials provided by publishers of L2 instructional materials. Language program directors and teachers should insist that publishers make use of evidence-based provisions such as these in designing digital course materials that include spoken input in order to facilitate L2 vocabulary learning on an ongoing basis.

Sample IBI Lessons

The following sample lessons demonstrate symbiosis between the IBI approach and MOI. The first lesson is focused on clothing and what students would choose to wear in different situations. It is designed for low-intermediate (first-year) students, as reflected by both the target vocabulary items and the degree of difficulty of different steps in the lesson. The second lesson also concerns clothing but in a substantially different manner. It focuses on the appearance of Gloria Steinem and other key figures during Fashion Week New York City in 2017. The target vocabulary and the nature of the lesson are appropriate for a much higher, upper-intermediate or advanced, level of L2 proficiency. Although presented in English here, the lessons could be adapted to basically any target L2. The communicative focus of Lesson 1 concerns preferences related to clothing. The topic of Lesson 2, on the other hand, concerns current news in the United States. To examine 14 additional sample lessons, the reader is referred to Barcroft's 2012 book on IBI vocabulary instruction.

Lesson 1: *What are your favorite clothes?*

Target Vocabulary.   Clothes, shirt, jeans, pants, shorts, shoes (running, tennis), socks, scarf, beige, pink, purple, blue-green, designer, brand, high-heel, hat, simple, fancy, wear, to wear it well, to make an impression, silk, cotton, comfortable, and other possible related vocabulary.

Materials.   Picture file with different types of clothing and outfits and a list of different situations for which people might dress in different ways.

Step 1. Use a picture file to show the students in your class different types of clothes. Name each type of clothing as you show the pictures and talk, using sufficiently comprehensible input, about what you think of these different types of clothes. Make sure to present target words *frequently* (within each input segment) and *repeatedly* (across multiple input segments over time). Go through the picture file multiple times and pronounce target vocabulary each time at different speaking rates, one time more slowly and other times more rapidly.

For example: *We're going to have a look at these pictures and see different types of* clothing *and talk about what you like and don't really like when it comes to different types of* clothing. *[Showing first picture] In this first picture you can see that the man is wearing a red* shirt *with* jeans *and* tennis shoes. *It is a relaxed look. I like it. What do you think? Do you like it? How many of you like the* shirt? *[Note student responses.] The jeans, here are the* jeans. *How many of you like the* jeans? *[Note student responses.] In this second picture you can see a very different look. This man is wearing* shorts *[pointing] and some very long* socks; *I think they'd be considered knee-high [pointing]* socks. *He's also wearing what I think are either* tennis shoes *or* running shoes, *which I kind of like, but the* socks *are really long. What do you think? Do you like the long* socks *[pointing] along with the* shorts *[pointing]? [Note student responses.] ...*

Step 2. Have students work in small groups. Provide each group with two pictures and ask them to decide which of the two outfits they like the most. After the students have had time to decide on their favorite of the two outfits, call on each small group and ask them to say which outfit they have chosen. Other students in the class should indicate by raising their hands whether they agree or disagree with each small group's assessment.

Step 3. Divide the class into pairs of students. Each student should describe to the other student in the pair what some student in the class is wearing, and the other student should attempt to guess which student is being described. The students in each pair take turns doing this about two or three times each. (*Optional*: After doing descriptions in pairs, the instructor can describe to the class what a few students are wearing and see whether students can correctly identify the students in question.)

Step 4. Have students work in groups of two or three. Give them a list of situations in which different types of outfits need to be selected and ask them what they suggest the person(s) in each situation should wear. For each situation, the students should work together to write out the type of clothing they suggest.

Step 5. As an extension activity to be completed outside of class, have each student write a brief essay about what the student likes to wear on different occasions. Provide a list of specific occasions to be considered, including, for example, a wedding, a day of hiking near a beach, the first day of the semester at the university, and a weekend night out on the town with friends.

Commentary

Note how this lesson is *input-first* (or *input-based*) when it comes to presenting target vocabulary and *incremental* when it comes to the use of target vocabulary in multiple contexts (along with providing different collocations for each word), as well as gradually and increasingly demanding when it comes to the types of tasks in which the learners engage. Steps 1–3 involve numerous exposures to target vocabulary in the input: in Step 1 using input presented by the instructor and in Steps 2 and 3 using input provided by fellow students. Note also that the students providing the input are not asked to do so during the initial stages of exposure to the novel target words. In those initial stages, learners are also not required to engage in semantic elaboration, particularly any redundant type of L1-based semantic elaboration, as supported by research demonstrating the negative effects of semantically elaborative tasks such as sentence writing. The learners are also not required to produce forced output without access to meaning (e.g., copying or choral repetition of target words), which is supported by experiments that revealed negative effects of word copying. Speaking-rate variability is also incorporated in Step 1, which is one of several types of acoustic variability that improve L2 vocabulary learning (others include talker and speaking-style variability). Steps 2 and 3 also provide students with opportunities to retrieve target words on their own, which research has found to facilitate vocabulary learning. Steps 4 and 5 increase demands on the learner while maintaining the focus on meaning, by providing learners with opportunities to express their own opinions about what they would and would not prefer to wear in a series of different situations.

Lesson 2: *What is Gloria Steinem doing at Fashion Week in New York City?*

Target Vocabulary.   *Resistance-minded, to lure, runway, twice-yearly, to showcase, platform, advocate, to swap, ribbon, row, body-diverse, to march, to knock off, to covet, flowing, range, to judge, to strut, pavement,* and other possible related vocabulary.

Materials.   *San Francisco Chronicle* article of September 11, 2017, by Tony Bravo entitled "The resistance-minded designer who lured Gloria Steinem to New York Fashion Week" (available online at http://www.sfchronicle.com/style/article/The-resistance-minded-designer-that-lured-Gloria-12189145.php).

Step 1. Let students know that they will be reading and discussing an article related to feminism and the political history of the United States. Ask students what they know about Gloria Steinem and the history of feminism in the United States. Have a brief conversation about this topic.

Step 2. Let students know that each student will be assigned to one or two vocabulary items that appear in the article or are related to it. Assign the vocabulary items to the students and instruct them that as an activity to do outside of class, they should define and exemplify the item in question in order to report back to the other students during the next day of class. Also ask them to repeat the item in question multiple times during their minipresentations.

Step 3. At the beginning of the next class, ask each student to present, define, and exemplify the terms that were assigned to them. Help to clarify any potential confusions about meanings and, when appropriate, note alternate definitions of the target items. For example, *Yes, to strut means to walk around in the way you just described. Interestingly, it is also a part of a car; it is a rod that forms part of the compression system of a car. Do you think the verb and the noun are kind of related in meaning?*

Step 4. Have all students read the news article in question. Additional prereading, during-reading, and postreading activities might be added at this point in order to support reading as a process.

Step 5. Have students form small groups. In each group, the students should discuss and write a list of reasons why, based on what they have read, Gloria Steinem attended Fashion Week in New York City in 2017.

Step 6. Have each group share their ideas from Step 5 with the rest of the class.

Step 7. Have the same groups from Step 5 plan to research (online, elsewhere, or both) the history of the feminist movement in the United States. Ask them to come up with a list of at least 10 facts about the history of the feminist movement in the United States and, when possible, to include items related to Gloria Steinem.

Step 8. At the beginning of the next class, give an unannounced practice quiz on the target vocabulary. Give definitions for target terms, ask students to attempt to retrieve and write the items in question, and then go over the answers to the practice quiz. When appropriate, mention alternative meanings, uses, or both for some of the target items.

Step 9. Have the same groups from Steps 5 to 7 share the facts that they have learned about the history of feminism in the United States. Have each group give one fact, and continue going over the facts one by one until no group has any additional fact to share.

Step 10. Ask the class what they find most interesting about what they have learned about the history of feminism in the United States and Gloria Steinem. Also ask them if they understand more about why Gloria Steinem might attend Fashion Week in New York City for the first time in 2017.

Step 11. Ask each student to write a one-half to one-page essay (to be turned in at the beginning of the next class) on what each student would suggest that Gloria Steinem do next in order to meet her long-term and current goals.

Commentary

Like Lesson 1, this lesson is also *input-first* and *incremental* in nature. Moreover, the meaning orientation and focus on content—in this case, the history of feminism in the United States and the life and work of Gloria Steinem—are clear and go well beyond preferences about clothing and thoughts about a fashion show in the lesson. Both the target vocabulary and the selected reading in this lesson lead learners toward tasks that require them to reflect upon their ideas about a sociopolitical movement and to learn about the history of feminism in the United States. In addition, on more than one occasion the lesson targets L2-specific meanings and uses of target vocabulary items that go beyond their most canonical and frequent uses, such as in the case of the target word *strut*, which although used as a verb in the reading in this lesson can also be used as a noun to refer to a part of an automobile. In this lesson, learners are also asked whether they can identify any relationship in meaning between the two uses. Finally, as with Lesson 1, this lesson provides learners with opportunities to attempt to retrieve target vocabulary items on their own after they have had substantial opportunity to process them as input. This type of sequencing is effective because it avoids requiring learners to repeat target words in a "parroted" way without access to meaning, as suggested by Principle 6, while instead allowing them to attempt to retrieve target words on their own at an appropriate time.

The Compatibility of IBI and MOI

As these two sample IBI lessons demonstrate, incorporating IBI vocabulary instruction in MOI allows language program directors and instructors to promote vocabulary acquisition in an effective manner in activities and tasks that are typical of MOI. All activities in Lesson 1 are meaning-oriented. Even when vocabulary learning is largely intentional and direct, such as when using a picture file, it is still meaning oriented because the purpose of conveying the meaning of the L2 word forms is to advance the learners' ability to understand and communicate while focusing on the topic at hand. Consistent with TBI, both lessons include a variety of meaningful tasks, such as selecting clothing for different situations in Lesson 1 and researching the history of feminism in the United States in Lesson 2. To the extent that learners were unfamiliar with the content of the newspaper article and the history of feminism in the United States, Lesson 2 also involves CBI. As can be seen in these examples, the IBI approach improves upon CLT in all of its instantiations, including TBI and CBI, by incorporating effective vocabulary instruction within them.

The IBI Approach and Language Program Direction: Six Recommendations

For language program directors and instructors interested in using the IBI approach, Table 9.3 provides six suggestions that may be helpful. Regarding the first two recommendations, the reader is referred to two books (Barcroft, 2012, 2015), the former for becoming familiar with all aspects of the approach (as exemplified by 14 sample lessons) and the latter for exploring research and theory related to lex-IP that underlies IBI vocabulary instruction. The third recommendation concerns assessing current instructional materials based on IBI principles, which can include asking questions about the existing instructional materials, such as the following: *In what ways are target words presented in the input? How frequently and repeatedly are target words presented? Are the vocabulary-related activities incremental in nature? Do they provide learners with opportunities to acquire multiple meanings and uses of target words?*

Table 9.3. Recommendations for Incorporating the IBI Approach

1.	Become familiar with all aspects of the approach.
2.	Explore pertinent theory and research.
3.	Assess instructional materials based on IBI principles.
4.	Incorporate the approach across multiple courses.
5.	Make effective vocabulary instruction a team effort.
6.	Stay apprised of pertinent research over time.

The fourth recommendation affirms that the IBI approach should be included in courses across multiple proficiency levels, including content-focused courses. More effective vocabulary instruction benefits learners regardless of their level. The fifth recommendation is to involve all instructors in the language program when incorporating the approach. The more that everyone is on board and contributing, sharing their ideas, expertise, and experience, the better. The sixth recommendation, as suggested by IBI Principle 10, continuing to stay as informed as possible about new research findings will give language program directors and instructors their best chance of providing the most effective vocabulary instruction possible. This goal can be met as part of the team effort as well, with different individuals sharing information about research findings from various sources, such as academic journals and pertinent presentations at academic conferences.

Summary and Conclusion

This chapter has highlighted the opportunity for language program directors and teachers to incorporate an evidence-based approach to vocabulary within different varieties of meaning-oriented instruction. It has focused on why meaning orientation is necessary for language acquisition and how communicative language teaching in general and task- and content-based instruction in particular, promote language acquisition. It has presented the 10 principles of IBI vocabulary instruction along with examples of research findings that support these principles. Two sample IBI lessons have also been presented, demonstrating how the IBI approach is consistent with different types of meaning-oriented instruction, along with six recommendations as to how the IBI approach can be incorporated effectively across multiple course levels within a language instruction program. Looking to the future, with reference to Principle 10 in particular, the IBI approach should continue to improve in its effectiveness as new research findings with direct implications for vocabulary instruction become available. These new findings should help language program directors and instructors to provide even more effective language instruction to their students.

References

Barcroft, J. (2002). Semantic and structural elaboration in L2 lexical acquisition. *Language Learning, 52,* 323–363.
Barcroft, J. (2004). Effects of sentence writing in L2 lexical acquisition. *Second Language Research, 20,* 303–334.
Barcroft, J. (2006). Can writing a new word detract from learning it? More negative effects of forced output during vocabulary learning. *Second Language Research, 22,* 487–497.
Barcroft, J. (2007). Effects of opportunities for word retrieval during second language vocabulary learning. *Language Learning, 57,* 35–56.

Barcroft, J. (2012). *Input-based incremental vocabulary instruction.* Alexandria, VA: TESOL International.

Barcroft, J. (2015). *Lexical input processing and vocabulary learning.* Amsterdam, Netherlands: Benjamins.

Barcroft, J., & Sommers, M. S. (2005). Effects of acoustic variability on second language vocabulary learning. *Studies in Second Language Acquisition, 27,* 387–414.

Brinton, D. (2003). Content-based instruction. In D. Nunan (Ed.), *Practical English language teaching* (pp. 199–224). New York, NY: McGraw Hill.

Brinton, D. M., Snow, M. A., & Wesche, M. B. (1989). *Content-based second language instruction.* New York, NY: Newbury.

Craik, F. I. M., & Lockhart, R. S. (1972). Levels of processing: A framework for memory research. *Journal of Verbal Learning and Verbal Behavior, 11,* 671–684.

De Groot, A. M. B. (2006). Effects of stimulus characteristics and background music on foreign language vocabulary learning and forgetting. *Language Learning, 56,* 463–506.

Ecke P. (2015). Parasitic vocabulary acquisition, cross-linguistic influence, and lexical retrieval in multilinguals. *Bilingualism: Language and Cognition, 18,* 145–162.

Hall, C. J. (2002). The automatic cognate form assumption: Evidence for the parasitic model of vocabulary development. *International Review of Applied Linguistics in Language Teaching, 40,* 69–87.

Hall, C. J., & Ecke, P. (2003). Parasitism as a default mechanism in L3 vocabulary acquisition. In J. Cenoz, B. Hufeisen & U. Jessner (Eds.), *The multilingual lexicon* (pp. 71–85). Dordrecht, Netherlands: Kluwer.

Hall, C. J., Newbrand, D., Ecke, P., Sperr, U., & Marchand, V. (2009). Learners' implicit assumptions about syntactic frames in new L3 words: The role of cognates, typological proximity, and L2 status. *Language Learning, 59,* 153–202.

Hulstijn, J. H. (1992). Retention of inferred and given word meanings: Experiments in incidental learning. In P. J. L. Arnaud & H. Béjoint (Eds.), *Vocabulary and Applied Linguistics* (pp. 113–125). London, UK: Macmillan.

Hulstijn, J. H., Hollander, M., & Greidanus, T. (1996). Incidental vocabulary learning by advanced foreign language students: The influence of marginal glosses, dictionary use, and recurrence of unknown words. *Modern Language Journal, 80,* 327–339.

Hymes, D. (1966). Two types of linguistic relativity. In Bright, W. (Ed.), *Sociolinguistics* (pp. 114–158). The Hague, Netherlands: Mouton.

Jiang, N. (2000). Lexical representation and development in a second language. *Applied Linguistics, 21,* 47–77.

Krashen, S. (1985). *The input hypothesis: Issues and implications.* New York, NY: Longman.

Lee, J. F., & VanPatten, B. (2003). *Making communicative language teaching happen* (2nd ed.). New York, NY: McGraw-Hill.

Long, M. (2015). *Second language acquisition and task-based language teaching.* Malden, MA: Wiley-Blackwell.

Lyster, R. (2011). Content-based second language teaching. In E. Hinkley (Ed.), *Handbook of Research in Second Language Teaching and Learning* (Vol. 2, pp. 611–630). New York: Routledge.

McNamara, D. S., & Healy, A. F. (1995). A generation advantage for multiplication skill training and nonword vocabulary acquisition. In A. F. Healy & L. E. Bourne, Jr. (Eds.), *Learning and memory of knowledge and skills: Durability and specificity* (pp. 132–169). Thousand Oaks, CA: Sage.

Morris, C. D., Bransford, J. D., & Franks, J. J. (1977). Levels of processing versus transfer appropriate processing. *Journal of Verbal Learning and Verbal Behavior, 16,* 519–533.

Nation, I. S. P. (2001). *Learning vocabulary in another language.* Cambridge, UK: Cambridge University Press.

Rott, S. (2007). The effect of frequency of input-enhancements on word learning and text comprehension. *Language Learning, 57,* 165–199.

Royer, J. M. (1973). Memory effects for test-like events during acquisition of foreign language vocabulary. *Psychological Reports, 32,* 195–198.

Savignon, S. J. (1972). *Communicative competence: An experiment in foreign-language teaching. Language and the Teacher,* Volume 12 [Series]. Philadelphia, PA: Center for Curriculum Development.

Sommers, M., & Barcroft, J. (2007). An integrated account of the effects of acoustic variability in L1 and L2: Evidence from amplitude, fundamental frequency, and speaking rate variability. *Applied Psycholinguistics, 28,* 231–249.

Willis, D., & Willis, J. (2007). Doing task-based teaching. Oxford, UK: Oxford University Press.

Wong, W., & Pyun, D. O. (2012). The effects of sentence writing on L2 French and Korean lexical retention. *The Canadian Modern Language Review, 68,* 164–189.

Editors

Peter Ecke (Ph.D., University of Arizona) is a Professor of Second Language Acquisition in the Department of German Studies and the Interdisciplinary Ph.D. Program in Second Language Acquisition and Teaching at the University of Arizona. His research areas are lexical development in multilingual speakers, language and intercultural competence development during study abroad, and the learning and teaching of German in the United States.

Susanne Rott (Ph.D., University of Illinois at Urbana-Champaign) is an Associate Professor of Germanic Studies and Linguistics and Head of the Department of Germanic Studies at the University of Illinois at Chicago. Her research focuses on the incremental development of individual words and collocations; the relationship between input factors, learning, and output; and computer-assisted language learning. Her publications have appeared in Applied Linguistics journals, such as *Language Learning*, *CALICO Journal*, and *Reading in a Foreign Language*.

Contributors

Joe Barcroft (Ph.D., University of Illinois at Urbana-Champaign) is a Professor of Spanish and Second Language Acquisition and Affiliate Professor of Psychological & Brain Sciences at Washington University in St. Louis. His research focuses on L2 vocabulary learning, input processing, and psycholinguistic approaches to L2 acquisition.

Denisa Bordag (Ph.D., Dr. phil. habil.) is an Associate Professor at Herder-Institute, University of Leipzig. Her areas of research interests focus on psycholinguistics and L2 acquisition, in particular the acquisition of vocabulary and grammar. In the recent years, she has conducted several projects exploring reading in native languages and L2s.

Jane F. Hacking (Ph.D., University of Toronto) is an Associate Professor of Russian and Linguistics at the University of Utah, where she codirects the Second Language Teaching and Research Center (L2TReC). Her research focuses on L2 phonology and the overall development of L2 proficiency. In 2017, she received an award for Outstanding Contribution to the Profession from the American Association of Teachers of Slavic and East European Languages.

Nan Jiang (Ph.D., University of Arizona) is currently a Professor of Second Language Acquisition at the University of Maryland. His research concerns second language processing. He is the author of *Conducting Reaction Time Research in Second Language Studies* (Routledge, 2012) and *Second Language Processing: An Introduction* (Routledge, 2018) and of numerous journal articles.

Amit Kirschenbaum (M.Sc.) is a Researcher and a Ph.D. Candidate at Leipzig University. His research interests span various aspects of language processing by humans and machines. His Ph.D. thesis (Institute of Computer Science, natural language processing or NLP) deals with automatic morphological analysis. In the recent years, he has been a research associate at the Institute of Applied Informatics (InfAI), where he applies knowledge combining NLP and Semantic Web technologies.

Nausica Marcos Miguel (Ph.D., University of Pittsburgh) is an Assistant Professor at Denison University, where she teaches Spanish language courses and linguistics. She is interested in learning and instruction of morphology and vocabulary. She has taught language courses in Spanish, English, and German.

Michael K. Olsen (Ph.D., University of Pittsburgh) is an Assistant Professor of Spanish at Tennessee Technological University. His primary research interests include second language acquisition of Spanish, classroom-based second language acquisition, and teacher talk in world language classrooms. He teaches Spanish language, linguistics, and language teaching methodologies courses. He also supervises student teachers in world languages.

Jamie Rankin (Ph.D., Harvard University) is a Senior Lecturer in the German Department of Princeton University, where he directs the Beginning German language sequence and mentors teaching assistants in L2 pedagogy. He is the coauthor with Larry Wells (late) of the *Handbuch zur deutschen Grammatik* (Cengage). In 2015, he was appointed Director of the Princeton Center for Language Study, which brings together students, instructors, and resources to enhance L2 teaching and learning. Research interests include L2 vocabulary, corrective feedback in the classroom, and developing new rubrics for assessing L2 written output.

Maria Rogahn (M.Sc.) is a Ph.D. Candidate at the University of Leipzig. She was a researcher at several projects addressing incidental vocabulary acquisition in native and second languages. Her additional area of interest is the first language acquisition.

Fernando Rubio (Ph.D., State University of New York at Buffalo) is an Associate Professor of Spanish Linguistics at the University of Utah, where he is also a Codirector of the Second Language Teaching and Research Center and Director of Online Curriculum Enhancement and Innovation. He currently serves on the ACTFL Board of Directors representing Higher Education and is the Chair of the ACTFL Research and Assessment Committee. He has authored textbooks, numerous journal articles, and book chapters on issues related to second language acquisition, assessment, and technology-enhanced language teaching.

Claudia Sánchez-Gutiérrez (Ph.D., Universidad de Salamanca, Spain) is an Assistant Professor at the University of California, Davis, where she teaches Spanish and Applied Linguistics while also working as the First-Year Spanish program coordinator. Her primary research interests include Spanish morphology as well as vocabulary teaching and learning.

Ulf Schuetze (Ph.D., University of British Columbia) is a Professor of Second Language Acquisition in the Department of Germanic & Slavic Studies at the University of Victoria, Canada, where he is also the Associate Director of the Digital Second Language Learning Lab. His research in computer-assisted language learning, lexical processing, and the sustainability of technology in second language acquisition has a direct application to teaching. His most recent publication, the monograph *Language Learning and the Brain: Lexical Processing in Second Language Acquisition* (Cambridge University Press, 2017) illustrates the dynamic environment involved when recording and producing words.

Erwin Tschirner (Ph.D., University of California, Berkeley) is Gerhard Helbig Professor of German as a Foreign Language at the University of Leipzig, Germany, and President of the Institute for Test Research and Test Development (ITT) in Leipzig. His main research areas are German linguistics, language assessment, and second language acquisition, focusing on the acquisition of vocabulary and grammar, speaking, listening, and reading proficiency.

Nina Vyatkina (Ph.D., Pennsylvania State University) is a Professor of German and Applied Linguistics and the Chair of the Department of Germanic Languages and Literatures at the University of Kansas. Her research interests include instructed second language acquisition, corpus-based language learning and teaching, and learner corpus research. Her articles have appeared in leading journals such as *Applied Linguistics*, and she serves on the Executive Board of the Computer-Assisted Language Instruction Consortium (CALICO) and the Editorial Boards of *Language Learning & Technology* and *International Journal of Learner Corpus Research*.

Alla Zareva (Ph.D., University of Georgia) is an Associate Professor in the Department of English at Old Dominion University and, currently, the Graduate Program Director of the M.A. Program in Applied Linguistics. Her research interests range from the organization of the mental lexicon of high proficiency ESL users to studying various language features of student academic presentations, based on small specialized corpora.